Child Rights in Humanitarian Crisis

This book demonstrates how a focus on children's rights can help practitioners to safeguard children during humanitarian crisis.

Child Rights in Humanitarian Crisis focuses on understanding and advancing child rights through practical applications of a child rights perspective in crisis response. The book establishes that with accessible, child-friendly participatory means, crisis response can improve from a child rights perspective and even advance children's rights whilst also supporting and furthering the development of a child's agency. The volume presents the reader with a clear focus on children from a range of backgrounds, including those most marginalised, such as children with disabilities. Drawing on expertise from the field as well as academia, and providing practical examples which link case studies to legal policies in recent and protracted humanitarian responses, such as in Turkey and at the Lithuania–Belarus border, this book is a treasure trove of advice from some of the humanitarian and development sector's most experienced professionals.

Combining insights from both research and practice, this book will be an essential read for humanitarian students and practitioners.

Rigmor Argren is a senior lecturer at Örebro University, Sweden. She holds a PhD and an LLM from Essex University, UK, and a MA in media and communications from Örebro University as well as a diploma in humanitarian leadership from the Centre for Humanitarian Leadership at Deakin University, Australia. She has formerly worked as Head of Surge Capacity Unit, Save the Children, Sweden. Her research focus is in the area of international humanitarian law and human rights law, often on topics such as freedom of information, right to information and gender issues.

Jessica Jonsson is senior lecturer at Örebro University, Sweden. She holds an LLD (PhD Law) from the European University Institute in Florence, Italy, and an LLM (Master of Laws) from the European Academy of Legal Theory in Brussels, Belgium. She is the former Director of the Child Rights Academy, Sweden and prior to that was Head of Mission War Child Canada in Uganda. She has been part of the international humanitarian community for well over a decade, working mainly with the UN in Africa. Her research focus includes topics such as child rights in international criminal justice and refugees' and asylum seekers' access to justice.

Routledge Humanitarian Studies Series

The Routledge Humanitarian Studies series in collaboration with the International Humanitarian Studies Association (IHSA) takes a comprehensive approach to the growing field of expertise that is humanitarian studies. This field is concerned with humanitarian crises caused by natural disaster, conflict or political instability and deals with the study of how humanitarian crises evolve, how they affect people and their institutions and societies, and the responses they trigger.

We invite book proposals that address, amongst other topics, questions of aid delivery, institutional aspects of service provision, the dynamics of rebel wars, state building after war, the international architecture of peacekeeping, the ways in which ordinary people continue to make a living throughout crises, and the effect of crises on gender relations.

This interdisciplinary series draws on and is relevant to a range of disciplines, including development studies, international relations, international law, anthropology, peace and conflict studies, public health and migration studies.

The Vulnerable Humanitarian
Ending Burnout Culture in the Aid Sector
Gemma Houldey

Humanitarian and Military Intervention in Libya and Syria
Parliamentary Debate and Policy Failure
Aran M. Lewis

Child Rights in Humanitarian Crisis
Improving Action and Response
Edited by Rigmor Argren and Jessica Jonsson

The Humanitarian Exit Dilemma
The Moral Cost of Withdrawing Aid
Chin Ruamps

For more information about this series, please visit: www.routledge.com/Routledge-Humanitarian-Studies/book-series/RHS

Child Rights in Humanitarian Crisis

Improving Action and Response

Edited by Rigmor Argren and Jessica Jonsson

Routledge
Taylor & Francis Group
LONDON AND NEW YORK

Designed cover image: AlexLinch @ iStock

First published 2023
by Routledge
4 Park Square, Milton Park, Abingdon, Oxon OX14 4RN

and by Routledge
605 Third Avenue, New York, NY 10158

Routledge is an imprint of the Taylor & Francis Group, an informa business

British Library Cataloguing-in-Publication Data
A catalogue record for this book is available from the British Library

ISBN: 978-1-032-03479-9 (hbk)
ISBN: 978-1-032-03477-5 (pbk)
ISBN: 978-1-003-18749-3 (ebk)

DOI: 10.4324/9781003187493

Typeset in Baskerville
by Apex CoVantage, LLC

Contents

List of Abbreviations vii
List of Figures ix
List of Tables x
List of Contributors xi
Preface xii
JESSICA JONSSON AND RIGMOR ARGREN

1 **Introduction: children's crisis response in need of improvement** 1
JESSICA JONSSON AND RIGMOR ARGREN

2 **Promoting children's rights to participation in humanitarian crises** 8
PHILIPPA HILL

3 **Making children's right to information meaningful in humanitarian crises** 37
RIGMOR ARGREN

4 **Digitalising children's humanitarian access: a way to enhance children's inclusion** 56
JESSICA JONSSON

5 **Strengthening the right to education in emergencies: normative change in humanitarian responses to children** 83
SONJA HÖVELMANN

6 **The right to self-determination and participation for refugee children with disabilities** 109
JAMIE BOLLING

7 **The child right's perspective in response to the humanitarian crisis at the Belarus-Lithuania border** 132
LAIMA VAIGĖ

8 **Forced migration, gendered violence and the child rights perspective: modalities of violence against marginalised groups in Turkey** 156
RUKAYA AL ZAYANI

9 **Child rights respect: global pandemics call for conscious change** 177
CORNELIA C. WALTHER

10 **Concluding remarks: where to next: closing gaps** 204
RIGMOR ARGREN AND JESSICA JONSSON

Index 209

Abbreviations

AAP	Accountability to Affected People
CHS	Core Humanitarian Standards
CPAT	Child Participation Assessment Tool
CPWG	Child Protection Working Group
CRC	UN Convention on the Rights of the Child
CRPD	UN Convention on the Rights of Persons with Disabilities
CVE	Countering Violent Extremism
DRW	Disabled Refugees Welcome
ECHO	Directorate-General for European Civil Protection and Humanitarian Aid Operations
ECHR	European Convention on Human Rights
ECtHR	European Court of Human Rights
EFA	Education for All
EiE	Education in Emergencies
HAP	Humanitarian Accountability Partnership
HPC	Humanitarian Program Cycle
IASC	Inter-Agency Standing Committee
ICCPR	International Convention on Civil and Political Rights
ICESCR	International Convention on Economic, Social and Cultural Rights
IHSA	International Humanitarian Studies Association
ICRC	International Committee of the Red Cross
IFRC	International Federation of the Red Cross
IDPs	Internally Displaced Persons
ILI	Independent Living Institute
INEE	Inter-Agency Network for Education in Emergencies
INGOs	International Non-Governmental Organisations
IOs	International Organisations
ISS	International Institute of Social Studies
LGBTIQ+	Lesbian, Gay, Bisexual, Trans, Intersex, Queer and Questioning+
MDGs	Millennium Development Goals
MSEE	Minimum Standards for Education in Emergencies
NGOs	Non-Governmental Organisations

NHRI	National Human Rights Institutions
NRC	Norwegian Refugee Council
OECD	Organisation for Economic Co-operation and Development
OPIC-CRC	Optional Protocol to the Convention on the Rights of the Child on a Communications Procedure
POZE	A new Perspective to life, the Optimization of interplays, the gradual pursuit of subsequent Zeniths, and Exposure to reality as it is
RTR	Real Time Review
SDGs	Sustainable Development Goals
UDHR	The Universal Declaration of Human Rights
UN	United Nations
UNESCO	United Nations Educational, Scientific and Cultural Organization
UNGA	United Nations General Assembly
UNHCR	United Nations High Commissioner for Refugees
UNICEF	United Nations International Children's Emergency Fund
UNSC	United Nations Security Council
WHO	World Health Organization

Figures

2.1 A photo of a child placing written feedback into a monster-shaped feedback box in Colombia 17
5.1 Timeline of important EiE frameworks. The size of the bubble is relative to the number of frameworks/events/funding that happened in each year. Left column: Humanitarian frameworks. Middle column: Total humanitarian funding for education per year (OCHA 2016). Right column: Important EiE frameworks, policy and events 103
9.1 Spiral soul to body 184
9.2 Spiral micro to meta 186
9.3 Spiral CRC pillars 195
9.4 Spiral R4 199
9.5 MindMap m4 and R4 201

Tables

5.1 Organisations chosen for document analysis 91
6.1 Refugee children with disabilities 126
8.1 The various forms of violence against cisgender Syrian women and girls and Syrian trans women 162

Contributors

Rukaya Al Zayani, MA, is a doctoral student in gender studies at Örebro University researching the modalities of violence against the queer community in Turkey. Rukaya holds an MA in international relations from Istanbul Bilgi University.

Jamie Bolling, MA, is the Director of the Independent Living Institute and Co-Chair of the European Network on Independent Living. She holds an MA in social anthropology from the University of Stockholm. She is considered an expert within the international independent living movement.

Philippa Hill, MSc, is Save the Children's Head of Humanitarian Child Rights, Participation & Accountability. Over the last decade, she has deployed to numerous crises, including protracted conflicts, epidemics, displacement and natural disasters. She holds an MSc in violence, conflict and development from SOAS University of London.

Sonja Hövelmann, MA, is a research fellow with the Centre for Humanitarian Action in Berlin. Her prior research centres around German humanitarian assistance and reform processes in the humanitarian sector. Previously, she was Academic Coordinator of the Joint Master Programme in Humanitarian Action (NOHA). Sonja holds a master's degree in social science from the Ruhr-University in Bochum.

Laima Vaigė, PhD, is a senior lecturer in law at Örebro University, Sweden. She has defended two doctorates in law, at Mykolas Romeris University (Lithuania) and Uppsala University (Sweden) and holds an LLM from Riga Graduate School of Law (Latvia). She is also a research associate at the Educational Disadvantage Centre at Dublin City University.

Cornelia C. Walther, PhD, following two decades with the United Nations, founded the POZE movement in Haiti, from where it has spread around the world. Based between Europe and the United States, she has published multiple books and presently concentrates on scaling POZE whilst offering executive coaching to non-profit leaders. Currently she is a Senior Research Fellow, and acting Managing Director at the Center for Social Norms and Behavioral Dynamics at the University of Pennsylvania.

Preface

A book of this kind is long overdue. The conception for the first edition of *Child Rights in Humanitarian Crisis: Improving Response* was created through the International Humanitarian Studies Association (IHSA) Conference, which took place at the International Institute of Social Studies (ISS) in The Hague, The Netherlands, on 27–29 August 2018. The panel was conceived with the understanding of examining the topic of children and improved crisis response through the three distinctive topics of international law, the impact of technology and changing realities. Representing the only panel with a child rights perspective, it drew a much broader audience than expected, with the opportunity to accommodate for more sessions next time and is indeed food for thought. The topic child rights in humanitarian crisis was again the subject of a panel entitled *Ethics of Humanitarian Action & Politics of Humanitarianism* on the subject of child rights complaints mechanisms at the IHSA conference 3–5 November 2021, this time run in hybrid form with participants in Science Po in Paris, France, and online.

The panels on child rights for children in humanitarian crises at the IHSA conferences in 2018 and 2021 allowed us to connect with other scholars who shared our view that this book had a gap to fill in the literature. Our determination to bring academics and practitioners closer to each other through this book project proved not always straightforward but consistently rewarding.

The plight of a still-growing number of children in need of access to and participation in their humanitarian response, the mentioned IHSA conference panel discussions, the creation of the treaty-based communication procedure for children and, of course, the interest shown from Routledge Publishing sparked the writing of this book. It is our sincere belief that continued discussions between those who work in academia and practitioners in the field meeting the beneficiaries together bring the required experience and knowledge to further improve the lives of children in humanitarian crises.

Örebro, Sweden
Jessica Jonsson and Rigmor Argren

1 Introduction

Children's crisis response in need of improvement

Jessica Jonsson and Rigmor Argren

Children on the move, displaced, violated or otherwise affected by humanitarian crises show that when adults fail and turmoil ensues, the next generation certainly is not immune to the consequences. Responding to the protection needs of children remains pertinent. As a consequence of humanitarian crisis, children face abuse, including physical, emotional and sexual abuse; neglect; trafficking; child marriage; female genital mutilation; child recruitment; slavery; and child labour. They may also find themselves separated from or unaccompanied by their family, often displaced or as refugees. It goes without saying that children with disabilities may be at even greater risks or face seemingly insurmountable challenges in such vulnerable circumstances. It must be acknowledged that in crisis situations, it is the family and community that will ultimately assist and protect the child most effectively, when possible, as all other structures, including neighbouring or receiving countries' structures, are substantially weakened, overloaded or no longer in operation.

In discussing the understanding and improvement of crisis response, the pertinent terminology refers to humanitarian actors – humanitarians, a broad encompassing term of those who seek to deliver assistance to people in times of crises (organisations and individuals involved in humanitarian response). Such actors hold power in decision and policy making, technology investment and development. Their features are increasingly diverse; they can be national or international, governmental or non-governmental, profit or non-profit.

Child rights perspective as a shared reasoning

The decision by the Office of the Secretary-General to develop a Guidance Note on Child Rights Mainstreaming, led by the Office of the High Commissioner for Human Rights, reflects the importance of reinforcing a holistic child rights perspective at all levels in line with a human rights–based

DOI: 10.4324/9781003187493-1

approach.[1] This book is written with a child-rights approach, where a child rights perspective serves as part of the chapters' shared reasoning.

In line with the 2030 Agenda for Sustainable Development and the rights of the child, a key commitment is to leave no one behind and reach those furthest behind first.[2] Governments and actors commit to prioritise reaching all children everywhere by focusing on those most excluded and at risk of being denied their rights.[3] The Human Rights Council resolution on the rights of the child requests inputs from a child rights perspective to the yearly thematic reviews of progress of the high-level political forum on sustainable development. With varying degrees of an often-lacking child rights perspective in crisis response in humanitarian contexts, the continued importance of an applied child rights perspective becomes apparent when the legal, political and moral foundations are understood. Human rights of the child can be argued to consist of three interconnected dimensions, a legal, political and moral dimension. These dimensions add justification for humanitarian access, participation and accountability and as a consequence a child rights perspective in the humanitarian response, where called for or relevant.

The legal dimension rests on the premise that children's rights be recognised as legitimate standards within legal systems, like the Convention on the Rights of the Child (CRC).[4] The political dimension rests on the claim that the idea of human rights for children is a global enterprise that provides settled norms of political discourse whereby states voluntarily accept relevant treaty obligations. These obligations will be the standards by which the legitimacy of their efforts to secure children's interests will be assessed.[5] The third dimension, the moral dimension, is needed, as there is still widespread disagreement as to the moral status of children's rights. It is needed to address the conceptual doubts about rights of children if children's rights are to command reasoned loyalty and establish a secure intellectual foundation. If there is no conceptual foundation

1 Letter from the Executive Office of the UN Secretary-General to Child Rights Connect, 19 October 2021. See Committee on the Rights of the Child, Eighty-Ninth Session, 31 January 2022.

2 Resolution of the Human Rights Council on the Rights of the Child (A/HRC/34/L.25). See also OHCHR report to the Human Rights Council entitled 'Protection of the Rights of the Child in the Implementation of the 2030 Agenda for Sustainable Development' (A/HRC/34/27).

3 Office of the High Commissioner for Human Rights, 'Input from a Child Rights Perspective to the High Level Political Forum on Sustainable Development "Review of Eradicating Poverty and Promoting Prosperity in a Changing World" ', July 2017, https://sustainabledevelopment.un.org/content/documents/16641OHCHR.pdf.

4 Convention on the Rights of the Child, G.A. Res. 44/25, Annex, 44 UN Gaor Supp. (No. 49), 167, entered into force on 2 September 1990 (1980).

5 John Tobin, 'Justifying Children's Rights', *International Journal of Children's Rights*, 21 (2013), 395–441, 398.

for children's rights, there is a risk that their rights will become invisible and be rejected by those to whom they are not self-evident. In light of these considerations, Tobin argues that there is a pressing need for a firm conceptual foundation and moral justification for the idea of the human rights of the child.[6] One such important measure, also advancing accountability, is the application of individual communication procedures, of which the authors find a need for further scholarly studies in the final chapter.

For rights to have meaning, rights-holders must have access to mechanisms that protect their rights and address violations at all levels (nationally and internationally) and in all contexts (development and humanitarian). Communication, feedback and accountability mechanisms are essential for the full realisation of children's rights. Alongside every major international human rights treaty, the CRC has its own individual communication or accountability mechanism.[7] The third optional protocol to the Convention, the 'Optional Protocol to the Convention on the Rights of the Child on a Communications Procedure', hereinafter OPIC-CRC, allows individual children, groups of children or their representatives to bring a complaint with regard to a rights violation to the Committee on the Rights of the Child.[8] Complaints can only be brought forward, however, if the country (where the violation took place) has ratified the protocol and if the national legal system has been unable to remedy the violation. The Committee on the Rights of the Child consists of 18 independent experts, tasked to monitor the implementation of the CRC and its three optional protocols. In addition to receiving individual complaints from individuals living in states that have acceded to the OPIC-CRC, the committee examines the reports that state parties to the CRC are obliged to submit on a regular basis.[9]

Further to the moral dimension, donors and aid organisations at the 2016 World Humanitarian Summit committed to include affected people profoundly in decisions pertaining to humanitarian crisis response. This workstream, referred to as the Participation Revolution under the Grand Bargain, strived to deliver timely, effective and efficient humanitarian responses – also to children. Children have the right to participate in matters that affect them, also following article 12 of the CRC – the child's right to be heard. It is the fundamental tenet for children's participation. As one of the four guiding principles of the CRC, participation is both connected

6 Ibid.

7 General Assembly Resolution A/RES/66/138 Optional Protocol to the Convention on the Rights of the Child on a Communications Procedure. 19 December 2011.

8 States are also able to bring complaints against each other through an inter-state communications procedure. Article 12 OPIC-CRC (inter-state communications) only applies to states.

9 A state must submit its first report after two years. Then periodic reports should be submitted every five years.

to and indivisible from all other rights enshrined in the Convention. There are a number of articles that specifically intersect with article 12 and directly help to define 'meaningful participation' of children and a 'child rights perspective'. These civil rights have been broadly conceptualised under the term 'participation' and include the right to freedom of expression, thought, conscience, religion, association, peaceful assembly, protection of privacy and access to information (articles 13–17 of the CRC).

A well-defined child rights perspective revolves particularly but not only around accessibility and participation of the child. The substantial rights of article12 mandate that due weight be given to the views of the child in accordance with the level of maturity and age of the specific child. By considering the actual views of the child together with an application of the best interest principle, the danger of the best interest principle being used to serve as a proxy for others' interests is diminished.[10]

The participatory rights of children have been described as the linchpin of the CRC and are a fundamental principle in elaborating and furthering the rights of children. Such participatory rights, as stated in article 12 of the CRC, therefore distinguish a rights-based approach to matters concerning children from traditional welfare approaches where children remain silent. It can here be pointed out that children with disabilities also have this participatory right. Furthermore, under the model of rights advanced under the CRC, children have a right to their best interest being a primary consideration in all matters affecting them under article 3(1). Through the right to participation, children can play an active role in determining their best interest.[11] The flexibility of the best interest principle allows, in the decision-making process, for an assessment of the particular circumstances of the individual child or group of children to render an outcome suitable for that child. This carries the risk that the subjective preferences of the decision-maker will affect the assessment of a child's best interest. On the other hand, a too-rigid concept or a predetermined formula for the sake of certainty would hamper the best interest of the child.[12]

10 Article 12 further states that children must be given the opportunity to be heard in any judicial and administrative proceedings affecting them. The views of the child will be a part in making an assessment of what is in the best interest of that particular child. The specific view of the child might not be in its best interest regarding the matter at hand; however, it is an important part of the process to establish the best interest. John Tobin (ed), *The UN Convention on the Rights of the Child: A Commentary* (Oxford: Oxford Commentaries on International Law, 2019); Michael Freeman, *A Magna Carta for Children? Rethinking Children's Rights* (Cambridge: Cambridge University Press, 2020).

11 Still, the assessment of the best interest of a child must also be informed by the other rights under the CRC, meaning that an outcome of a decision cannot be considered in the best interest of a child if it is contrary to another right under the CRC. Ibid., Tobin (n 10), 591.

12 Ibid.

Improving humanitarian response

This book offers a critical inquiry into the safeguarding of child rights during humanitarian response as applied to a broadly defined context of humanitarian crises. Such crises require immediate attention. Examples include natural disasters, armed conflict zones, civil unrest and other violent settings. Humanitarian crises furthermore include disease outbreaks and displaced people. Humanitarian responses are not only experienced and necessary in the first phase of response, usually at the site of the first outbreak of the emergency, they can also be found necessary in recipient territories, when those who flee from the original crisis over-stretch systems and resources in other places. Child protection efforts in these settings are often urgent. The responses require a systems-based child rights approach, bringing together numerous entities to provide the care and support that children and their families require.

Key focuses of the book

Child Rights in Humanitarian Crisis: Improving Response focuses on understanding and advancing child rights through a practical application of a child rights perspective in crisis response. The book furthermore establishes that with accessible, child-friendly participatory means, crisis response can improve from a child rights perspective and even advance child rights and support and further the development of a child's agency. The book presents the reader with a clear focus on children, including those most marginalised, children with disabilities. Humanitarians' field experiences are linked to legal policies in order to further the relevance of child rights law.

The book undertakes a critical review of child rights in humanitarian crises, focused on the ability to provide response mechanisms from a child rights perspective. The text offers a critique of crisis response and provides recommendations for improvement, encompassing perspectives from the field at the site of crises as well as in (presumed) harbours of safety in recipient countries. It investigates national and international responses for children in humanitarian situations, including efforts of receiving states and the usage of modern technology. Key achievements and challenges are identified in the form of good practices and lessons learned, which provide a basis for further development of global practice guidelines. The book demonstrates practical wisdom and unique insights from very experienced professionals working in the humanitarian and development sector. The book gathers contributors both from academia and the world of practitioners to examine the overall aim of ensuring child rights in humanitarian crisis.

The materials examined throughout the chapters of this book span traditional legal materials, such as treaties, case-law and general comments from the Committee of the Rights of the Child, as well as the Committee on the Rights of Persons with Disabilities. Additional materials include policies and guidelines from expert organisations and involved business sectors working in the field of humanitarian response and doctrine.

The structure of the book

In Chapter 2, Philippa Hill explores how aid agencies can support children's rights to participation during humanitarian responses. This is done based on learning from Save the Children and applied throughout the humanitarian programme cycle.

In Chapter 3, Rigmor Argren argues that children's right to information, and the way it is protected under the Convention on the Rights of the Child, has unique features and therefore, when children are concerned, must be approached in a manner distinctively separate from how the right to information applies in its adult-centric form.

In Chapter 4, Jessica Jonsson discusses the importance of ensuring that children in crises have access to responses, health services and basic information, which may only be possible through today's digital environment by being connected, able to access and utilise digital technologies.

In Chapter 5, Sonja Hövelmann applies a discursive analysis and examines how humanitarian actors have put education in emergencies on the international agenda by arguing in favour of inclusion of education in core humanitarian responses.

In Chapter 6, the perspective shifts to a recipient country. Jamie Bollinger highlights the area of crisis response for refugee children with disabilities. The key for success in this work, Bollinger argues, is to apply the social model of disability, which reframes disability in terms of the right to participation and accessibility.

In Chapter 7, Laima Vaigė critically examines the humanitarian crisis at the border of Lithuania and Belarus that started in the summer of 2021. Due to severe legislative changes, thousands of asylum seekers remained stranded in the border zone as the authorities ventured into the semantical paradox of providing 'accommodation' that stopped them from entering Lithuania.

In Chapter 8, Rukaya Zayani discusses the modalities of violence in the lives of Syrian refugees in Turkey in relation to intersecting social identities. The author adopts a broadened perspective on gendered violence and takes into account different social identities such as gender, sex and sexual orientation.

In Chapter 9, Cornelia Walther takes on a decisively forward-looking approach and looks at interactions that are conducive to the respect of children's legal entitlements (enshrined rights) and their actual manifestation, or the gap between theory and practice.

In the final tenth chapter, the editors, Jonsson and Argren, provide concluding remarks on where to next, identifying three main gaps in relation to improving crisis response from a child rights perspective.

List of references

2019 Edition of the Minimum Standards for Child Protection in Humanitarian Action (CPMS) (2019). The Alliance for Child Protection in Humanitarian Action (alliancecpha.org).

Committee on the Rights of the Child Opens Eighty-Ninth Session 31 January 2022 at Treaty bodies Sessions (ohchr.org) accessed 9 February 2022.

Convention on the Rights of the Child, G.A. Res. 44/25, Annex, 44 UN Gaor Supp. (No. 49), 167, entered into force on 2 September 1990 (1980).

Freeman, M, *A Magna Carta for Children? Rethinking Children's Rights*. Cambridge: Cambridge University Press, 2020.

General Assembly Resolution A/RES/66/138 Optional Protocol to the Convention on the Rights of the Child on a communications procedure. 19 December 2011.

Letter from the Executive Office of the UN Secretary-General to Child Rights Connect, 19 October 2021 at letter_asg_response.pdf (childrightsconnect.org) accessed 30 October 2021.

Office of the High Commissioner for Human Rights, 'Input from a child rights perspective to the High Level Political Forum on Sustainable Development "review of eradicating poverty and promoting prosperity in a changing world" ', July 2017. https://sustainabledevelopment.un.org/content/documents/16641OHCHR.pdf

Office of the High Commissioner for Human Rights, 'Protection of the rights of the child in the implementation of the 2030 Agenda for Sustainable Development' (A/HRC/34/27).

Resolution of the Human Rights Council on the rights of the child (A/HRC/34/L.25).

Tobin, J (ed), *The UN Convention on the Rights of the Child: A Commentary*. Oxford: Oxford Commentaries on International Law. 2019.

Tobin, J, 'Justifying Children's Rights', *International Journal of Children's Rights*, 21, 395–441, 2013.

2 Promoting children's rights to participation in humanitarian crises

*Philippa Hill**

1. Introduction

> The Syrian people are in need of more than aid. We are in need of people who can feel the same as us and understand. We are so happy that you are trying to understand us and feel what we feel.
>
> Abdallah, 15–17 years, Eastern Ghouta, Syria[1]

Children have the right to participate in matters that affect them. Article 12 of the UN Convention on the Rights of the Child (CRC) – the child's right to be heard – is the fundamental tenet for children's participation. As one of the four guiding principles of the CRC, Article 12 is both connected to and indivisible from all other rights enshrined in the Convention. There are additional articles that specifically intersect with Article 12 and directly help to define the meaningful participation of children. These civil rights have been broadly conceptualised under the term 'participation' and include the right to freedom of expression, thought, conscience, religion, association, peaceful assembly, protection of privacy, and access to information (Articles 13–17 of the CRC).

Children's rights are universal (everyone under 18 has the rights contained in the CRC) and inalienable (those rights cannot be taken away from children). In humanitarian crises, children inevitably experience breaches of their rights; for example, children's right to healthcare may be compromised by the destruction and slow rehabilitation of health centres, or children's right to be protected during war may be compromised by parties to

* Philippa Hill is Save the Children's Head of Humanitarian Child Rights, Participation & Accountability. The author of this chapter is grateful for her current and former colleagues across the world who submitted case studies of their efforts to promote child participation: Titilope Eluwa, Warda Ashraf, Budhi Utama, Ronald Apunyo, Maria Camila Palacios, Iñaki Borda, and Luis Caroprese. Thanks also to Eline Severijnen and Alana Kapell for helpful comments and continual inspiration.

1 McDonald, A. 'Invisible Wounds: The Impact of Six Years of War on the Mental Health of Syria's Children' (2017) Save the Children 9.

DOI: 10.4324/9781003187493-2

a conflict. However, barriers to the realisation of children's rights in their entirety may also be posed by humanitarian actors themselves – the very organisations that seek to support children during crises. There can sometimes be a misconception that children's rights to participation can be set aside in the pursuit of ensuring other rights (for example, to protection, education, or health) are realised, that participation is a luxury that can be considered later in a response when other rights have been met. This not only risks participation never being promoted (as it may be years or decades until children have adequate protection, education, or healthcare in many crises) but overlooks the fact that children's rights are indivisible (rights cannot be separated from each other) and interdependent (one set of rights cannot be fully realised without the other). From a human rights perspective, no hierarchy of rights exists. Realising children's right to participation strengthens the realisation of other rights.[2]

Therefore, humanitarian organisations must seek to advance children's rights to participation within and through their aid efforts. Within Save the Children, for something to be considered child participation, there must be an opportunity for children to express their views, those views must be taken seriously, there must be the opportunity to influence decision-making, and children must see the results of their participation.[3] As Feinstein and O'Kane state,

> When children, especially the most marginalized, have opportunities to express their views, access information, form associations, participate in decisions that affect them, and take action to fulfil their rights, they are often more able to protect themselves, claim their rights, and hold adults accountable.[4]

Accountability mechanisms are essential for the full realisation of children's rights. Alongside every major international human rights treaty, the CRC has its own form of a 'feedback' or accountability mechanism. The CRC's 3rd Optional Protocol[5] is a communications (or complaint) procedure that allows children, groups of children, or their representatives to bring a complaint/rights violation to the Committee on the Rights of the

2 C Willow, 'United They Stand: Moving beyond the Participation–Protection Divide' (2021) Save the Children, Discussion Paper 10.

3 Save the Children, 'The Nine Basic Requirements for Meaningful and Ethical Children's Participation' (2021), 2, https://resourcecentre.savethechildren.net/library/nine-basic-requirements-meaningful-and-ethical-childrens-participation, accessed 22 February 2022.

4 C Feinstein and C O'Kane, 'Children's and Adolescent's Participation and Protection from Sexual Abuse and Exploitation', Innocenti Working Paper 2009–09, UNICEF Innocenti Research Centre, 5.

5 Optional Protocol to the Convention on the Rights of the Child on a Communications Procedure.

Child.[6] Complaints can only be brought forward, however, if the country (where the violation took place) has ratified the Protocol and if the national legal system was unable to remedy the violation. This provision of an appeal process is a vital example of the child's right to be heard being respected and fulfilled. For rights to have meaning, rights-holders must have access to mechanisms that protect their rights and address violations at all levels (nationally and internationally) and in all contexts (development and humanitarian).

Within the humanitarian sector, feedback mechanisms (either established by individual organisations or increasingly set up as inter-agency systems) are one of the most widespread processes by which crisis-affected people, including children, can express their views regarding the aid effort and one element of what is referred to as accountability to affected populations (AAP; see next section). As such, interrogating the extent to which these feedback mechanisms work for children and uphold the rights to participation as set out in the CRC is vital.

Some aid agencies may use the term 'complaints mechanism', and indeed the Core Humanitarian Standard refers to 'complaints.' However, Save the Children recognised that in many countries, the use of the word 'complaint' was deterring people from sharing feedback and suggestions. It can also be a barrier to people reporting safeguarding concerns, because sometimes it can make people think they need to find evidence to prove the concern is true before reporting it. Therefore, Save the Children is moving towards use of the term 'feedback' to cover all issues.[7]

This chapter will focus on exploring learning from Save the Children's experiences establishing child-friendly feedback mechanisms in humanitarian contexts before reflecting more broadly on child participation across the humanitarian programme cycle. We will conclude with reflections on child participation during the coronavirus pandemic and finally end with some key learning on how to promote children's participation in humanitarian response.

2. From beneficiaries to rights-holders?

In recent years, the aid sector has acknowledged that the tendency to treat people living in crisis-affected areas as 'beneficiaries' or mere 'recipients' of aid and not provide them with adequate opportunities to participate and influence the aid response undermines both the dignity and rights of those

6 States are also able to bring complaints against each other through an inter-state communications procedure. Article 12 (inter-state communications) only applies to states.

7 Save the Children also welcomes country offices engaging with the communities with whom they work to determine the most appropriate term to use – for example, in the Philippines, following consultations with children and adults, the term 'comment' was decided to be the most appropriate.

crisis-affected people and the effectiveness of the response itself. Over the past two decades, accountability to affected people (AAP) has become a well-recognised principle of humanitarian action. In 2007 the Humanitarian Accountability Partnership (HAP) established an inter-agency standard on humanitarian accountability and quality management.[8] The HAP standard was later incorporated into the Core Humanitarian Standard (CHS), launched in 2014, which sets out nine commitments that organisations and individuals involved in humanitarian response can use to improve the quality and effectiveness of the assistance they provide. Two of these commitments closely relate to the principle of participation: that '4. Communities and people affected by crisis know their rights and entitlements, have access to information, and participate in decisions that affect them' and that '5. Communities and people affected by crisis have access to safe and responsive mechanisms to handle complaints'.[9] In 2011, the Inter-Agency Standing Committee (the highest-level humanitarian coordination forum of the UN system) endorsed five commitments on AAP: 1. leadership; 2. transparency; 3. feedback and complaints; 4. participation; and 5. design, monitoring, and evaluation.[10] Following the 2016 World Humanitarian Summit, donors and aid agencies signed up to the Grand Bargain. Under one of the Grand Bargain workstreams, the Participation Revolution, donors and aid organisations committed to include people affected by humanitarian crises in decisions to ensure that humanitarian response is relevant, timely, effective, and efficient.[11]

The humanitarian sector therefore has a set of commitments that place communities and people affected by crisis at the centre of humanitarian action and acknowledge their right to participation; these standards or related principles have been accepted by most major aid providers. However, the connections between AAP and the rights of the child have not always been fully recognised. Many people working within the aid sector are not aware that children have legal rights to participation. Often AAP is conceptualised and applied in an age-blind manner, which in practice results in approaches and systems that are not appropriate for children and do not uphold children's rights to participation. Even within child-focused organisations, AAP is sometimes not widely understood as an approach that, at its core, seeks to uphold and promote the rights of children and adults. AAP is

8 Humanitarian Accountability Partnership, 'HAP Standards' (2008), https://reliefweb.int/report/world/guide-hap-standard-humanitarian-accountability-and-quality-management-0, accessed 26 August 2021.

9 Core Humanitarian Standard Alliance, 'Core Humanitarian Standard' (2015), https://corehumanitarianstandard.org/the-standard, accessed 26 August 2021.

10 Inter-Agency Standing Committee (IASC) website, https://interagencystandingcommittee.org/iasc-task-force-on-accountability-to-affected-people-closed, accessed 26 August 2021.

11 Grand Bargain website, https://interagencystandingcommittee.org/grand-bargain, accessed 26 August 2021.

instead considered primarily as a way of improving the effectiveness of aid or even merely a way of meeting donor requirements.

Furthermore, despite commitments within the humanitarian sector, meaningful participation of affected people (including children) has remained a challenge. Within the humanitarian sector, feedback mechanisms (either established by individual organisations or increasingly set up as inter-agency systems) are one of the most widespread processes established with the aim of enabling crisis-affected people, including children, to express their views regarding the aid effort – though feedback mechanisms alone should not be considered sufficient for fully realising children's participation rights within humanitarian responses. Other opportunities for advancing children's rights to participation across the humanitarian programme cycle are discussed later in the chapter. Within this chapter, *feedback mechanisms* are defined as

> the overall system that includes ways for children and adults to share feedback, concerns, and complaints (feedback channels), the systems and processes an organisation has for managing and analysing feedback, and the processes the organisation has for using feedback data to inform decisions and for closing the feedback loop (informing feedback providers of any actions taken as a result of feedback).

Feedback channels are defined as 'ways for children and adults to share questions, provide feedback, and report concerns they may have about an organisation's programmes and the behaviour of their staff and representatives, or that of other organisations'.[12] These definitions will be generally understood across the humanitarian sector, though occasionally feedback mechanisms are conceptualised by some as being limited to feedback channels alone (rather than the holistic system of receiving, managing, and responding to feedback).

In 2018, Ground Truth Solutions and the Organisation for Economic Co-operation and Development (OECD) conducted surveys with crisis-affected people in Afghanistan, Bangladesh, Iraq, Haiti, Lebanon, Uganda, and Somalia. While there was an increase from similar studies conducted in previous years, only 41% of respondents felt that aid providers took affected peoples' views into account when providing aid, and typically only just over half of respondents knew how to provide feedback to aid agencies.[13] It should be noted that those surveys conducted by Ground Truth Solutions

12 P Hill and E Severijnen, 'Creating an Inclusive and Accessible Feedback and Reporting Mechanism', Save the Children (2020), https://resourcecentre.savethechildren.net/library/save-children-feedback-and-reporting-mechanism-guidance, 6.

13 Ground Truth Solutions and OECD, 'The Grand Bargain: Perspectives from the Field' (2019), https://groundtruthsolutions.org/wp-content/uploads/2018/06/GTS-Grand-Bargain-briefing-note-June-2018.pdf, 21–22.

were not always disaggregated by age, and where they are, they show only adult respondents. It is thus to be assumed that only adults were asked to respond, despite the analysis speaking about the perspectives of crisis-affected people in general. While these studies do offer valuable insights into the opinions of affected adults, the failure to consult with children as part of this process is indicative of how children's perspectives are often overlooked in humanitarian action.

When it comes to child-friendly feedback mechanisms, it is likely that the challenges and lack of access are more significant. A 2015 inter-agency review of feedback mechanisms[14] found several common challenges: that existing agency-established (or national) mechanisms are often not accessible for children most impacted by discrimination and inequality, there is often low awareness among children of feedback mechanisms, children often do not feel comfortable accessing the existing mechanisms, there may be a lack of accessible and child-friendly information about what children can hold agencies to account for (for example, codes of conduct are not known or understood by children), and sometimes agencies lack capacity to respond in a timely manner to feedback received.[15] The following section reflects on learning from establishing and managing feedback mechanisms for children in humanitarian contexts.

3. Child-friendly feedback mechanisms in humanitarian crises: challenges and solutions

3.1. Establishing feedback mechanisms

A recurring challenge across the humanitarian sector when it comes to establishing feedback mechanisms to support the participation of crisis-affected children and adults is related to setting up mechanisms that are appropriate for the context and accessible to all. All too often, feedback mechanisms are established which do not consider technological, social, or other barriers that people may face in providing feedback. Furthermore, even when feedback mechanisms are established that are appropriate for adults, there is often limited consideration of what would work for children. However, aid agencies are increasingly understanding the importance of analysing context and considering inclusivity when designing feedback mechanisms.

14 The feedback channels reviewed by the study included telephone hotlines, direct telephone calls to staff, social media groups, feedback boxes, face-to-face communication with staff (including help desks, surveys, and group discussions), community representatives, monitoring and evaluation processes, and work with child and youth groups/committees.

15 A Wood, 'Interagency Study on Child-Friendly Feedback and Complaint Mechanisms within NGO Programmes' (2015), https://resourcecentre.savethechildren.net/library/interagency-study-child-friendly-feedback-and-complaint-mechanisms-within-ngo-programmes.

Since 2017, extreme violence in Myanmar has driven hundreds of thousands of Rohingya people across the border into Bangladesh. The refugees were settled in the Cox's Bazar district, most being housed within refugee camps. The Rohingya refugee response in Bangladesh is a very challenging context for feedback mechanisms. An assessment by Internews in October 2017 found that over 70% of both host and refugee population were illiterate. The Rohingya language, which is the primary language of communication for 96% of the refugee population, has no written script. Only 54% of refugee households had access to a mobile phone, and it was technically illegal for refugees to purchase a SIM card. Furthermore, several parts of the camps were not covered by any mobile phone network.[16] Save the Children's initial decision about what feedback channels to use in the response was not based on an adequate assessment of the context or the affected population's preferences. This led to several of the initial feedback channels being generally inappropriate: feedback boxes were not used, as most people could not write, and the telephone hotline was rarely used due to low access to phones, barriers to SIM purchase, and poor signal in camps. Feedback was collected through help desks and post-distribution monitoring, but that only captured feedback related to aid distributions and not feedback related to service provision. Other aid organisations similarly struggled to initially implement mechanisms that suited Rohingya refugees, in particular women and children.[17]

The Save the Children Bangladesh Rohingya Response team recognised that they needed to diversify their feedback channels and make them more appropriate for the context. The team added new feedback channels, including listening groups, voice recording options, exit interviews at health facilities, and capturing feedback that community mobilisers heard. These channels all built on Rohingya refugees' preferences for verbal and face-to-face communication. However, it was observed that children were not accessing these channels, and less than 1% of the total feedback received came from children. In response, the team designed and piloted child-friendly feedback discussions, using a combination of different child-friendly tools, including dot voting, risk mapping and a 'yes, no, maybe' activity. The pilot showed that proactively collecting and responding to feedback from children was relevant and effective. The sessions conducted with children brought out several issues that were not previously known – including child safeguarding concerns and other serious issues. Children also gave feedback that programme teams took on board to improve the quality of activities, which led to actions including refresher training for

16 Internews, 'Information Needs Assessment: Cox's Bazar – Bangladesh' (2017), https://internews.org/resource/information-needs-assessment-coxs-bazar-bangladesh, 10.

17 Christian Aid and Gana Unnayan Kendra, 'Accountability Assessment Rohingya Response Bangladesh' (2018), www.christianaid.org.uk/sites/default/files/2018-03/Response-Accountability-Assessment-Feb-2018.pdf, 4–6.

medical and teaching staff. A girl from one of the sessions said, 'We enjoyed sharing our opinions, and we liked the picture voting system. The facilitators encouraged us to talk, which made us feel good. We would like to do more of these sessions!' In this context, it was found that children were much more comfortable sharing things when they were proactively asked about them through an organised consultation process.

Similarly, in north-eastern Nigeria, an area that has been experiencing conflict since 2009, Save the Children thought they had set up a strong feedback mechanism, with a toll-free hotline and help desks. However, when they analysed the feedback they were receiving, they recognised a problem. For example, in the last quarter of 2018, over 1000 complaints and feedback were received. Ninety-nine percent of the feedback providers were adults, and only 1% were children. The Nigeria team realised that their feedback mechanism was not child friendly. The team decided to diversify their feedback channels and consult with children to hear directly from them about what feedback channels they would prefer to use. Through discussions with children, they learned that children wanted staff members to sit with them and discuss issues – this made them feel more dignified. The team established feedback sessions with the children using participatory activities. After starting these feedback sessions with children, the proportion of feedback received from children rose to 11% of total feedback. As a result of the Nigeria team's approach, children's voices have become more pronounced in the programme, and their feedback led to specific changes. For example, children complained about lack of water at child-friendly spaces and schools, which made management push for water and sanitation facilities in these places. Children also reported that they felt unsafe and did not attend some of the child-friendly spaces because of snakes in the playground. After this was reported, the team were able to respond and make the playground safe for children. These examples demonstrate the importance of analysing context and consulting with children to inform the design of feedback mechanisms.

Despite the emerging evidence within the sector that it is not possible to establish accessible and inclusive feedback mechanisms without the active involvement of crisis-affected people, we still sometimes see reluctance when it comes to involving children in those processes. One barrier to overcome when establishing or adapting feedback mechanisms is an assumption that children will not have adequate understanding to be able to assess what channels may be appropriate. However, it is clear from experience that when given the opportunity, children can assess for themselves what feedback channels would work well and what the potential barriers to accessing them may be.

In 2019 Cyclone Idai struck Mozambique, Malawi, and Zimbabwe. The cyclone caused widespread flooding and left devastation in its wake – homes, schools, and hospitals were ripped apart, whole communities were cut off, and agricultural land was completely submerged. Shortly after, Mozambique was hit by a second cyclone in the north of the country. During the establishment of their Mozambique emergency response, Save the Children ran consultations with children to better understand what feedback channels might be appropriate for them. In Manica province, Save the Children ran consultations with girls and boys between the ages of 6 and 14 years. Children discussed and voted on what feedback channels they felt would be most appropriate. The discussions yielded nuanced assessments of relative benefits and downsides of different channels. For example, group feedback discussions were a preferred option of many children. Children mentioned that sharing feedback via group discussions would allow children to collaboratively come up with ideas and solutions, and others felt that it was a transparent way of airing issues. However, children were aware that speaking in a group setting was not confidential and so had some concerns about sharing feedback about abuse as well as worries that they could be bullied by other children as a result of sharing feedback. They therefore also recommended that Save the Children establish opportunities to speak to staff face to face individually so that children could share feedback they would be less comfortable talking about in a group setting. Children remarked that sometimes they found it hard to talk to staff who only visited intermittently, as they were like strangers. To feel comfortable with the staff collecting feedback, children recommended that Save the Children set up help desks at child-friendly spaces (spaces established in emergency responses where children can take part in psychosocial support and recreational activities) and that the same staff would operate those help desks regularly so that children could grow to trust them. Children were also able to explain when a feedback channel would be less appropriate. For example, children liked the idea of feedback boxes (where written feedback can be deposited), as they are a confidential channel, but explained that many children in those communities could not read or write well enough to use them. Children also said that they would like to be able to give feedback via a telephone hotline, but most children did not have access to a phone. Children suggested that phones could be installed in child-friendly spaces. This suggestion is an example of the importance of ongoing dialogue – as it may not have been possible due to budgetary or other constraints to establish such a network of phones. Consulting with children to understand their preferences need not entail organisations always doing exactly what children request – but we have a duty to listen to their ideas seriously and explain to children when and why we may not be able to enact them all, in line with the CRC. By listening to children's preferences regarding feedback channels and considering them alongside assessments of the context and feasibility of various options, we can establish more accessible and inclusive feedback mechanisms. We can also identify important considerations regarding *how to manage* feedback mechanisms in a child-friendly way, not only what channels to use.

Beyond informing which feedback channels to use, supporting child participation in the process of establishing a feedback mechanism can have wider benefits in terms of acceptance and uptake. Since 2015, political and socio-economic developments in Venezuela have led to soaring inflation, unemployment, widespread food and medical shortages, and violence, devolving into a humanitarian crisis and triggering an outflow of Venezuelans into neighbouring countries such as Colombia and beyond. Save the Children Colombia began conducting humanitarian interventions in areas along the border with Venezuela in 2016. At the start of the response, there was a desire to set up a feedback mechanism. The response team organised consultations to ensure the communities felt involved; to learn what feedback channels would work best for children and adults; and to encourage communities to provide feedback, whether positive or negative. Following these consultations, four feedback channels were identified as appropriate for the context: a telephone hotline, email, feedback boxes, and feedback forms filled out either in person or online using a digital data collection tool (Kobo Toolbox). To help ensure that children were interested in using the feedback mechanism, Save the Children involved children in the design of the feedback boxes. Children submitted ideas and worked collaboratively with a designer to come up with a final design – a monster-shaped feedback box in both girl and boy variations and feedback forms shaped like cookies.

The team found that this design was entertaining and recognisable for children and that children were eager to 'feed' their feedback to the

Figure 2.1 A photo of a child placing written feedback into a monster-shaped feedback box in Colombia

monster. By involving children in the design and rollout phases of a feedback mechanism, their ownership of the mechanism may increase and thus their willingness to provide feedback. Furthermore, children's willingness to dedicate time and energy to the design process demonstrates that children value both the opportunity to provide feedback in general and a desire to co-develop such mechanisms.

3.2. Ensuring feedback informs action

Establishing inclusive child-friendly feedback mechanisms is only part of the challenge; perhaps the bigger challenge is ensuring that feedback and other forms of participation inform action. While across the humanitarian sector it has been much more common for aid organisations to have feedback mechanisms, the 2019 Grand Bargain Annual Independent Report found a 'lack of progress on ensuring that feedback from affected populations is integrated into the design, delivery and review of programmes'.[18] Article 12 of the CRC requires actors to give due weight to children's views – however, in practice, children's views are often disregarded by aid actors. This may not be a result of any specific intent to disregard children's views – one finding from a learning event convened by the International Rescue Committee was that feedback information in general is often 'crowded out' from decision-making processes because it is competing with other, higher prioritised information such as expenditure, procurement, output, and activity-monitoring data.[19] Feedback sometimes comes in forms that are hard to quantify and thus requires greater effort to analyse and consider its implications. At other times, feedback analysis may not be easily visible to decision-makers within an organisation, or there may be limited incentives to respond to feedback. When this is the case, changes to internal systems may support improved use of feedback data, as Save the Children found in Nigeria and Afghanistan. In Nigeria, separate project-level feedback databases were scrapped in favour of a cloud-based database that covered all of Save the Children's activities in the country; this database, with different levels of access to ensure confidentiality, enabled decision-makers to view feedback analysis with ease and take appropriate action. Changes to feedback management systems may also tackle incentives for staff to act upon feedback. In Afghanistan, the team was struggling with how to systematically track feedback from communities and how to engage programme teams to close the feedback loop in a timely manner. They decided to develop a dashboard that visualised the status of feedback cases across different projects.

18 V Metcalfe-Hough et al., Grand Bargain Annual Independent Report 2019. (2019) HPG/ODI, London, 45

19 International Rescue Committee, 'Client Voice and Choice Learning Exchange Event Report' (2016), www.rescue.org/report/client-voice-and-choice-learning-exchange, 3.

They found that following this, project teams started resolving feedback more quickly, perhaps to get their projects off the dashboard.

A further challenge is ensuring that feedback not only informs immediate reactions to specific challenges (for example, adding a child to a school enrolment list when they had been wrongly left off) but also is used to inform adaptation at strategic and policy levels. A study by CDA of World Vision and national partners' feedback mechanisms in Ethiopia, India, Pakistan, Somaliland, Tanzania, and Zimbabwe found that most feedback loops were closed at the field or project level, with few individual pieces of feedback referred upwards for decisions.[20] While local-level decisions can enable timely response to feedback, the fact that feedback was never analysed at a higher level limits the opportunity for it to be used for learning and strategic decision-making.

There is also a risk that if staff think that feedback cannot be responded to, it may never get reported to those who are better able to influence strategic and policy decisions. For example, in the early days of the Rohingya refugee crisis, feedback from children and adults requesting access to formal education could not be addressed directly by Save the Children, as the government of Bangladesh did not allow for such education to be provided at that time. In this situation, there could be a temptation to just disregard the feedback. However, logging such feedback could be useful for informing advocacy, as it would help demonstrate the level of demand for formal education from refugees and potentially be used to contribute to further advocacy for wider access to education.

Barriers to children's feedback informing decision-making processes may be greater than those of adults, due to common perceptions and negative attitudes towards children, their rights, and their capabilities within many societies. These social conditions may push adults to disregard the opinions of children.[21] In addition, greater effort may be required to interpret the feedback of children, especially younger children. These challenges cannot be easily overcome by a change in database or establishment of a dashboard; they require ongoing investment in instilling an understanding of children as rights-holders and active citizens with valuable opinions, as well

20 World Vision and CDA, 'Using Beneficiary Feedback to Improve Development Programmes: Findings from a Multi-Country Pilot' (2016), http://feedbackmechanisms.org/findings/, 9.

21 See J Moran-Ellis and EKM Tisdall, 'The Relevance of "Competence" for Enhancing or Limiting Children's Participation: Unpicking Conceptual Confusion' (2019) *Global Studies of Childhood* for a discussion of how different conceptualisations of competence might help or hinder children's participation in decision-making processes (not specific to the humanitarian sector). Of particular interest is a conclusion, based on analysis of many studies, that 'Children risk being judged as competent [to participate] only when they are compliant and their views accord with adults (professionals or researchers), leaving little room for children to act or think in ways contrary to what is expected', and that, 'Only very rarely is adults' competence called into question in the articles'.

as ensuring that adequate time and human resources are dedicated to collecting and analysing children's feedback.

Besides the rights-based imperative to listen to children and take their opinions into consideration, listening to and responding to all feedback from children, however minor it may seem, can help keep children safe. Children may test whether they can trust adults or organisations by sharing what could be seen as minor feedback (for example, expressing dissatisfaction with education materials) prior to deciding whether to disclose a more serious issue (such as physical or sexual abuse). Children who have had negative experiences of providing feedback in the past and it not being taken seriously or it being treated in a manner that was not confidential may be less likely to report serious concerns. Children may also express serious issues as partial disclosures initially (for example, saying that they do not like a certain member of staff); if these seemingly unsubstantiated or minor issues are dismissed, children may feel unable to disclose the full extent of abuse they may have experienced.[22] Thus the process of listening to children regardless of the subject or seriousness of their feedback, taking appropriate action, and letting children know what happened as a result of their feedback are essential for building trust between children and aid agencies that can help keep children safe. This therefore emphasises the importance of what is called 'closing the feedback loop.'

3.3. Closing the feedback loop

In Save the Children, we define 'closing the feedback loop' as informing children and adults of how their feedback has influenced Save the Children's work; what actions or changes have been made as a result of their feedback; and, in some cases, the reasons Save the Children has not been able to act on their feedback. Children and adults who share feedback with aid organisations or other duty bearers have a right to know how the information they have shared has been used and what effect it has had. Closing the feedback loop is a key aspect of a quality feedback mechanism, as it enables children and other feedback providers to understand how their views have contributed to change. Properly closing the feedback loop supports the promotion of the dignity and agency of the children and adults we serve. It demonstrates that we have listened to the person's opinion and respected it enough to consider how to respond, and it shows affected people that they can influence our work. Closing the feedback loop also has a positive impact on other programmatic activities, as it builds trust and encourages acceptance within the communities we serve.

22 NSPCC, 'Recognising and Responding to Abuse', https://learning.nspcc.org.uk/child-abuse-and-neglect/recognising-and-responding-to-abuse, accessed 26 February 2021.

Not closing the feedback loop can have negative consequences. People who provide feedback may feel that feedback mechanisms do not work or that the organisation does not take feedback seriously. This can harm relationships between the organisation and communities by undermining trust. If people do not see change after providing feedback nor understand how feedback is used, they are likely to become less willing to share feedback in the future. As mentioned previously, this may also lead to children and adults being less willing to disclose incidents of abuse. In addition, children's experiences with participation, including feedback mechanisms, may also help or hinder their recovery after experiencing traumatic events or abuse. The process of being heard and respected after negative experiences can help support the child's self-confidence, esteem, and resilience, as well as building their trust in society's protective mechanisms. Conversely, failing to listen and respect a child can further disempower and victimise them. Fundamentally, not closing the feedback loop also reduces the extent to which feedback mechanisms can be considered a means of promoting participation.

It should be noted, however, that aside from potential reputational risk (which could hinder future funding opportunities), there are limited systems within the humanitarian sector that can compel agencies to close the feedback loop. In some responses, common feedback platforms exist to which a person could theoretically elevate their feedback should they feel that an individual agency had failed to respond to it adequately. However, these platforms do not include means to compel aid agencies to act (aside from the risk of being named and shamed). Since the late 1990s there have been discussions about creating a humanitarian ombudsman to investigate complaints, but to date these have not come to fruition.[23]

There may be times when aid agencies or other duty bearers are unable to resolve all feedback they receive; for example, a request for assistance may be outside an organisation's remit. However, sharing information with the person who provided feedback, referring them to other services, or providing an explanation that we are unable to provide that type of assistance and why in a timely manner is important. This demonstrates that we have listened to the person's feedback. A study led by CDA focusing on World Vision projects in Ethiopia found that response to feedback was the cornerstone of trust between community members and World Vision. A community member from the Amhara region was quoted as saying, 'They hear us. They listen to us. They do all that they can and tell us what they can't do. And they give us respect'.[24] Reflections on the wider CDA and World Vision study found that where feedback loops were closed, people

23 I Christoplos and J Mitchell, 'A Humanitarian Ombudsman Revisited?' (2018) ALNAP, www.alnap.org/blogs/a-humanitarian-ombudsman-revisited, accessed 14 November 2021.

24 S Cechvala and I Jean, 'Feedback Loops Case Study' (2016) CDA Collaborative Learning Projects and World Vision Ethiopia, 24.

in targeted communities valued the feedback mechanisms, regardless of whether their specific concerns could be acted upon (World Vision and CDA, 2016, p. 8). Likewise, in 2016 children affected by Cyclone Roanu in Sri Lanka gave governments and others extensive advice about future emergency assistance. Within these recommendations, the children said that, 'Even [if] you can't give us any donations, we urge you to speak to us respectfully and kindly'.[25] This shows that, like adults, children place value on respectful and open communication, even if it is not accompanied by provision of requested assistance.

3.4. Monitoring and continual improvement

A final important reflection from Save the Children's experience of strengthening child-friendly feedback mechanisms is that it is vital to continually monitor feedback mechanisms to understand whether they are effective, inclusive, and accessible. A lack of feedback from children could be a result of many issues. For example, in some contexts it may be that (as discussed before) feedback channels may work for adults but not be accessible for children. It may be that awareness of the feedback mechanism has not been raised among children and children are unaware that they are welcome to provide feedback. It may be that children are unaware of the standards of behaviour or quality they should expect from aid providers and so do not know what they might complain about. Or it may be that children fear retribution, either from aid providers or from community members, if they provide feedback. At times, especially if they have not been listened to in the past, children simply may not trust aid organisations' promises to listen to feedback and thus see engaging with feedback mechanisms as a waste of time. Therefore, it is vital to never assume that a lack of feedback from children means that everything is going well; it is instead essential that aid organisations monitor feedback mechanisms to ensure they are operating well.

Following an earthquake and tsunami in Central Sulawesi, Indonesia, in 2018, Save the Children's national partner Yayasan Sayangi Tunas Cilik (YSTC) launched a humanitarian response. The team consulted with children and adults and engaged with the inter-agency Communicating with Communities working group to inform the design of their feedback mechanism. They created a diversified set of feedback channels, including children's feedback consultations, a hotline, feedback boxes, post-distribution monitoring, speaking directly to YSTC staff, community meetings, speaking to community leaders, SMS, and WhatsApp. Despite setting up a strong mechanism, the team recognised it was important to monitor how satisfied

25 M Scharenguivel and B Withana, 'Our Voices Matter. The Views of Children on Emergency Preparedness and Response in Sri Lanka' (2017) Save the Children International Sri Lanka Country Office, https://reliefweb.int/report/sri-lanka/our-voices-matter-views-children-emergency-preparedness-and-response-sri-lanka, 27.

people were with the feedback mechanism. After six months, the team identified an opportune moment to review the mechanism through consultation with girls, boys, women, and men and see what could be improved.

The monitoring process found that often people were not aware of all the feedback channels open to them or that children were welcome to provide feedback. The team also learned that speaking directly to YSTC would be a preferred way of providing feedback for both children and adults. Children shared that they would like opportunities to speak one to one with YSTC staff to share feedback they want to be kept confidential. They said they sometimes felt too shy to share their feelings during children's feedback consultations. As only 8% of feedback in YSTC's database came from people speaking to staff face to face, the team decided they needed to improve their efforts to capture feedback received through that channel. There were also some surprising findings. For example, some participants were worried they might get sent to jail or be accused of defamation if they gave negative feedback to YSTC. The team committed to continue and intensify messaging that there would be no negative consequences of providing feedback to YSTC. It would have been easy for YSTC not to have monitored their feedback mechanism – at a glance, it was successful, with girls, boys, women, and men all providing feedback. However, through taking time to check with children and adults about their feelings towards the feedback mechanism, the team was able to make it more effective and respond to misconceptions.

4. Child participation across the humanitarian programme cycle

While most of this chapter has focused on learning related to feedback mechanisms, we wish to highlight that feedback mechanisms are not the only ways to advance children's right to participation within humanitarian responses, nor should they be considered sufficient by themselves. Children should be supported to participate in multiple forms across all phases of a humanitarian response – whether that is through working with and influencing aid agencies or by leading efforts in their own right. The Inter-Agency Standing Committee (IASC) Guidelines on Working with and for Young People in Humanitarian and Protracted Crises use the framework of the humanitarian programme cycle (HPC) to identify opportunities for children and young people to participate across a response.[26] The HPC contains five key phases (1. needs assessment and analysis, 2. strategic planning, 3. resource mobilisation, 4. implementation and monitoring, and 5.

26 Inter-Agency Standing Committee, 'IASC Guidelines on Working with and for Young People in Humanitarian and Protracted Crises' (2020), https://interagencystandingcommittee.org/events/iasc-guidelines-working-and-young-people-humanitarian-and-protracted-crises, 68.

operational peer review and evaluation). In the following section, we will reflect briefly on examples of how children's participation could be promoted across the HPC.

4.1. Assessment and analysis

In order to understand how children have been affected by a crisis, it is vital that they be considered within needs assessment and analysis processes. This includes those processes that may not involve direct participation of children (such as ensuring that child-focused analysis of secondary data is undertaken), but importantly there must also be opportunities for children to be meaningfully engaged as both respondents and partners in the assessment and analysis process.[27] In general, current needs assessment processes across the humanitarian sector do not ensure the systematic consultation of children. While at times understandable given how needs assessments may take place in the very early days of a response when there is limited time and there may be few staff with skills in child participation within the response team, this commonly results in the outputs of such needs assessments failing to include the unique perspectives and experiences of children. This not only means that needs and issues specific to children can often fail to be given the weight they deserve but also that valuable contributions to the overall relief effort from the perspective of children are ignored. Failure to listen to children's perspectives and opinions about the response to the crisis not only ignores children's own agency and ability to participate in decision-making processes that affect their lives but can be further defined as no less than a rights violation.

Recognising this, several child-focused aid agencies (most commonly Save the Children, Plan, and World Vision) have joined forces during many of the large-scale humanitarian crises since 2013 to consult with children to understand how they have been affected and what they recommend. These children's consultations have taken place after Typhoon Haiyan in the Philippines, during the Ebola epidemic in Sierra Leone, following the 2015 Nepal earthquakes, in Bangladesh with Rohingya refugees, and following the Central Sulawesi earthquake and tsunami in Indonesia.[28] These consultations have allowed aid agencies to understand children's perspectives and gather information to inform both humanitarian programming and advocacy. While generally limited to consultative participation, children have been able to be more closely involved in some of the consultations: in Sierra Leone, young facilitators were drawn from children's clubs to support with the design of data collection tools and the facilitation of consultations, and

27 Ibid.

28 Consultation reports available at: https://resourcecentre.savethechildren.net/document-collections/inter-agency-childrens-consultations-emergencies.

in Nepal and Indonesia, children used the findings of the consultations to engage in advocacy with local government and other decision-makers. Further effort is required to ensure that such consultations happen in all crises.

4.2. Strategic planning and resource mobilisation

With regard to the next phases of the HPC, strategic planning and resource mobilisation, it is less common to see children's participation in the phases themselves, but effort should be undertaken to ensure that strategic plans build in opportunities for participation into later phases of the response and take into account feedback and learning from past participatory processes (for example, using recommendations already collected from children through feedback mechanisms, monitoring, or previous consultations). In the initial phases of rapid onset crises, it may be challenging to enable children's participation during strategic planning due to the rapid pace of action (often with deadlines of less than 24 hours) and potentially the lack of measures needed to ensure meaningful and safe child participation. However, in later phases of crises or in protracted emergencies, there should be no excuse for not supporting child participation in strategic planning. For example, in the occupied Palestinian territories, Save the Children invited children to participate in strategic development and planning for a multi-year project; this involved consultative sessions with children, involvement in meetings with the senior management team, and working with children on project design ideas.

With regard to resource mobilisation, a primary objective should be ensuring that there are sufficient resources to support meaningful child participation throughout the remainder of the response. This could include training in child participation for staff, supporting children to act as peer educators, or sub-grants directly to child-led organisations to support children's own self-directed initiatives.[29]

4.3. Implementation and monitoring

The implementation and monitoring phase of a response offers significant opportunities for meaningful participation. Children's perspectives are hugely valuable as services are established or adapted. For example, in response to a recognition that sanitation services set up in crises are often not appropriate for the needs or preferences of children, Save the Children worked with a user-centred design agency to develop an approach

29 Inter-Agency Standing Committee, 'IASC Guidelines on Working with and for Young People in Humanitarian and Protracted Crises' (2020), https://interagencystandingcommittee.org/events/iasc-guidelines-working-and-young-people-humanitarian-and-protracted-crises, 79.

for supporting child participation in latrine design.[30] This approach combined interactive digital surveys and co-creation sessions to explore children's preferences for latrines, uncover root causes of problems related to sanitation, and collaboratively arrive at a list of ideas for how to best address them. The initial two pilots within Rohingya refugee camps in Bangladesh and internally displaced persons' camps in Iraq both demonstrated good consultation and identification of the varied challenges girls and boys faced. However, the final outcomes were influenced by the willingness and ability of the organisation to act on children and their caregivers' suggestions and explain their decisions. In Bangladesh, an external evaluation found there was strong follow-through on the children's and caregivers' solutions, which contributed to high satisfaction with the new latrines and increased latrine usage; additionally, participants expressed pride that they had been able to contribute to improvements in sanitation for their community. Conversely, in Iraq, there was much weaker follow-through on the children's and caregivers' solutions, which led to lower satisfaction and frustration from some affected people with the process.[31] Learning from the shortcomings and strengths of the initial pilots has gone on to inform further application of the approach in Ethiopia with Save the Children and in Peru with Plan.

Another approach used by Save the Children to support child participation in the implementation of services is called *Improving Learning Environments Together in Emergencies*.[32] This approach was developed after recognising that while children may be consulted during learning environment assessments in emergencies, it was rare for assessment findings to be shared directly with children and for children to be involved in the development of school improvement plans. The approach thus sought to embed child participation within three stages of design and implementation: assessment, findings feedback, and school improvement plan development. The approach, implemented in humanitarian contexts including Syria and northern Uganda, has supported improvements in learning environments based on the expressed needs and creative solutions of students themselves.

While aid actors (and indeed this chapter) often focus on actions facilitated by humanitarian agencies, children often engage in child-led action in crises and may independently implement their own solutions to the challenges their communities face. For example, in late November 2010, Côte

30 Eclipse Experience and Save the Children, 'User-Centred Community Engagement' (2018), www.eclipse-experience.com/user-centred-community-engagement/case-studies, accessed 3 August 2021.

31 P Sandison, 'We're Listening: An Evaluation of User-Centred Community Engagement in Emergency Sanitation' (2019) Oxfam, https://policy-practice.oxfam.org/resources/were-listening-an-evaluation-of-user-centred-community-engagement-in-emergency-620617/.

32 Save the Children, 'Improving Learning Environments Together in Emergencies' (2018), https://resourcecentre.savethechildren.net/library/improving-learning-environments-together-emergencies-ilet-package.

d'Ivoire plunged into a political-military crisis during the political election process. The National Coordination of the Working Children and Youth Associations of Côte d'Ivoire (which is part of a wider African movement of working children and youth) started their actions before the violence and the socio-economic and political situation escalated. These actions included using radio to share messages of peace and tolerance and organising leisure activities aimed at forming positive bonds across potential societal divisions. The working children and youth associations also carried out humanitarian and solidarity actions. During the response phase, this included identifying and housing displaced children and youth and organising sports and leisure activities to support children's psychosocial wellbeing.[33] Child-led actions around the world often focus on disaster risk reduction, readiness, and prevention. However, their efforts during emergencies have included providing first aid, teaching younger children, family tracing, food distribution, and more.[34] Child-led actions will often be more responsive, start more rapidly, and be more adaptable than efforts of larger humanitarian agencies. It is essential that adult-led agencies seek to support and strengthen the efforts of child led initiatives through partnerships, funding, and capacity strengthening and bridging.

With regard to participation in monitoring, feedback mechanisms, as discussed previously, are one of the most common opportunities for child participation. However, children may be involved in monitoring responses in other ways. For example, in Lebanon, Jordan, Syria, and Palestine, UNICEF has worked in partnership with NGOs and young people to involve adolescent girls and boys in monitoring their programme. Adolescents use online tools to input data on programme coverage, programme quality, experiential learning, and behaviour change to reflect whether implementation has been going to plan. This then enables UNICEF and its partners to adapt and improve programmes, as well as tracking long-term progress.[35]

4.4. Operational peer review and evaluation

It is vital that children's perspectives be considered during the evaluation and review of humanitarian interventions. Without hearing directly from children about their experiences of receiving and being engaged in humanitarian aid, we cannot truly understand its effectiveness and appropriateness,

33 C O'Kane, 'Review of Children's Participation in Humanitarian Programming' (2013) Save the Children, 23, https://resourcecentre.savethechildren.net/library/review-childrens-participation-humanitarian-programming.

34 A West, 'The Participation of Children and Young People in Emergencies' (2007) UNICEF, 35.

35 Inter-Agency Standing Committee, 'IASC Guidelines on Working with and for Young People in Humanitarian and Protracted Crises' (2020), https://interagencystandingcommittee.org/events/iasc-guidelines-working-and-young-people-humanitarian-and-protracted-crises, 83.

nor learn for future crises. However, children's perspectives are not always adequately considered within evaluatory processes.

In Save the Children, Real Time Reviews (RTRs) are conducted within all large-scale emergency responses. RTRs are internal evaluations which aim to provide feedback at the early stage of an emergency response, to help support course correction with the goal of being adaptable and changing activities and whole areas of focus if that is what is in the best interests of affected children and their communities. Prior to 2015, most RTRs involved very limited child participation – at best, there would be a small number of focus group discussions not tailored to be child friendly or genuinely participatory. Some RTRs did not speak to any children at all. Children's consultations were not recognised as a key source of data to triangulate findings from other sources, nor was it recognised that we can only truly understand the effects and impact of our work by talking to children. The problem was thus twofold: children were not being given the opportunity to tell us what was going well and what wasn't, and response decision-makers were missing out on vital information that would have enabled them to course correct and improve the response. During the 2015 Nepal earthquake response, the team made the decision to commission a set of community consultations to inform the RTR – including numerous consultations with children. Based on learning from that experience, simple tools and guidance were developed to support consultations with children within RTRs, and from 2016 it became mandatory that all RTRs include consultations with children.

As well as ensuring children's perspectives inform reviews of the whole response, children should also be supported to participate in evaluations of humanitarian projects. For example, in 2015 InsightShare worked with a team of young people in Côte d'Ivoire to conduct a participatory evaluation of two interventions intended to respond to the repeated socio-political crises that have affected the country: peace clubs established by Search for Common Ground and a citizenship and communication project supported by the International Centre for Transitional Justice. During the evaluation, the young people used video production and story circles to listen to their peers and then used the most significant change method to analyse how and why any changes had taken place. After analysing the barriers to and enablers of positive change, the young people created a final video report to share the results; this was screened for key decision-makers in government, NGOs, and the United Nations.[36] Such an approach helps us better understand the effects of a programme from the perspective of those it is intended to support, as well as helping children and young people to develop new skills.

36 R Herrington, 'Emerging Practices in Design, Monitoring, and Evaluation for Education for Peacebuilding Programming: Practice Guide', *Search for Common Ground*, Washington, D.C., 51 (2015), www.sfcg.org/wp-content/ uploads/2016/06/Emerging-PracticeGuide.pdf, accessed 19 September 2021.

As with feedback mechanisms, it is critical that the learning from evaluations be used to inform action. In this manner, children's participation in the evaluation phase can not only help us understand the extent to which completed humanitarian projects were appropriate and effective but also inform the development and delivery of higher-quality humanitarian aid for children in the future.

4.5. Building on existing foundations for participation

Despite a common tendency within the humanitarian sector to disregard systems, structures, or information from before the start of a crisis, the foundations that have been laid before a crisis emerges can be one of the greatest enablers of child participation during humanitarian response. If children's networks exist, and in particular if those groups have experience of working with aid agencies, it becomes much easier to support child participation early in a response and across the whole HPC. If government policies, legislation, and budgets support children's participation rights and children have been supported to establish sustainable networks and initiatives prior to an emergency, children will be better prepared to meaningfully participate in the response – either working independently or alongside humanitarian agencies. For example, in southern India, a local NGO (the Voluntary Health Association of Kanyakumari) supported children to develop children's neighbourhood parliaments to strengthen their role in community action. During the Asian tsunami in 2004, these neighbourhood parliaments worked as forums to provide relief, to provide additional nutrition support and psychosocial care to children, to encourage children to take charge of children's rights, and to inform the development of community-based child protection mechanisms.[37]

In crisis-prone contexts, children might be supported to participate in disaster risk reduction and emergency preparedness processes, thus directly helping to lay the foundations for child participation in humanitarian response. However, any process or structure that meaningfully supports children's participation rights will help to foster the understanding among children and the wider society that children's perspectives matter and that children are active citizens who can contribute to solving problems in their communities. This acknowledgement of children's capacities by children themselves as well as their communities, combined with the support of aid agencies for participation, will enhance the potential for meaningful child participation across the HPC.

37 C O'Kane, 'Review of Children's Participation in Humanitarian Programming', Save the Children, 20 (2013), https://resourcecentre.savethechildren.net/library/review-childrens-participation-humanitarian-programming.

This last section has sought to offer a snapshot of opportunities to incorporate children's participation within the work of humanitarian aid agencies across the HPC. We wish to close with some reflections on child participation during the furthest-reaching crisis in recent history – the COVID-19 pandemic – including an important reminder that while we have focused on how aid agencies can promote child participation within their work, children may independently take action within humanitarian crises.

5. Closing reflections – child participation in the Covid-19 pandemic

In 2020 as COVID-19 spread across the world, aid organisations faced many dilemmas – both around how to respond to the disease itself and how to maintain existing programming without putting lives at risk. As countries went into lockdown, the opportunities for face-to-face engagement between aid organisations and crisis-affected children became more and more limited. Many feedback channels had to be put on hold – for example, feedback boxes closed due to fears of transmission of coronavirus, and feedback discussions stopped as it was no longer possible for staff to visit communities or to gather groups of people together. Furthermore, sometimes concerns about ensuring children's safety led to doubts and procrastination – even opposition to child participation. However, actions by children themselves as well as by aid organisations ensured that participation continued, though often in different forms to usual.

COVID-19 changed children's lives dramatically – children's spaces of playing, learning, and participation rapidly shut down across much of the globe. In this context, it was vital to listen to children's perspectives and hear their solutions to the challenges that they and their communities were facing. Recognition of this contributed to initiatives such as *#covidunder19*, where Terre des Hommes, in collaboration with the UN and around 30 organisations, surveyed over 26,000 children across 137 countries to understand children's experiences of the pandemic.[38] The pandemic also brought with it what the World Health Organisation termed an 'info-demic' – an over-abundance of information, including accidental misinformation as well as deliberate attempts to disseminate wrong information to undermine the public health response and advance alternative agendas of groups or individuals.[39] In this context, children's right to information was at risk.

38 Terres des Hommes, '#covidunder19 Initiative' (no date), www.tdh.ch/en/projects/covidunder19, accessed 18 September 2021.

39 World Health Organisation, 'Managing the COVID-19 Infodemic: Promoting Healthy Behaviours and Mitigating the Harm from Misinformation and Disinformation' (2020), www.who.int/news/item/23-09-2020-managing-the-covid-19-infodemic-promoting-healthy-behaviours-and-mitigating-the-harm-from-misinformation-and-disinformation, accessed 2 September 2021.

Across the world, children jumped into action to promote accurate and child-friendly information. For example, in March 2020 in the very early days of the pandemic (before many large adult-led organisations had taken much action), children in Togo who were part of the child-led network 'Movement of African Working Children and Youth' (Mouvement Africain des Enfants et Jeunes Travailleur) produced a video that used the idea of football/soccer red cards to call out behaviours that could spread coronavirus.[40] In Mali, members of the National Children's Parliament and members of the National Advisory Council of Children and Youth of Mali developed a television awareness-raising spot on coronavirus, which was broadcast on national television.[41] In Nicaragua, members of a children's movement produced a radio segment on how to prevent COVID-19 transmission. In Cambodia, children produced short videos about handwashing and other prevention measures, which they shared across social media networks and within their local child and youth network. In Sudan, the Sudanese National Society for Deaf and Save the Children supported children with disabilities to design, perform, photograph, and edit a video that used sign language to raise awareness of COVID-19 among groups who might otherwise struggle to access information. The video was shared on national and international media outlets, including Al Jazeera TV.[42] These are just five examples of how children around the world, sometimes supported by adult-led organisations but also sometimes in an entirely child-led manner, played an active role in counteracting misinformation on coronavirus.

However, many of the approaches that supported continued child participation during the coronavirus pandemic – at least at the national, regional, or global level – relied on children having access to technology. On the one hand, COVID-19 pushed aid organisations to recognise the power of technology and social media for engaging with children and promoting their participation, including in countries affected by crisis. On the other, the increased reliance on technology reinforced and exacerbated the exclusion from spaces of participation that children most affected by inequality and discrimination face. This thus sets out a challenge to aid organisations – that we must capitalise on technology where appropriate to support the participation of children in crisis-affected countries, but we must always consider how to ensure that all children have access to those participatory processes. For example, in Colombia, to help children without access to the internet still be able to participate, access information, and provide

40 MAEJT, 'le MAEJT contribue à la sensibilisation contre le COVID19' (2020), www.youtube.com/watch?v=Gwq_XV1fTl8, accessed 28 August 2021.

41 Conseil Consultatif National des enfants et Jeunes du Mali, 'Un message de sensibilisation sur les gestes barrières contre le coronavirus' (2020), www.facebook.com/ccnejmali/videos/319810622319878/ accessed 26 August 2021.

42 Sudanese National Society for Deaf and Save the Children, 'Coronavirus Awareness Raising Video' (2020).

feedback, Save the Children set up a 'post person' system. With safety measures in place, a staff member gave children information and an envelope so that they could share their feedback; this feedback was then collected and analysed to inform action. Children's rights to participation must never become rights that can only be realised by children from affluent or privileged backgrounds, and thus aid organisations must seek to ensure that considerations of inclusivity and accessibility are at the forefront when designing any participatory process.

6. Conclusion

For rights to have meaning, rights-holders must have access to mechanisms that protect their rights and address violations at all levels. This is reflected at the global level through mechanisms such as the CRC's 3rd Optional Protocol. Measures need to be taken to institutionalise accountability mechanisms across all contexts, including humanitarian action. However, the CRC's 3rd Optional Protocol has limited precedent to date – being ratified by fewer than 50 countries,[43] with children only being able to use it if all national options have been exhausted, and the first oral hearings having only occurred in 2021[44] – and there is no humanitarian ombudsman. Therefore, the current most practicable opportunities for advancing children's ability to hold humanitarian responders and aid agencies to account for fulfilling their rights lie in strengthening the single and inter-agency systems for child participation within humanitarian responses and supporting child participation within societies pre-crisis through policies, systems, legislation, and budgets at all levels.

From our experiences supporting child participation throughout the Humanitarian Program Cycle and establishing and managing child-friendly feedback mechanisms in humanitarian contexts, we wish to highlight some key learning.

- Work with staff and volunteers at all levels of humanitarian aid organisations to ensure that they understand the importance of children's participation rights and have the skills required to support quality processes.
- Evidence demonstrates that children's participation can most easily be supported early in the humanitarian programme cycle when there are

43 As of 17 November 2021, 48 countries have ratified the Optional Protocol to the Convention on the Rights of the Child on a communications procedure; see for up-to-date figures, https://treaties.un.org/Pages/ViewDetails.aspx?src=TREATY&mtdsg_no=IV-11-d&chapter=4.

44 Child Rights Connect, 'Historic Ruling by the UN Committee on the Rights of the Child in the Climate Change Case Brought by 16 Child Petitioners under the OPIC' (2021), https://opic.childrightsconnect.org/historic-ruling-by-the-un-committee-on-the-rights-of-the-child-in-the-climate-change-case-brought-by-16-child-petitioners-under-the-opic-2/ accessed 17 November 2021.

existing children's networks and initiatives that have been established pre-emergency. We must therefore encourage development or multi-mandate organisations and governments to promote policies, systems, legislation, and budgets at all levels that support child participation before a crisis strikes.

- Support child participation in the design and establishment of feedback mechanisms. Children can analyse their context and understand what options might work for them and their peers. They will be able to analyse risks associated with different feedback channels and provide suggestions about how they can best be managed.
- Consider how feedback will be managed, analysed, and presented to inform action before the collection of feedback begins. Understand and respond to what incentives support, or limit, children's feedback being used to inform decision-making.
- Treat children with respect and ensure that they receive a response to their feedback – even if that response is explaining why it is not possible to implement their suggestions. This not only affords children the respect they deserve but also builds trust in the feedback mechanism and organisation.
- Monitor the feedback mechanism to ensure that it is effective, inclusive, and accessible. Do not assume that because you have received feedback that the mechanism is working for every girl and boy.
- Ensure that any participatory process supports the participation of children most impacted by inequality and discrimination – paying particular attention to how increasing technology use may enable but also hinder the participation of some children.
- Challenge negative attitudes and address the perceptions that many adults still have regarding children and their rights in general. This includes the perceptions of adults within crisis-affected communities but also the perceptions of staff working within the humanitarian system.
- Apply internationally recognised standards for quality child participation in any initiative with children. The UN Committee's Nine Basic Requirements for Meaningful and Ethical Child Participation provides us with a roadmap to quality, inclusive, and safe participation.[45]

More broadly, we suggest that not only is it the responsibility of aid organisations to promote child participation across their work throughout the whole humanitarian programme cycle – it is also the responsibility of aid organisations to seek out, support, and promote child-led action in

45 Save the Children, 'The Nine Basic Requirements for Meaningful and Ethical Children's Participation' (2021), 2, https://resourcecentre.savethechildren.net/library/nine-basic-requirements-meaningful-and-ethical-childrens-participation, accessed 22 February 2022.

humanitarian crises. Children are not merely beneficiaries of humanitarian aid – they are rights-holders and active citizens who play a key role in ensuring that humanitarian aid is effective and appropriate for people of all ages, genders and identities.

7. List of references

Literature

Cechvala, S and Jean, I, 'Feedback Loops Case Study' (2016). CDA Collaborative Learning Projects and World Vision Ethiopia, 24.

Feinstein, C and O'Kane, C, 'Children's and Adolescent's Participation and Protection from Sexual Abuse and Exploitation' (2009). Innocenti Working Paper 2009-09, UNICEF Innocenti Research Centre.

Finnegan, L, 'After Yolanda: What Children Think, Need and Recommend' (2013). Save the Children, World Vision, UNICEF, and Plan International.

McDonald, A, 'Invisible Wounds: The Impact of Six Years of War on the Mental Health of Syria's Children' (2017). Save the Children.

Metcalfe-Hough, V, et al., Grand Bargain Annual Independent Report 2019 (2019). HPG/ODI, London.

Moran-Ellis, J and Tisdall, EKM, 'The Relevance of "Competence" for Enhancing or Limiting Children's Participation: Unpicking Conceptual Confusion' (2019). Global Studies of Childhood.

Other sources

Child Rights Connect, 'Historic Ruling by the UN Committee on the Rights of the Child in the Climate Change Case Brought by 16 Child Petitioners under the OPIC' (2021). https://opic.childrightsconnect.org/historic-ruling-by-the-un-committee-on-the-rights-of-the-child-in-the-climate-change-case-brought-by-16-child-petitioners-under-the-opic-2/ accessed 17 November 2021.

Christian Aid and Gana Unnayan Kendra, 'Accountability Assessment Rohingya Response Bangladesh' (2018). www.christianaid.org.uk/sites/default/files/2018-03/Response-Accountability-Assessment-Feb-2018.pdf.

Christoplos, I and Mitchell, J, 'A Humanitarian Ombudsman Revisited?', ALNAP (2018). www.alnap.org/blogs/a-humanitarian-ombudsman-revisited, accessed 14 November 2021.

Conseil Consultatif National des enfants et Jeunes du Mali, 'Un message de sensibilisation sur les gestes barrières contre le coronavirus' (2020). www.facebook.com/ccnejmali/videos/319810622319878/ accessed 26 August 2021.

Core Humanitarian Standard Alliance, 'Core Humanitarian Standard' (2015). https://corehumanitarianstandard.org/the-standard, accessed 26 August 2021.

Eclipse Experience and Save the Children, 'User-Centred Community Engagement' (2018). www.eclipse-experience.com/user-centred-community-engagement/case-studies, accessed 3 August 2021.

Empatika, 'Let's Get Back to Our Routine': Listening to Children Who Were Affected by Central Sulawesi Earthquake and Tsunami' (2018). Yayasan Sayangi Tunas Cilik/Save the Children Indonesia, Wahana Visi Indonesia/World Vision Indonesia, Yayasan Plan International Indonesia/Plan International Indonesia, and UNICEF.

Grand Bargain website. https://interagencystandingcommittee.org/grand-bargain, accessed 26 August 2021.

Ground Truth Solutions and OECD, 'The Grand Bargain: Perspectives from the Field' (2019). https://groundtruthsolutions.org/wp-content/uploads/2018/06/GTS-Grand-Bargain-briefing-note-June-2018.pdf, 21–22, accessed 26 August 2021.

Herrington, R, 'Emerging Practices in Design, Monitoring, and Evaluation for Education for Peacebuilding Programming: Practice Guide' (2015). 51 Search for Common Ground, Washington, DC. www.sfcg.org/wp-content/uploads/2016/06/Emerging-PracticeGuide.pdf, accessed 19 September 2021.

Hill, P and Severijnen, E, 'Creating an Inclusive and Accessible Feedback and Reporting Mechanism' (2020). Save the Children. https://resourcecentre.savethechildren.net/library/save-children-feedback-and-reporting-mechanism-guidance.

Humanitarian Accountability Partnership, 'HAP Standards' (2008). https://reliefweb.int/report/world/guide-hap-standard-humanitarian-accountability-and-quality-management-0, accessed 26 August 2021.

Inter-Agency Standing Committee (IASC) website. https://interagencystandingcommittee.org/iasc-task-force-on-accountability-to-affected-people-closed, accessed 26 August 2021.

Inter-Agency Standing Committee, *IASC Guidelines on Working with and for Young People in Humanitarian and Protracted Crises* (2020). https://interagencystand ingcommittee.org/events/iasc-guidelines-working-and-young-people-humanita rian-and-protracted-crises.

International Rescue Committee, 'Client Voice and Choice Learning Exchange Event Report' (2016). www.rescue.org/report/client-voice-and-choice-learning-exchange.

Internews, 'Information Needs Assessment: Cox's Bazar–Bangladesh' (2017). https://internews.org/resource/information-needs-assessment-coxs-bazar-bangladesh.

MAEJT, 'le MAEJT contribue à la sensibilisation contre le COVID19' (2020). www.youtube.com/watch?v=Gwq_XV1fTl8, accessed 28 August 2021.

NSPCC, 'Recognising and Responding to Abuse'. https://learning.nspcc.org.uk/child-abuse-and-neglect/recognising-and-responding-to-abuse, accessed 26 February 2021.

O'Kane, C, 'Review of Children's Participation in Humanitarian Programming' (2013). Save the Children. https://resourcecentre.savethechildren.net/library/review-childrens-participation-humanitarian-programming.

Risso-Gill, I and Finnegan, L, 'Children's Ebola Recovery Assessment: Sierra Leone' (2015). Save the Children, Plan, World Vision and UNICEF.

Sandison, P, 'We're Listening: An Evaluation of User-centred Community Engagement in Emergency Sanitation' (2019). Oxfam. https://policy-practice.oxfam.org/resources/were-listening-an-evaluation-of-user-centred-community-engagement-in-emergency-620617/.

Save the Children, 'Improving Learning Environments Together in Emergencies' (2018). https://resourcecentre.savethechildren.net/library/improving-learning-environments-together-emergencies-ilet-package.

Save the Children, 'The Nine Basic Requirements for Meaningful and Ethical Children's Participation' (2021), 2. https://resourcecentre.savethechildren.net/library/nine-basic-requirements-meaningful-and-ethical-childrens-participation, accessed 22 February 2022.

Scharenguivel, M and Withana, B, 'Our Voices Matter. The Views of Children on Emergency Preparedness and Response in Sri Lanka' (2017). Save the Children

International Sri Lanka Country Office. https://reliefweb.int/report/sri-lanka/our-voices-matter-views-children-emergency-preparedness-and-response-sri-lanka.

Steinbock, L and Severijnen, E, 'Childhood Interrupted: Children's Voices from the Rohingya Refugee Crisis' (2018). Save the Children, Plan International and World Vision.

Sudanese National Society for Deaf and Save the Children, 'Coronavirus Awareness Raising Video' (2020).

Terres des Hommes, '#covidunder19 Initiative' (no date). www.tdh.ch/en/projects/covidunder19, accessed 18 September 2021.

West, A, 'The Participation of Children and Young People in Emergencies', UNICEF (2007).

Willow, C, 'United They Stand: Moving beyond the Participation-protection Divide' (2021). Save the Children, Discussion paper.

Withers, L and Dahal, N, 'After the Earthquake: Nepal's Children Speak out' (2015). Save the Children, Plan, World Vision and UNICEF.

Wood, A, 'Interagency Study on Child-Friendly Feedback and Complaint Mechanisms Within NGO Programmes' (2015). https://resourcecentre.savethechildren.net/library/interagency-study-child-friendly-feedback-and-complaint-mechanisms-within-ngo-programmes.

World Health Organisation, 'Managing the COVID-19 Infodemic: Promoting Healthy Behaviours and Mitigating the Harm from Misinformation and Disinformation' (2020). www.who.int/news/item/23-09-2020-managing-the-covid-19-infodemic-promoting-healthy-behaviours-and-mitigating-the-harm-from-misinformation-and-disinformation, accessed 2 September 2021.

World Vision and CDA, 'Using Beneficiary Feedback to Improve Development Programmes: Findings from a Multi-country Pilot' (2016). http://feedbackmechanisms.org/findings/.

3 Making children's right to information meaningful in humanitarian crises

*Rigmor Argren**

In humanitarian crises, children's right to information is crucial. Some children lack family protection and must fend for themselves. They may no longer reside in their usual environment and need to adapt to new situations. This inevitably has implications for their access to information. International law protects children's right to information as an integral part of freedom of expression under Article 13 of the Convention on the Rights of the Child[1] (CRC). The right to information is also protected by several treaties, notably Article 19 of the International Covenant on Civil and Political Rights[2] (ICCPR). However, because this provision is inherently adult-centric,[3] it becomes necessary to identify what is unique about a *child's* right to information under Article 13 of the CRC. This analysis is essential, since the right to information seems to be historically intertwined with society's political functions, such as taking part in public debate and holding public office. These activities presuppose a certain level of maturity. Filtering out the adult-centric features of the right to information creates scope to establish the purpose of a child's right to information in humanitarian crises.

Section 1 therefore begins with an overview of the historical underpinnings of freedom of expression. The distinctively adult-centric elements of this right are pointed out, and the concept of 'childhood' is discussed, with particular reference to the challenges to a child's evolving maturity and agency that humanitarian crises may pose. Section 2 examines the right to information and argues that the greatest possible protection of a child's right to information in humanitarian crises requires an approach in which

* Rigmor Argren is a senior lecturer in law, School of Law, Psychology and Social Work, Örebro University, Sweden.

1 1980 Convention on the Rights of the Child, G.A. Res. 44/25, Annex, 44 UN Gaor Supp. (No. 49), 167, entered into force on 2 September 1990.

2 1966 International Covenant on Civil and Political Rights, entered into force on 23 March 1976; 999 UNTS 171.

3 The term is borrowed from Marc Jans, 'Children as Citizens: Towards a Contemporary Notion of Child Participation', *Childhood*, 11(1) (2004), 27–44, 27. He does, however, argue that in modern society, adulthood cannot be separated from childhood as a distinctive standard, but the transition into adulthood should, rather, be recognised as a fluid process.

DOI: 10.4324/9781003187493-3

information is understood to have three distinctive and deliberate layers. Section 3 then suggests that the right to information is made meaningful for children in humanitarian crises when Article 13 of the CRC is read in conjunction with other provisions in the treaty. Last, section 4 presents the conclusions of the discussion.

1. Right to information with historical underpinnings

This section first examines the historical and ideological origins of the right to information as set out in the general context of freedom of expression. Next, given the adult-centric features of the classic perceptions of freedom of expression, the distinction between childhood and adulthood is outlined. In this discussion, the emphasis is on children's essential right to develop their own agency. Having recognised that the humanitarian context has certain particular features, this section closes by introducing the notion of paternalism in humanitarian action and discusses what this means for children's right to information in humanitarian crises.

1.1. Freedom of expression as the linchpin of liberalism and a democratic society

At the outset, freedom of expression was not perceived as a right with relevance for children.[4] For instance, neither the 1924 Geneva Declaration on the Rights of the Child nor the Declaration of the Rights of the Child adopted by the General Assembly in 1959 contained provisions on freedom of expression.[5] One explanation put forward in the literature is that freedom of expression was initially perceived as an autonomous right, protected through non-interference by public authorities.[6] Child rights, on the other hand, were perceived as requiring intervention by the authorities in order to be realised. Such intervention by authorities is commonly referred to as a positive obligation for the state.[7] As further illustrated in the following, state obligations requiring non-interference for their fulfilment can be traced back centuries. This perception, that a state protected a right by abstaining from action, was first systematically challenged in the 1980s.[8]

The dichotomous construction that some rights (generally speaking, civil and political rights protected by the ICCPR) were costless because all they

4 Geraldine Van Bueren, *The International Law on the Rights of the Child* ([paperback edition], The Hague: Martinus Nijhoff, 1998), 131.
5 Geneva Declaration of the Rights of the Child of 1924, adopted 26 September 1924, League of Nations O.J. Spec. Supp. 21, at 43 (1924) and Declaration of the Rights of the Child, G.A. res. 1386 (XIV), 14 U.N. GAOR Supp. (No. 16) at 19, U.N. Doc. A/4354 (1959).
6 Van Bueren (n 4), 132.
7 Ibid.
8 David Jason Karp, 'What Is the Responsibility to Respect Human Rights? Reconsidering the "Respect, Protect, and Fulfill" Framework', *International Theory*, 12 (2019), 83–108, 86.

required was non-interference, whereas other rights (such as economic, social and cultural rights protected by the International Covenant on Economic, Social and Cultural Rights (ICESCR))[9] required state investment is a flawed distinction and a misconception.[10] It is now commonly accepted in the human rights discourse that all rights are associated with a full spectrum of duties on behalf of the state. The full spectrum of state obligations is commonly referred to as to 'respect, protect and fulfil'.[11] Although it is accepted that all rights give rise to a full spectrum of obligations, it is worth dwelling briefly on the historical backdrop to the right to information and freedom of expression in preparation for the discussion in this chapter.

The perception of freedom of expression as an autonomous right, to be protected by state non-interference, can readily be traced back to the European Enlightenment. In this regard, Schabas reminds us of the English Bill of Rights from 1688, which declared: 'That the freedom of speech and debates or proceedings in Parliament ought not to be impeached or questioned in any court or place out of Parliament'.[12] In addition to emphasising government non-interference as the protective measure, this also illustrates the close ties with politics.

In his 19th-century writings, John Stuart Mill argued that the powers of the state should be kept at a minimum.[13] Liberalism clearly was perceived as *freedom from* state interference, while political rights were perceived primarily as an individual's right to autonomy.[14] Mill also noted that the freedom of the press was so well established that arguments in its favour were no longer necessary. He held that the purpose of the press – to be a means 'of securities against corrupt or tyrannical government'[15] – was clear. Freedom of expression was thus seen as an indispensable instrument for the development of a democratic society founded on public debate.

This view of freedom of expression as a 'classic civil and political right'[16] is also included in the European Convention on Human Rights[17] (ECHR), here expressed in the landmark case of *Handyside v the United Kingdom*

9 International Covenant on Economic, Social and Cultural Rights, 993 UNTS 3, entered into force on 3 January 1976 (1966).

10 John Tobin and Aisling Parkes, 'Article 13: the Right to Freedom of Expression', in John Tobin (ed), *The UN Convention on the Rights of the Child: A Commentary* (Oxford: Oxford University Press, 2019), 435–474, 451.

11 Ibid. For a critical review of these concepts from a political science perspective, see David Jason Karp (n 8).

12 William A Schabas, *The European Convention on Human Rights: A Commentary* (Oxford: Oxford University Press, Incorporated, 2015), 444.

13 John Stuart Mill, *On Liberty* (London: Andrews UK, 2011), 132.

14 Kyle Vella, 'Power, Paternalism and Children on the Move', *Journal of International Humanitarian Action*, 1(3) (2016), 1–12, http://doi.org/10.1186/s41018-016-0003-y.

15 Mill (n 13), 32.

16 Tobin and Parkes (n 10), 436.

17 1950 Convention for the Protection of Human Rights and Fundamental Freedoms, adopted on 3 September 1953, 213 UNTS 222.

before the European Court of Human Rights (ECtHR): 'freedom of expression constitutes one of the essential foundations of [democratic] society, one of the basic conditions for its progress and for the development of every man'.[18] The purpose of this adult-centric freedom of expression is to link the 'development of man' and the aspect of a public 'marketplace of ideas'.[19] In this regard, mass media have the 'task of purveyor of information and public Watchdog'.[20] The ECtHR has consistently provided strong protection for publications or modes of communication (notably mass media) that serve the purpose of social and political debate.[21] It must be noted that commentators have also established that the discourse on freedom of information is predominantly depicted as concerning information for political purposes.[22] Political objectives of information requests are, at face value, twofold: either 'to question the government, or to be informed, typically as a pre-political act'.[23] In other words, both purposes are adult-centric. The ECtHR highlights the importance of fundamental freedom of expression for public debate in a democratic society:

> Freedom of expression constitutes one of the essential foundations of a democratic society. Subject to paragraph 2 of Article 10, it is applicable not only to 'information' or 'ideas' that are favourably received or regarded as inoffensive or as a matter of indifference, but also to those that offend, shock or disturb. Such are the demands of pluralism, tolerance and broadmindedness without which there is no 'democratic society'.[24]

These aspects of political debate and the governance of a democratic society that the right to freedom of expression seeks to safeguard are intrinsically adult-centric, in that they rest on the assumption of a certain maturity. Human rights treaties, such as the ICESCR, ICCPR or ECHR, apply to adults and children alike, but practical circumstances may prevent children from fully enjoying these rights, given these treaties' adult-centric origins

18 *Handyside v the United Kingdom* (Application no. 5493/72) Judgment, 7 December 1976, para 49.
19 Tobin and Parkes (n 10), 436.
20 *Barthold v Germany* (Application no. 38734/79), Judgment, 25 March 1985, para. 58.
21 Clare Ovey and Robin White, *Jacobs and White: The European Convention on Human Rights* (4th edition, Oxford: Oxford University Press, 2006), 320.
22 Gregory Michener and Ben Worthy, 'The Information-Gathering Matrix: A Framework for Conceptualizing the Use of Freedom of Information Laws', *Administration & Society*, 50 (2015), 476–500, 477.
23 Ibid.
24 *Fressoz and Roire v France* [GC] (Application no. 29183/95), 1999 Judgment, 21 January 1999, para 44. The Court is here quoting the famous case of *Handyside v the United Kingdom*.

and elements.[25] It is therefore now time to become better acquainted with the concept of childhood.

1.2. Conceptualising childhood

The concepts of both adulthood and childhood are social constructs.[26] Implicitly, it is assumed that the child is 'a vulnerable, weak, and dependent creature, bereft of those capacities that entitle adults to be regarded as full members of our society' and therefore 'citizens in waiting'.[27] The notion of childhood is not static; rather, it changes through history and over time in a fluid way.[28] For several thinkers of the European Enlightenment, the notion of children as vulnerable and in need of protection was central to their arguments.[29]

Mill explicitly stated that his doctrine on the need to limit society's control over its individual subjects to a minimum 'is meant to apply only to human beings in the maturity of their faculties. We are not speaking of children, or of young persons below the age that the law may set as that of manhood or womanhood'.[30] In other words, the not yet fully fledged 'maturity of faculties' implicitly calls for particular behaviour from those who have reached maturity vis-à-vis those who have not: adults are expected to provide protection for the non-adults. This requires a balancing act between the protective and the empowerment approach.[31] Adding to the challenge here is that the child's state of mind or mental development is far from static. Furthermore, recognising progressive autonomy for the child is the starting point for understanding children's civil and political rights.[32]

Under international law, the Universal Declaration of Human Rights (UDHR) and the twin covenants of the ICCPR and the ICESCR seek to protect children. Additionally, children must enjoy specific rights, as prescribed in the preamble of the CRC, since they may still be in the process of

25 John Tobin and David Archard, 'Article 1: The Definition of a Child' in John Tobin (ed), *The UN Convention on the Rights of the Child: A Commentary* (Oxford: Oxford University Press, 2019), 21–40, 22, note 6.

26 Van Bueren (n 4), 32; for a discussion on the history of childhood as a notion, see Marc Jans, 32–33.

27 Vella (n 14), 1–12, 2.

28 Kay Bennett, 'Concepts of Childhood: A Discussion of the Development, through History', in Basu Chandni and Vicky Anderson-Patton (eds), *Children and Childhood: Practices and Perspectives* (Publishers location: Oxford, 2019), 3–14, 3.

29 Gamze Erdem Türkelli, Wouter Vandenhole and Jan Wouters, 'Introducing New Frontiers in Children's Rights: From Protection to Empowerment', *Nordic Journal of Human Rights*, 39 (2021), 103–12, 104.

30 Mill (n 13), 26.

31 JC Buitelaar, 'Child's Best Interest and Informal Self-Determination: What the GDPR Can Learn from Children's Rights', *International Data Privacy Law*, 4(8) (2018), 293–308, 293.

32 Usang Maria Assim, 'Civil Rights and Freedoms of the Child', in Ursula Kilkelly and Ton Liefaard (eds), *International Human Rights of Children* (Singapore: Springer, 2019), 389–417, 399.

developing the required maturity.[33] While lacking provisions for the child's right to freedom of expression, the aforementioned 1924 and 1959 Child Rights Declarations were early manifestations of a desire to protect the child.[34] But despite this reference to protecting the child, Thorgeirsdóttir mentions that during the drafting of the CRC, the proposed title, 'A Draft Convention on the Protection of the Child', was rejected.[35]

The notion of a child has also been framed as a comparative negative: someone who is not yet adult.[36] This definition, in terms of what a child is not, can partly be explained by considering that the notion of childhood is mediated, which means that it is defined by someone else – a conveyer, normally an adult.[37] Neither the 1924 nor the 1959 Child Rights Declaration explicitly defines 'child'.[38] The CRC has an age-based approach: Article 1 states that 'for the purpose of this Convention, a child means every human being below the age of eighteen years unless under the law applicable to the child, majority is attained earlier'.[39]

Defining a child and answering the question of whether a child *is* entitled to rights and, if so, which, are deeply contested.[40] Suffice it here to note that the ideological and historical foundation underpinning freedom of expression contains features that are inherently adult-centric. As Thorgeirsdóttir puts it, children are not widely 'factual' bearers of political rights.[41] Nor are classic autonomous rights for political purposes traditionally seen as child's play. On the other hand, children are most certainly entitled to empowerment and self-fulfilment.

The notion of *agency* may be defined as 'the ability of an actor to exert influence, affect the outcome of a process or event, to make happen or prevent an event or action'.[42] Tobin adds that in the process of becoming an autonomous individual, self-fulfilment is central and entails the 'capacity to choose and pursue a worthwhile life'.[43] This entails a certain amount of power over 'the production, in and through social relations, of effects that shape the capacities of actors to determine their circumstances and fate',[44]

33 CRC, preamble.
34 1924 and 1959 Declarations on the Rights of the Child.
35 Herdís Thorgeirsdóttir, *A Commentary on the United Nations Convention on the Rights of the Child, Article 13: The Right to Freedom of Expression* (Leiden: Brill, 2006), 19.
36 Van Bueren (n 4), 33.
37 Vella (n 14), 3.
38 Tobin and Archard (n 25), 22.
39 CRC, Article 1.
40 Tobin and Archard (n 25), 23.
41 Thorgeirsdóttir (n 35), 2.
42 Adriana Sinclair, 'Why We Should See International Law as a Structure: Unpicking International Law's Ontology and Agency', *International Relations*, 35 (2020), 216–235, 217.
43 Tobin and Parkes (n 10), 435–474, see footnote 9 and accompanying text previously.
44 Vella (n 14), 4.

which includes the capacity to take decisions 'on one's behalf and on behalf of others'.[45]

It may be assumed that anyone who requires special protection, by law or otherwise, lacks full agency. A humanitarian crisis notoriously involves change, unintentional as well as deliberate and negative as well as positive. Scope for a child's agency may thus shift rapidly and unpredictably. Again, this may vary greatly among individuals, with some suddenly shouldering the burden of wider responsibilities – as children do when they head households – and facing the challenge of increased agency, while others may see their area of influence shrink.

1.3. Upholding agency in a context of paternalism

In humanitarian crises, caring may inadvertently turn into control. Humanitarian relief work is inspired by the ethics of care and seeks a degree of control over the lives of others.[46] There are situations when humanitarian interventions resemble imposition. Although there is consent from beneficiaries, such consent can be driven by their helpless situation.[47] The ethics of care easily become ethics of control.[48] This means that humanitarian interventions can have unintentional features of paternalism. Providing aid and support (be it to all those in need during a humanitarian crisis, or to help parents care for their children) is seen as inherently beneficial. Nevertheless, when caring reaches a tipping point and turns into control, the situation changes and reveals the paradox of paternalism. *Caring* therefore has the potential to be both constructive and destructive.[49]

This section has outlined the deep roots of the human right to freedom of expression in public life, political debate, citizenship and autonomy, based on the maturity of the individual. These political rights also require access to information, at least for two purposes that, in turn, have helped to shape the role of the mass media. First, the mass media exist to ensure an informed public. Second, the mass media serve as checks and balances to the powers that be, act as a watchdog and safeguard democracy. In essence, this implies that freedom of expression is adult-centric and was not originally perceived as anything to do with children.

Fulfilling children's right to information therefore becomes a delicate balancing act between protection (or care) and empowerment (or agency). This balancing act becomes even more complex in humanitarian crises, owing to paternalistic undercurrents of humanitarian interventions. The underlying *purpose* of the information is essential for children in

45 Assim (n 32), 392.
46 Vella (n 14), 2.
47 Ibid., 5.
48 Ibid.
49 Ibid.

humanitarian crises for upholding the child's agency. Furthermore, it must also provide scope for the child to develop such agency and gain autonomy. Such autonomy is closely tied to the core of human dignity.[50] Every human being possesses dignity by virtue of being human.[51] A child's right to information serves the twofold purpose of upholding dignity and simultaneously providing support for developing the child's agency.

2. Examining the right to information

Article 13 of the CRC largely mirrors the provisions of Article 19 of the ICCPR. Given that the discussion here is focused on protecting the rights of the child, it is worth recalling that Article 19 of the ICCPR should also apply to children. As will be argued here, the context of CRC article extends the right to information (as already protected under Article 19) with complementary, distinctly different scope for children, particularly in humanitarian crises. Article 19 of the ICCPR protects the right to seek, receive and impart information.[52] A comparison reveals a marked difference in focus on the object of protection between freedom of expression (the right to impart information) and the right to information (to seek and receive what others voluntarily share).[53] The former is designed to protect the individual disseminating information: the sender. The latter, on the other hand, focuses on the recipient of information.[54] Under Article 13 of the CRC, children also have the right to *seek* information. This means that the child is seen as active, rather than just passively receiving whatever information authorities or non-governmental organisations (NGOs) wish to share.[55]

In the literature pertaining to children's access to information, research focuses on the right to information for children in vulnerable situations. Specifically, two areas – both relating to public authorities – can be identified. Attention is paid to refugee children (unaccompanied as well as accompanied)[56] and child-friendly justice systems.[57] The latter area has

50 Ibid.
51 Assim (n 32), 390.
52 ICCPR, Article 19.
53 By contrast, the provisions in the ECHR does not explicitly include the right to seek information: 'Everyone has the right to freedom of expression. This right shall include freedom to hold opinions and to receive and impart information and ideas without interference by public authority and regardless of frontiers'. Article 10(1), ECHR.
54 Maeve McDonagh, 'The Right to Information in International Human Rights Law', *Human Rights Law Review*, 13 (2013), 25–55, 29.
55 Tobin and Parkes (n 10), 444.
56 See, for example, SE Rap, 'The Right to Information of (Un)Accompanied Refugee Children: Improving Refugee Children's Legal Position, Fundamental Rights' Implementation and Emotional Well-Being in the Netherlands', *The International Journal of Children's Rights*, 28 (2020), 322–51.
57 Helen Stalford, Liam Cairns and Jeremy Marshall, 'Achieving Child-Friendly Justice through Child-Friendly Methods – Let's Start with the Right to Information', *Social Inclusion*, 5(3) (2017), 207–218.

useful approaches concerning a right to information that will be discussed further in Section 2.2. First, however, it is necessary to examine the difference between *opinion* and *view* and its potential implications for a child's right to information. Second, it is suggested that a distinctive child-centric reading of the right to information can be achieved if the purpose of information is examined in three distinctive layers.

2.1. Distinguishing 'opinion' from 'view'

A fundamental difference between Article 19 of the ICCPR and Article 13 of CRC already appears in the first provision. In the former, the first paragraph safeguards freedom to hold opinions without interference. This provision is not included in Article 13 of the CRC. Should we assume that the CRC does not protect children's right to hold opinions freely? The right to express one's opinion was, in fact, seen as inherent in the right to freedom of expression in the CRC draft.[58] This may support authors who argue that children's right to hold an opinion should be seen as subsumed under the right to freedom of expression.[59]

This author, however, finds it more plausible to assume that, for adults and children alike, the right to hold an *opinion* is protected by Article 19 of the ICCPR. Nevertheless, it is lacking in the identical form under Article 13 of the CRC, because the CRC seeks to consider children's varying but evolving maturity. Furthermore, the variable scope of a child's right to information is due to the fact that the CRC permits parents, as well as authorities, to restrict a child's rights if this is perceived as necessary to protect the best interests of the child.[60] This feature of the CRC, which has been termed 'paternalistic', is seen as justified vis-à-vis children in a manner that would not apply to adults.[61]

The right to hold an opinion under Article 19 of the ICCPR is absolute and so central as to be non-derogable. As far as the CRC is concerned, this treaty provides for no derogation clause at all.[62] The CRC mentions opinions, but not in relation to the right to information. Rather, it is cited as one of several impermissible grounds for discrimination mentioned in the preamble and further elaborated in Article 2. The provision makes it clear that the CRC applies to a child 'irrespective of the child's or his or her parent's or legal guardian's race, colour, sex, language, religion, political or other *opinion*, national, ethnic or social origin, property,

58 Office of the United Nations High Commissioner for Human Rights and Save the Children Sweden, *Legislative History of the Convention on the Rights of the Child* (New York: United Nations, 2007), para 236.

59 Gerison Lansdown and Ziba Vaghri, 'Article 13: The Right to Freedom of Expression', in *Monitoring State Compliance with the UN Convention on the Rights of the Child* (Cham: Springer, 2022), 65–73, 66.

60 Tobin and Parkes (n 10), 441.

61 Ibid.

62 Van Bueren (n 4), 398.

disability, birth or other status.'[63] This list is the same as those of major non-discrimination clauses in human rights treaties, with the additional grounds of disability and ethnic origin.[64] Although fairly extensive, the listing in Article 2(1) is considered purely exemplary.[65] The CRC seemingly envisions two kinds of opinion, either 'political' or 'other'. Article 2(2) confirms that opinions (be they 'political' or 'other' in nature) are normally associated with adulthood, with reference to the child's parents. The provision requests states to ensure that children are protected from 'all forms of discrimination or punishment on the basis of . . . expressed opinions, . . . of the child's parents, legal guardians, or family members'.[66] Clearly, the provision shields children from matters that are linked to their parents, but it does so by reinforcing the premise that expressing opinions is primarily associated with adulthood. In the drafting history of the CRC, the right to hold an opinion was separated from the right to expression at the second reading, but it was still seen as closely linked with the right of expression.[67]

By contrast, the term assigned in the CRC to children's thoughts is 'views'. Forming one's own views, irrespective of age, is the purpose of the right to seek, receive and impart information and ideas of all kinds enshrined in Article 13 of the CRC. It has been stated that 'views without information are as worthless as a speech without an audience'.[68] The connection between expressing a view and having an audience is further established by Article 12, often referred to as the child's 'right to be heard'. Although this right was made a separate provision under the CRC, it immediately precedes Article 13, and this relationship is not only sequential but material, since children who are heard also need the right to form views. Interestingly, Article 12 is narrower in scope than Article 1 of the CRC. In particular, two limiting aspects must be noted: a) it applies only to 'all matters affecting the child',[69] and b) it requires the child to be 'capable of forming his or her own views'.[70] This expressly emphasises the underlying assumption that children's views are distinctively different from adults' opinions.[71]

63 CRC, Article 2(1). Emphasis added.

64 Samantha Besson and Eleonor Kleber, 'Article 2: The Right to Non-Discrimination', in John Tobin and Philip Alston (eds), *The UN Convention on the Rights of the Child: A Commentary* (Oxford: Oxford University Press, 2019), 41–72, 48.

65 Ibid., 53.

66 CRC, Article 2(2).

67 Office of the United Nations High Commissioner for Human Rights and Save the Children Sweden, para 236.

68 S Detrick, *A Commentary on the United Nations Convention on the Rights of the Child* (The Hague: Martinus Nijhoff Publishers, 1999), 233.

69 CRC, Article 12(1).

70 Ibid.

71 Tobin and Parkes (n 10), 455.

As illustrated by the adult-centric rights protected by Article 19 of the ICCPR, the drafters acknowledged that the potential power of the right to express opinions in public could not be unfettered. But the criteria for permissive limitation are firmly and explicitly crafted into the right itself, to afford the most extensive protection for it. The human rights instruments (except for the African Charter[72] and the Arab Charter)[73] contain limitations to freedom of expression, detailed and exhaustive, through a cumulative test with three elements: the limitation must be a) prescribed by national law, b) for the listed grounds only and c) necessary and proportionate to that need.[74]

Duties and responsibilities under Article 19(3) pertain to the rights enshrined in Article 19(2) (referring to freedom of expression, not freedom of opinion). No such duties or responsibilities exist in Article 13 of the CRC. Tobin asserts in his commentary to the CRC that there is little documentation on why the notions of duties and responsibilities were omitted in Article 13.[75] In fact, they were never part of the draft Article 13, although one might think the child's evolving sense of responsibility could have prompted such inclusion. Instead, delegates appeared to be more concerned with protecting parents' rights than with safeguarding the child's evolving capacities. Nevertheless, this omission further illustrates that the protected *views* of the child under the CRC distinctively differ from the *opinions* protected by Article 19, ICCPR. It was simply not deemed necessary to intertwine duties and responsibilities with children's right to express their views.

72 The provisions under the African Charter hold that measures restricting freedom of expression have to be 'within the law'. The African Commission on Human and Peoples' Rights has expressed its view that 'within the law' should mean within International Human Rights Law. See *Media Rights Agenda and Constitutional Rights Project v Nigeria,* Twelfth Annual Report', reprinted in Rachel Murray and Malcolm D Evans (eds), *Documents of the Africa Commission on Human and People's Rights* (Oxford: Hart Pub, 2001), para 66. 'Media Rights Agenda, Constitutional Rights Project, Media Rights Agenda and Constitutional Rights Project v Nigeria, Twelfth Annual Report', in Rachel Murray and Malcolm D Evans (eds), *Documents of the Africa Commission on Human and People's Rights* (Oxford: Hart Pub., 2001).

73 For an introductory analysis of the Arab Charter, see Mervat Rishmawi, 'The Revised Arab Charter on Human Rights: A Step Forward?', *HRLR,* 5 (2005), 361–376.

74 There are two types of situation in which restrictions on adult-centric freedom of expression are permitted. The first category allows limitations for the purpose of respecting the rights or reputations of others. The second is for the protection of national security or public order, or public health and morals. The relevant provision in Article 10(2) of the ECHR reads: 'in the interests of national security, territorial integrity or public safety, for the prevention of disorder or crime, for the protection of health or morals'. The word 'protection' in the ECHR, in contrast to 'respect' in the ICCPR, may show that the ECHR, at least, can be applied to relations among non-state actors; that is, it may have some horizontal effect. This, in turn, implies that the ECHR provision is wider in scope than the corresponding provision (Article 19(3)(b)) of the ICCPR.

75 Tobin and Parkes (n 10), 455.

2.2. *Analysis of the child's right to information in humanitarian crises*

The discussion now turns to in-depth understanding of Article 13 in the CRC. From a child rights perspective, it is essential to analyse the right to information in terms of the presumed result of the information – that is, its purpose. Lansford and others have developed an instructive approach in relation to the requirements of a child-friendly justice system and meaningful implementation of participatory rights.[76] They suggest interpreting information as consisting of three cumulative layers, all of which must be provided for the child's right to information to be fulfilled. Here, it is suggested that the three-layered information approach is equally useful for protecting children's right to information in humanitarian crises.

The first layer identified is *practical and procedural information.*[77] In the humanitarian context, this refers to information about any procedures with implications for the child. Examples are registration in refugee settings, arrangements for food distribution, enrolment in education in emergencies and support for unaccompanied minors.

The second layer is *foundational rights-based information.*[78] This is information that helps the child to understand what *ought to* happen. In other words, this layer concerns the normative rules for which key actors should be accountable. In humanitarian settings, actors such as Save the Children and UNICEF have done extensive work in this regard.[79] This second information layer is about repackaging relevant documents and policies into child-friendly versions, which generally share two features, First, the documents are given simpler language, while drawings, images, colour and the like are used to make the information more appealing.[80] However, research has shown that since human and children's rights are rather abstract concepts, presenting information about rights in an attractive guise is not enough.[81] The reality is that *more* is required before children understand how their rights may be applied in practice to their specific situation. The bureaucratic language of public documents, together with other technicalities, can become effective barriers to intelligent use of information.[82]

Information, including that from digital sources, must therefore be adapted to guarantee that it is user friendly, functional and accessible.[83]

76 See generally Stalford, Cairns and Marshall (n 57).
77 Ibid., 211.
78 Ibid.
79 For an account of Save the Children International's work in this regard, see Philippa Hill's contribution to this book.
80 Stalford, Cairns and Marshall (n 57), 211.
81 Ibid., 212.
82 Paulo Morais, Jose Caramelo Gomes and Noemia Rute Peres de Bessa Vilela, 'Government Transparency: Reality or Mirage?', *Lex localis – Journal of Local Self-Government*, 15 (2017), 725–736, 727.
83 Ibid., 728.

Given that there will be children (and adults) with different skill levels as well as varying degrees of maturity, the information must be of such a kind as to facilitate everyone's meaningful actions for their lives based on the information. Child-friendly materials are a good starting point, but where making rights relevant and substantive is concerned, they tend to remain a somewhat superficial measure.[84]

To make the right to information truly meaningful for children, Stalford and others suggest that a third layer of information is required: *agency-asserting information*.[85] They argue that

> [i]t is at this point that the right to information is understood not merely as conveying facts to the child, but as a process of contextualising that information, presenting genuine choices, defining what support is available to enable the child to exercise those choices, calibrating expectations in the light of other factors that influence decisions about the child, and presenting realistic and clear projections as to what outcomes might arise from different courses of action.[86]

In other words, until the right to information is realised through its third layer of agency, asserting information[87] (which allows the child to simultaneously exercise and develop its agency), the right to information in humanitarian crises cannot be considered fulfilled. In the following, we explore how the child's right to information during humanitarian crises can be made meaningful by additional provisions in the CRC.

3. Further provisions that make the right to information meaningful

The previous section clarified that the right to information for children is an enabling right – that is, one with a purpose. Information in a vacuum, not integrated into a person's field of agency, does not contribute to the development of the child's capacities. The purpose of children's right to information is to enable them to take, and learn to take, meaningful action for their lives based on that information.

This section first highlights the CRC's unique provision pertaining to the role of mass media for the child's development and well-being. Second, it examines the particularities of the right to development enshrined in the CRC. It then argues that for the right to information to be appropriately

84 Stalford, Cairns and Marshall (n 57), 212.

85 Ibid.

86 Ibid.

87 See 'Digitalising Children's Humanitarian Access', the later chapter by Jessica Jonsson in this book.

protected for children in humanitarian crises, the right to information needs to be seen in conjunction with the right to development.

3.1. Use of mass media to disseminate information

Article 17 of the CRC focuses not primarily on the child's right to information but on the *role of mass media* vis-à-vis children. It has been pointed out that this provision has specific, unique features that mean there is no jurisprudence under international law to draw upon in seeking to interpret the meaning of Article 17.[88] The gist of this provision is to create a conducive environment in which children can enjoy their right to (intellectual) development. The provision explicitly points out the mass media is a resource when it comes to children's access to information. Furthermore, such access, apart from being through diverse channels, should promote the 'spiritual and moral well-being and physical and mental health'[89] of the child. This emphasis on the child's well-being has meant that the intersection of media, law and children is often approached through restrictions on the dissemination of information presumed to be potentially harmful to the child.[90] Article 17 is designed to favour and promote mass media. The CRC drafters appear to have been determined to safeguard a positive perception of the mass media, not least in terms of children.[91]

The provision enjoins states to 'encourage' mass media activities in five outlined areas.[92] But 'encourage' is a fairly weak word that imposes no substantive obligations on states.[93] Rather, Article 17 comes across as more of a task list for the mass media than anything else. The third-party actor at the heart of this provision, the 'mass media', remains undefined, nor was it the

88 John Tobin and Elizabeth Handsley, 'Art.17 the Mass Media and Children: Diversity of Sources, Quality of Content, and Protection against Harm', in John Tobin (ed), *The UN Convention on the Rights of the Child: A Commentary* (Oxford: Oxford University Press, 2019), 600–645, 602.

89 CRC, Article 17.

90 Tobin and Handsley (n 88), 602.

91 Ibid., 607.

92 The five areas are as follows:
(a) encouraging the mass media to disseminate information and material of social and cultural benefit to the child and in accordance with the spirit of Article 29;
(b) encouraging international co-operation in the production, exchange and dissemination of such information and material from a diversity of cultural, national and international sources;
(c) encouraging the production and dissemination of children's books;
(d) encouraging the mass media to have particular regard to the linguistic needs of the child who belongs to a minority group or an indigenous people;
(e) encouraging the development of appropriate guidelines for the protection of the child from information and material injurious to his or her well-being, bearing in mind the provisions of Articles 13 and 18. CRC, Article 17, para (a)–(e).

93 Tobin and Handsley (n 88), 603.

subject of particular discussion among the convention's drafters.[94] The provision covers public as well as private mass media.[95] As a concluding note, it must be mentioned that Article 17 seems to concentrate substantially on the child-friendly aspects, termed the 'second layer' in the previous section. It now remains to find out what further obligations are in place to ensure that children enjoy the third layer of information during humanitarian crises as well as in other times. The discussion therefore now turns to Article 6(2) in the CRC and the rights it protects.

3.2. The right to development and the child's agency

If the provision concerning Article 17 is *sui generis* in human rights law, then the right to survival and development, as protected under Article 6, may be even more of an odd one out in the human right discourse. Under Article 6, the right to life is accompanied by rights to survival and development.[96] The historical differences with respect to the right to life (a negative obligation: not to kill) and the right to survive (a positive obligation: to keep alive) have increasingly diminished, to the point where they are arguably no longer relevant.[97] Rather, it has been suggested that these three distinctive rights may be seen as a continuum.[98] The addition of the right to survival and development in Article 6 reflects a long-term commitment to child development under international law.[99] First, the UN Child Rights Committee[100] has embraced Article 6 as one of four guiding principles under the Convention that informs the understanding of each of its provisions.[101] It should be seen as a holistic right that protects both process and outcome.[102] Second, the child's right to development must be seen as composite, covering the progressive elements of all the rights protected in the CRC.[103] Third, the right to development must be understood as a dynamic concept.[104] As such, it seeks to capture something different from the threshold test that is

94 Ibid., 604.
95 Ibid.
96 John Tobin and Noam Peleg, 'Art.6 the Rights to Life, Survival, and Development', in John Tobin (ed), *The UN Convention on the Rights of the Child: A Commentary* (Oxford: Oxford University Press, 2019), 186–236, 189.
97 Ibid., 221.
98 Noam Peleg, 'International Children's Rights Law: General Principles', in Ursula Kilkelly and Ton Liefaard (eds), *International Human Rights of Children* (Singapore: Springer, 2019), 135–157, 144.
99 Tobin and Peleg (n 96), 189. The 1990 World Declaration on the Survival, Protection and Development of Children offers an insight into the risk factors to child survival and by implication the right to survival.
100 See also Chapter 1, concerning the role and function of the committee.
101 Ibid., 220.
102 Peleg (n 98), 147.
103 Ibid.
104 Van Bueren (n 4), 293.

otherwise common in human rights law. The right to development in Article 6(2) does not primarily concern the collective right to development in a society; rather, its focus is the child's personal development.[105]

The Draft Convention on the Right to Development,[106] to be presented in the final revised version in May 2022, does not define the right to development.[107] The foremost reason is that restricting the meaning of the right to development to a singular definition would have defeated the people-centred aspect of the right to development, which implied authorship that varies from one context to another.[108] Second, existing descriptions of development, as expressed in the 1986 UN Declaration on the Right to Development, are held to suffice.[109] In the declaration, the right to development is described as a process that should be assessed in terms of outcomes as well as means of achieving them.[110] Third, although the right to development in the draft convention is distinctive and separate from the provisions in CRC Article 6(2), it cannot be denied that there is a nexus between the collective aspects of development in society and the individual child's right to development.[111] Fourth, the notion of a child's development must not be reduced to the 'process of transformation from childhood to adulthood'. Should this happen, children would be seen merely as 'human becomings' rather than human beings.[112] This would reduce the right to development to a right to become adult.[113]

Considering the child's rights to information and to development together makes the right to *purposeful* information clearer. It not only unpacks the element of a child's evolving agency but also provides a counterbalance to the perception that the right to information, integral to freedom of expression, deals only with autonomy and non-interference by the state.

4. Conclusions

This chapter has argued that, to be meaningful for children in humanitarian crises, the right to information as protected under the CRC must be given a distinctive and unique interpretation. In this regard, it is worth recalling that Article 19 of the ICCPR also applies to children, despite its somewhat adult-centric origins. It has been suggested that Article 13 of the

105 Tobin and Peleg (n 96), 223.
106 Human Rights Council, *Draft Convention on the Right to Development, with Commentaries*, A/HRC/WG.2/21/2/Add.1. 20 January 2020.
107 Ibid., 7.
108 Ibid.
109 Declaration on the Right to Development, G.A. res. 41/128, annex, 41 U.N. GAOR Supp. (No. 53) at 186, U.N. Doc. A/41/53 (1986), adopted on 4 December 1986.
110 Draft Convention on the Right to Development, 8.
111 Tobin and Peleg (n 96), 224.
112 Ibid., 226.
113 Ibid.

CRC, which particularly protects the rights of the child, must be given its own distinctive meaning in order to enhance the legal protection of the child. For children in humanitarian crises, this can be achieved when Article 13 of the CRC is read in conjunction with the provisions in Article 6(2) that protect the child's right to survival and development. But, as this chapter argues, this is not enough: it does not make the right to information distinctively meaningful for children in humanitarian crises. Only when the child has access to information comprising three purposeful layers can one safely assume that the right to information has become meaningful for a child in a humanitarian crisis.

The three layers consist of instructive information, foundational rights information and agency-asserting information. In a situation of humanitarian crisis, it is critical for a child that these three layers of information be provided. This is because humanitarian interventions, even if they are unintended, may have paternalistic features. The desire to care and assist is a benevolent one but may unintentionally undermine the development of the child's own agency. For children in humanitarian crises, due attention must be paid to *purposeful* information in order to make their right to information meaningful.

Bibliography

Treaties

Convention for the Protection of Human Rights and Fundamental Freedoms, adopted on 3 September 1953, 213 UNTS 222 (1950).

Convention on the Rights of the Child, G.A. Res. 44/25, Annex, 44 UN Gaor Supp. (No. 49), 167, entered into force on 2 September 1990 (1980).

Declaration of the Rights of the Child, G.A. res. 1386 (XIV), 14 U.N. GAOR Supp. (No. 16) at 19, U.N. Doc. A/4354 (1959).

Draft Convention on the Right to Development, with commentaries, A/HRC/WG.2/21/2/Add.1.20 January 2020.

Geneva Declaration of the Rights of the Child of 1924, adopted on 26 September 1924, League of Nations O.J. Spec. Supp. 21, at 43 (1924).

International Covenant on Civil and Political Rights, 660 UNTS 171, entered into force on 23 March 1976 (1966).

International Covenant on Economic, Social and Cultural Rights, 993 UNTS 3, entered into force on 3 January 1976 (1966).

Universal Declaration of Human Rights, G.A. res. 217A (III), U.N. Doc A/810 at 71 (1948).

World Declaration on the Survival, Protection and Development of Children (1990).

Case law

Barthold v Germany (Application no. 38734/79), Judgment, 25 March 1985.

Fressoz and Roire v France [GC] (Application no. 29183/95), 1999 Judgment, 21 January 1999.

Handyside v the United Kingdom (Application no. 5493/72), Judgment, 7 December 1976.

Media Rights Agenda, Constitutional Rights Project, Media Rights Agenda and Constitutional Rights Project v Nigeria, 'Twelfth Annual Report', in Murray, Rachel and Evans, Malcolm D (eds), *Documents of the Africa Commission on Human and People's Rights.* Oxford: Hart Pub. 2001.

Literature

Assim, Usang Maria, 'Civil Rights and Freedoms of the Child', in Kilkelly, Ursula and Liefaard, Ton (eds), *International Human Rights of Children.* Singapore: Springer. 2019, 389–417.

Bennett, Kay, 'Concepts of Childhood: A Discussion of the Development, through History' in Chandni, Basu and Anderson-Patton, Vicky (eds), *Children and Childhood: Practices and Perspectives.* Oxford: Brill. 2019, 3–14.

Besson, Samantha and Kleber, Eleonor, 'Article 2: The Right to Non-Discrimination', in Tobin, John and Alston, Philip (eds), *The UN Convention on the Rights of the Child: A Commentary.* Oxford: Oxford University Press. 2019, 41–72.

Buitelaar, JC, 'Child's Best Interest and Informal Self-Determination: What the GDPR Can Learn from Children's Rights', *International Data Privacy Law,* 4(8), 293–308, 2018.

Detrick, S, *A Commentary on the United Nations Convention on the Rights of the Child.* The Hague: Martinus Nijhoff Publishers. 1999.

Erdem Türkelli, Gamze, Vandenhole, Wouter and Wouters, Jan, 'Introducing New Frontiers in Children's Rights: From Protection to Empowerment', *Nordic Journal of Human Rights,* 39, 103–112, 2021.

Jans, Marc, 'Children as Citizens: Towards a Contemporary Notion of Child Participation', *Childhood,* 11(1), 27–44, 2004.

Jason Karp, David, 'What is the Responsibility to Respect Human Rights? Reconsidering the "Respect, Protect, and Fulfill" Framework', *International Theory,* 12, 83–108, 2019.

Lansdown, Gerison and Vaghri, Ziba, 'Article 13: The Right to Freedom of Expression', *Monitoring State Compliance with the UN Convention on the Rights of the Child,* 65–73, 2022.

McDonagh, Maeve, 'The Right to Information in International Human Rights Law', *Human Rights Law Review,* 13, 25–55, 2013.

Michener, Gregory and Worthy, Ben, 'The Information-Gathering Matrix: A Framework for Conceptualizing the Use of Freedom of Information Laws', *Administration & Society,* 50, 476–500, 2015.

Mill, John Stuart, *On Liberty.* London: Andrews UK. 2011.

Morais, Paulo, Caramelo Gomes, Jose and Rute Peres de Bessa Vilela, Noemia, 'Government Transparency: Reality or Mirage?', *Lex localis – Journal of Local Self-Government,* 15, 725–736, 2017.

Office of the United Nations High Commissioner for Human Rights and Save the Children, Sweden, *Legislative History of the Convention on the Rights of the Child.* New York: United Nations. 2007.

Ovey, Clare and White, Robin, *Jacobs and White: The European Convention on Human Rights* (4th ed.). Oxford: Oxford University Press. 2006.

Peleg, Noam, 'International Children's Rights Law: General Principles', in Kilkelly, Ursula and Liefaard, Ton (eds), *International Human Rights of Children.* Singapore: Springer. 2019, 135–157.

Rap, SE, 'The Right to Information of (Un)Accompanied Refugee Children: Improving Refugee Children's Legal Position, Fundamental Right, Implementation and Emotional Well-Being in the Netherlands', *The International Journal of Children's Rights,* 28, 322–351, 2020.

Rishmawi, Mervat, 'The Revised Arab Charter on Human Rights: A Step Forward?', *HRLR,* 5, 361–376, 2005.

Schabas, William A, *The European Convention on Human Rights: A Commentary.* Oxford: Oxford: Oxford University Press, Incorporated. 2015.

Stalford, Helen, 'Child-Friendly Justice through Child-Friendly Methods –Let's Start with the Right to Information', *Social Inclusion,* 5(3), 207–218, 2017.

Thorgeirsdóttir, Herdís, *A Commentary on the United Nations Convention on the Rights of the Child, Article 13: The Right to Freedom of Expression.* Leiden: Brill. 2006.

Tobin, John and Archard, David, 'Article 1: The Definition of a Child', in Tobin, John (ed), *The UN Convention on the Rights of the Child: A Commentary.* Oxford: Oxford University Press. 2019, 21–40.

Tobin, John and Handsley, Elizabeth, 'Article 17: The Mass Media and Children: Diversity of Sources, Quality of Content, and Protection against Harm', in Tobin, John (ed), *The UN Convention on the Rights of the Child: A Commentary.* Oxford: Oxford University Press. 2019, 600–645.

Tobin, John and Parkes, Aisling, 'Article 13: The Right to Freedom of Expression', in Tobin, John (ed), *The UN Convention on the Rights of the Child: A Commentary.* Oxford: Oxford University Press. 2019, 435–474.

Tobin, John and Peleg, Noam, 'Article 6: The Rights to Life, Survival, and Development', in Tobin, John (ed), *The UN Convention on the Rights of the Child: A Commentary.* Oxford: Oxford University Press. 2019, 186–236.

Van Bueren, Geraldine, *The International Law on the Rights of the Child* [paperback edition]. The Hague: Martinus Nijhoff. 1998.

Vella, Kyle, 'Power, Paternalism and Children on the Move', *Journal of International Humanitarian Action,* 1, 1–12, 2016.

Other source

United Nations Treaty Collection. https://treaties.un.org/, accessed 31 March 2022.

4 Digitalising children's humanitarian access

A way to enhance children's inclusion

*Jessica Jonsson**

1. Introduction

> Innovations in digital technologies affect children's lives and their rights in ways that are wide-ranging and interdependent – even children who do not themselves access the Internet. Meaningful access to digital technologies can support children to realize the full range of their civil, political, cultural, economic and social rights. However, if digital inclusion is not achieved, existing inequalities are likely to increase, and new ones may arise.[1]

In relation to this quote from the UN Committee on the Rights of the Child, children's rights and digital space may have been given little consideration during the drafting of the Convention on the Rights of the Child (CRC)[2] but, since 1989 and especially in the past decade, internet connectivity and digital technology have been influencing children's ways of exercising their rights in the modern world.[3] With COVID-19, this influence received yet another impetus as various communications, services and education moved online. Meaningful access through digital inclusion lacks any express provision in the CRC to recognise children's right to access and use technology or digital space, but the growing importance of digital technology in their

* Jessica Jonsson, Senior Lecturer at Örebro University, holds an LLD (PhD in law) from the European University Institute and an LLM (master's in law) from the European Academy of Legal Theory.

1 UN Committee on the Rights of the Child, *General Comment No. 25 on Children's Rights in Relation to the Digital Environment,* CRC/C/GC/25, (2021) para 4.

2 1980 Convention on the Rights of the Child, General Assembly Resolution 44/25, Annex, 44 UN *General Assembly Official Records* (GAOR) Supplement No. 49, 167, entered into force 2 September 1990.

3 'Internet access' is used throughout to denote internet connectivity, also known as the 'right to broadband' or 'freedom to connect' (to Wi-Fi and the internet, cellular connection, ethernet and Bluetooth). 'Universal access' usually means access to publicly available communication network facilities and services, typically provided by such means as pay telephones, community telecentres and community internet access terminals.

DOI: 10.4324/9781003187493-4

lives makes this access essential and called upon by UN Resolutions and General Comments.[4]

The UN Committee on the Rights of the Child General Comment No. 25 on children's rights in relation to the digital environment ('the General Comment') makes it clear that new modes and methods of warfare are not the only challenges to how we perceive and conceptualise humanitarian response. In addition, the digital potential for the children concerned (beneficiaries) to use present-day digitalised opportunities, with digital technologies and big data transforming our societies and crisis responses, is significant. Harnessing the power of technology and digital innovation may bring digital public goods that promote digitalised humanitarianism and, with it, accelerated inclusion in more effective and transparent crisis responses.

Once evaluations of innovations, case studies and best practice standards are completed, understanding of potential benefits will improve. Yet most studies focus on integration and future growth. Nonetheless, innovations combined with swift changes and risks at times of emergency entail unknown vulnerabilities for beneficiaries. Progress in artificial intelligence (AI) and automated data processing, for example, is also rapid and may pose threats to privacy and protection rights in the private sphere. This places a heavy responsibility on governments, the business sector and humanitarian actors to ensure, through legislation, regulation and policies, that children are protected from further violations while benefiting from access and digital inclusion.

The aim of this chapter is modest. It offers a critical inquiry into certain aspects of digitalised humanitarianism, illustrated by a few of the many emerging digital technologies involved in humanitarian response. The perspective is that of the Committee on the Rights of the Child ('the Committee') in its recent emphasis on the importance of children's access to digital technologies and digital inclusion, within the context of humanitarian response.[5] While recognising certain potential benefits of our contemporary digitalised humanitarianism, the chapter discusses some key challenges. The author maintains that technology must do no harm and that the current digitalised drive towards accountability, with a potential paradigm shift towards anticipation, is still in the making.

Since global problems, such as disease outbreaks and refugee crises, have been growing and proliferating at an ever-faster rate, innovative new ways to respond to challenges affecting children in humanitarian crises are seen as an important driver in further digitalisation of humanitarian interventions. The humanitarian crisis in Ukraine has involved a society in which technology is more readily available and the business sector more cooperatively

4 See, for example, CRC/C/GC/25 (n 1) paras 4, 28–29.
5 Ibid., para 4.

inclined than, for example, in the Syrian context.[6] In these vulnerable situations, children's access to the digital environment is important, and research has shown how separated children's access to digital technologies is especially so.[7]

This chapter opens with a few illustrations of the humanitarian sector's digital transformation by humanitarian actors utilising humanitarian technologies and a discussion of why children's digital inclusion and access to the digital environment should be inserted in the legal framework. Many global challenges, including crisis mapping and security monitoring applications, can now be found within the scope of what this chapter recognises as humanitarian digital technologies. Thanks to substantial investments from UN agencies, donor governments, businesses and large organisations, digitalised humanitarian assistance now exists that benefit from various forms of automated data processing, information and communication technologies, humanitarian applications and digitalised processes. Digitalised tools and processes comprise far more than the internet: they encompass content, software and applications too. These products may be in written, verbal, visual and/or auditory form – through mobile applications, for example, usually accessed on a smartphone or tablet – from public, commercial and/or other providers.

Possible implications of humanitarian digitalisation, such as further marginalisation of beneficiaries, are then addressed. The recent General Comment, designed to enable, protect and enforce active participation in the digital environment rather than mere passive inclusion, is cited throughout regarding digital access and inclusion and their implications.

The chapter ends with a few concluding remarks on the widespread use of digital innovations in the quest for improved accountability, on an observed shift towards more anticipatory digitalised humanitarianism and on the relevance of the developing legal framework of children's access to and inclusion in the digital environment in a humanitarian context.[8]

6 Offshore Technology, 'I'm Not Planning to Die, Ukraine's Besieged Tech Workers and the Response from Their Colleagues around the World', www.offshore-technology.com/special-focus/Im-not-planning-to-die-Ukraines-besieged-tech-workers-and-the-response-from-their-colleagues-around-the-world/ accessed 29 May 2022; Department for International Development, 'The Use of Mobile Technology for Humanitarian Programming in Syria: Potential and Constraints', 29 March 2017, https://reliefweb.int/sites/reliefweb.int/files/resources/20170324%20SIM%20O3%20Research%20Report%201_Mobile%20Technology%20%281%29.pdf, accessed 1 May 2022.

7 CRC/C/GC/21 UN Committee on the Rights of the Child, *General Comment No. 21 on Children in Street Situations,* CRC/C/GC/21 (2017), para 35.

8 Mark Lowcock, *Anticipation Saves Lives: How Data and Innovative Financing Can Help Improve the World's Response to Humanitarian Crises* (2019). Speech delivered at the London School of Economics. London, 2 December, https://reliefweb.int/report/world/mark-lowcock/under-secretary-general-humanitarian-affairs-and-emergency-relief, accessed 2 May 2022.

Consistent definitions of 'child' and 'digital environment' are needed for any inquiry into children's digitalised humanitarian access. According to the CRC, a 'child' is anyone aged below 18. (In most industrialised countries, 18 is the age of majority, and a 'minor' is thus synonymous with the CRC definition of a 'child'.) In line with the General Comment, the 'digital environment' is 'constantly evolving and expanding, encompassing information and communications technologies, including digital networks, content, services and applications, connected devices and environments, virtual and augmented reality, artificial intelligence, robotics, automated systems, algorithms and data analytics, biometrics and implant technology'.[9] In terms of children's access, the Committee refers interchangeably to the 'digital environment', 'digital technology' and 'connectivity'.

2. Digitalised humanitarian access

While acknowledging that the digitalisation of technology ranges far and wide and that humanitarian crisis responders are not unfamiliar with technology facilitation, our focus remains on access to digital technologies that serve to fulfil or enable provision of humanitarian response – that is, essential means of exercising various fundamental child rights.[10] Information and communication technologies are recognised as critical forms of crisis response, without which disaster survivors cannot access response services; make the best decisions for themselves and their communities; or participate at local, national and/or international levels.[11] The importance of the legal framework and digitalised humanitarian technology on children's access to the digital environment is explored in the following sections.

2.1. Meaningful access to digital technologies

Children report that the digital environment represents vital opportunities for their voices to be heard in matters that affect them, and this is particularly true of children in humanitarian crises.[12] Children's right of access to

9 CRC/C/GC/25 (n 1) para 2.

10 Whereas technology has always had a role in humanitarian response, in the mid-1990s, humanitarian technology was added to the international policy agenda. See Robin Stephenson and Peter S. Anderson, 'Disasters and the Information Technology Revolution', *Disasters*, 21(4) (1997), 305–334, and on digitisation aimed at beneficiaries and communications with communities (CwC), see United Nations Office for the Coordination of Humanitarian Affairs (2013), *OCHA on Message: What Is Communication with Communities?*

11 UN Committee on the Rights of the Child, *General Comment No. 14 on the Right of the Child to Have His or Her Best Interests Taken as a Primary Consideration* (art. 3, para. 1), 29 May 2013, CRC/C/GC/14 (2013), paras 89–91.

12 Amanda Third and Lilly Moody, *Our Rights in a Digital World: A Report on the Children's Consultations to Inform UNCRC,* General Comment 25 (London and Sydney: 5Rights Foundation and Western Sydney University, 2021), 25, 95.

information in the humanitarian enterprise, as asserted in a previous chapter, represents a unique opportunity in the digital environment.[13] For children in armed conflicts, migrant and separated children and children in other vulnerable situations or remote locations, access to digital technologies is even more crucial.[14] Research indicates how children in low-income, rural settings and vulnerable situations tend to see internet access as a basic need that should constitute a right, and some see it as a right. To some, access to technology is the central issue and a precondition for realising a right to the internet, given that it is the principal means of communication today – sometimes the only one – and a life saver. In this context, most children consider access to a connected smartphone a basic need.[15]

This section serves to identify the significance of children's access to the digital environment, illustrated mainly by the legal framework.

2.1.1. Access to the digital environment

In a public emergency or a health or humanitarian crisis, using digital technologies to access health services and information may be the only option.[16] Available and easily accessible technologies, such as mobile telephony and content in humanitarian applications, have provided a valuable space.[17] As illustrated by the Syrian and Ukrainian conflicts, mobile applications and messaging services such as Facebook Messenger, WhatsApp, WeChat, KakaoTalk and Telegram have become integral to present-day responses to humanitarian crises. The ability of many individuals in affected areas to post images, videos and texts about a specific situation in a particular area on various social media platforms has changed not only crisis response but also the speed at which many beneficiaries can react.[18] Fast access to crisis response services has been the idea behind many types of humanitarian applications as well.[19]

13 See preceding chapter, by Rigmor Argren.
14 CRC/C/GC/25 (n 1), paras 87,121, and see CRC/C/GC/21 (n 7), para 35.
15 Third and Moody (n 12), 14.
16 CRC/C/GC/25 (n 1), para 93.
17 Kristin Bergtora Sandvik, 'The Humanitarian Cyberspace: Shrinking Space or an Expanding Frontier?', *Third World Quarterly*, 37(1) (2016), 219–242.
18 Kristin Bergtora Sandvik, M Gabrielsen Jumbert, J Karlsrud and M Kaufmann, 'Humanitarian Technology: A Critical Research Agenda', *International Review of the Red Cross*, 96(893) (2014), 223.
19 The Humanitarian Kiosk application, for example, was designed because, after the Haiti earthquake, humanitarians took to visiting, and downloading the latest information at, the physical reception centre ('humanitarian kiosk') managed by the UN Office for the Coordination of Humanitarian Affairs (OCHA). The application enables humanitarians to share up-to-date information that is readily available for download from a mobile device for offline use. Humanitarians can provide and access concrete information about crises and engage constructively in coordination mechanisms. Senior UN managers and donors can make urgent decisions about funding and programme priorities based on current

Some of the rights and freedoms realised during the pandemic, for example, were facilitated by internet access and availability of digital technology, freedom of expression, access to health services and the right to education and information. The digital environment and human rights have become inseparable in recent scholarly and legal policy commentaries, and scholars including Land and Çalı have put forward arguments for a human right to internet access that is also derived from other fundamental human rights protected by international law.[20] Whereas no explicit right to internet access has yet been recognised,[21] a series of UN resolutions have been passed on the subject. In 2016 the UN General Assembly passed a resolution that declared internet access a human right.[22] The resolution inspired further pressure for the recognition of the right to internet access as an ancillary right but failed to address governmental responsibility to provide universal access.[23] The Council of Europe Recommendation of 2018 also refers to access to the digital environment and connectivity in relation to fulfilling rights and principles for the child.[24] It highlights access to digital technology as an operational principle and a measure to respect, protect and fulfil the rights of the child in the digital environment.[25]

The most recent UN resolution goes further, emphasising the importance of applying a human-rights–based approach to internet access and calling on all stakeholders

> to bridge digital divides within and between countries, with particular attention to the poorest and those in the most vulnerable situations, as

---

information. Beneficiaries can get a better idea of the crisis and the availability of response services by selecting the closest humanitarian kiosk to their own location. *Humanitarian Kiosk* application: https://itunes.apple.com/us/app/humanitarian-kiosk/id546482411.

20 Başak Çalı, 'The Case for the Right to Meaningful Access to the Internet as a Human Right in International Law', in A Von Arnauld, K Von der Decken and M Susi (eds), *The Cambridge Handbook of New Human Rights: Recognition, Novelty, Rhetoric* (Cambridge: Cambridge University Press, 2020), 276–284; Molly Land, 'Toward an International Law of the Internet', *Harvard International Law Journal*, 54(2) (2013), 393–458. See also A Pettrachin, 'Towards a Universal Declaration on Internet Rights and Freedoms?', *International Communication Gazette*, 80(4) (2018), 337–353. See e.g. the Universal Declaration of Human Rights, 10 December 1948 (UN GARES 217 A), Article 19; International Covenant on Civil and Political Rights, Article 19(2), opened for signature on 19 December 1966, 999 *United Nations Treaty Collection* (UNTC) 171 (entered into force on 23 March 1976), see also Articles 22 and 25.

21 Articles 9 and 21 of the *Convention on the Rights of Persons with Disabilities* do, however, expressly refer to access to the Internet for people with disabilities, including through the use of accessible formats.

22 A/HRC/32/L.20 (2016); A/HRC/RES/32/13 and see A/HRC/47/L.22 (2021).

23 Stephen Tully, 'A Human Right to Access the Internet? Problems and Prospects', *Human Rights Law Review*, 14(2) (June 2014), 175–195.

24 CM/REC(2018)7 of the Committee of Ministers to the member states: *Guidelines to respect, protect and fulfil the rights of the child in the digital environment*, 13.

25 Ibid.

well as women and children, and to promote affordable and reliable connectivity, digital access and digital inclusion, and the expansion of accessible and inclusive public services, distance-learning solutions and digital health services'[26]

While non-binding, and not explicitly mentioning legal obligations to provide the infrastructure necessary for internet access, it nonetheless marks a significant step towards greater legal recognition of an internet access right.

Given that the ever-changing digital environment is vital in enabling fundamental human rights, access to digital technologies has become all the more important, and this is also recognised as a right through state practice in a growing number of nations.[27] Four out of five individuals believe internet access is a fundamental right, according to a survey by the BBC.[28] Hamelink suggests that a recognition of the freedom of expression as an express right would enhance the claim to a right to access, since, by implication, related entitlements to facilities for the exercise of this right would be included.[29] He also supports a collective right of internet access for certain vulnerable groups who are otherwise often denied access.

Whereas the UN Human Rights Council, in resolution 48/13 of October 2021, recognises that a clean, healthy, and sustainable environment is a human right, internet access remains an enabling right for the time being. The trend towards recognising the right to access to digital technologies is rooted in the principles of indivisibility and interdependence of fundamental human rights, as referred to in all major human rights treaties, and a characteristic of children's rights in particular.[30] Here, the comprehensiveness of the recent General Comment is encouraging. The rights of the child must be respected, protected and fulfilled in the digital environment, just as they must be offline. Children's rights in the digital environment are thus different from digital rights. In the General Comment, this is reflected, for example, in the statement that access to digital technologies can enable children 'to realise the full range of their civil, political, cultural, economic

26 A/HRC/47/16, para 6.

27 Estonia classified internet access as a human right in 2001, after which Finland, Sweden, Canada, Germany, Greece, Costa Rica and France followed suit. In 2013, Mexico also declared such access a human right. CRC/C/GC/25 (n 1), para 28; Vint Cerf, *Internet Is Not a Human Right* (2012), www.nytimes.com/2012/01/05/opinion/internet-access-is-not-a-human-right.html?_r=1, accessed 29 April 2022. A commentary from Joy Liddicoat of APC may be found at www.apc.org/en/news/access-internet-and-human-rightsthanks-vint, accessed 12 June 2022.

28 BBC News, 'Internet Poll', http://news.bbc.co.uk/2/shared/bsp/hi/pdfs/08_03_10_BBC_internet_poll.pdf, accessed 1 May 2022.

29 Cees Hamelink, 'Human Rights in Cyberspace', in *Cyberidentities: Canadian and European Presence in Cyberspace* (Ottawa. Les Presses de l'Université d'Ottawa | University of Ottawa Press, 1999).

30 ICCPR Article 2 states that nations must take steps to give immediate effect to the enumerated rights.

and social rights'.[31] To enable realisation of the full range of child rights, this digital technology access is required to be *meaningful*.[32]

2.1.2. *Meaningful access*

According to the Human Rights Committee's General Comment No. 34 and the report of the Special Rapporteur of the Human Rights Council, governments have a positive duty to promote and provide both infrastructure and hardware for enabling access.[33] 'Given that the Internet has become an indispensable tool for realising a range of human rights, combating inequality and accelerating development and human progress, ensuring universal access to the Internet should be a priority for all States.'[34] La Rue acknowledges that disadvantaged groups 'often face barriers to accessing the Internet in a way that is meaningful, relevant and useful to them in their daily lives'.[35]

For children as a vulnerable group, the United Nations 2003 World Summit on the Information Society recommended that national e-strategies address the special requirements of older people, persons with disabilities, children (especially marginalised children) and other disadvantaged and vulnerable groups by means including appropriate educational, administrative and legislative measures, to ensure their full inclusion in the Information Society.[36] The UN secretary-general has called on states, NGOs and private entities to enable universal coverage.[37] If meaningfulness depends on universal access, full digital inclusion that extends beyond rights of access must be achieved. Digital inclusion is recognised as necessary not only to promote equality of access to content and services but also to overcome and prevent inequalities that may impede the ever-growing impact of the digital environment on children's lives. Even in countries where connectivity per se is not an issue, children report that their lack of digital inclusion can be problematic.[38]

31 CRC/C/GC/25 (n 1), para 4.

32 Ibid., para 4, states are required to ensure all children equal and effective access to the digital environment, paras 9, 28; see also CRC/C/GC/9 (2006), paras 37–38; *Report of the Special Rapporteur on the Promotion and Protection of the Right to Freedom of Opinion and Expression*, Frank La Rue, Human Rights Council, UN Document A/HRC/17/27 (16 May 2011), paras 61, 87.

33 Human Rights Committee, General Comment No. 34 on Article 19: Freedoms of Opinion and Expression, 15, UN Doc. CCPR/C/GC/34 (12 September 2011); ibid., La Rue.

34 La Rue (n 32) para 85, 22 and see further 17, https://www2.ohchr.org/english/bodies/hrcouncil/docs/17session/a.hrc.17.27_en.pdf.

35 Ibid., para 61.

36 World Summit on the Information Society: *Plan of Action*, para 9(e), WSIS-03/GENEVA/DOC/5-E, 2003.

37 UN Report of the Secretary General. Roadmap for Digital Cooperation (June 2020).

38 Amanda Third, S Livingstone and G Lansdowne, 'Recognising Children's Rights in Relation to Digital Technologies: Challenges of Voice and Evidence, Principle and Practice',

A lack of meaningful access may be due to a variety of factors. Financial constraints (not only in low-income countries), gender and other bases of discrimination are among the more common factors, seldom absent in a humanitarian setting.[39] The Committee addresses issues for children who are affected by armed conflicts, those who are internally displaced, migrants, asylum seekers and refugees, unaccompanied minors, children living in street settings and those affected by natural disasters. In these vulnerable situations, states parties should ensure safe, secure, private and beneficial access for such children to the digital environment.[40] The potential of digitalisation must be recognised, and individuals' aspirations and sometime belief that internet access is a right must not be ignored. In dire situations of humanitarian crisis, digital access is considered as valuable as a meal or more so, because it enables people to stay connected and search for family members.[41]

This context necessitates international and regional cooperation, owing to the cross-border and transnational nature of the digital environment and the stakeholders alike. This cooperation can ensure that nations, businesses and other actors effectively enable access to both internet and the requisite digital technologies to assist in providing the content of the crisis response, to respect, protect and fulfil children's rights.[42] The Committee goes as far as to state that it is vital for all parties involved to cooperate, both bilaterally and multilaterally.

The business sector's role is emphasised and explained where responsibilities are shared among states parties and enterprises, including non-profit organisations,[43] that provide products and services associated with digital technologies. There is official recognition of the sector's obligations to conduct due diligence regarding child rights and also to apply self-regulatory policies and codes of conduct so as to prevent and respond to risks and associated harm.[44] State parties are responsible, through legislation, regulation and policies, to ensure that businesses fulfil their obligations. Mobile

---

in B Wagner, MC Kettemann and K Vieth (eds), *Research Handbook on Human Rights and Digital Technology: Global Politics, Law and International Relations* (Cheltenham, UK: Edward Elgar Publishing, 2019), 376–410; Third and Moody (n 12), 16.

39 Third and Moody (n 12), 25, 18.

40 CRC/C/GC/25 (n 1), para 121.

41 A population desperate to connect, refugee voices. UNHCR *Connectivity for Everyone*, www.unhcr.org/innovation/connectivity-for-everyone/, accessed 3 June 2022.

42 (n 1) para 123.

43 (n 1) para 35, 6–7.

44 Policy and codes of conduct initiatives for using technology innovations in humanitarian work exist: UNHCR, UNICEF, the GSM Association and Deloitte, for example, have codes of conduct for innovation-related-interventions. Whereas response to humanitarian crises is regulated by a range of general standards, such as Sphere and the Humanitarian Accountability Partnership Standard, there is no specific set of principles related to innovation. See Jonathan Corpus Ong and Pamela Combinido, 'Local Aid Workers in the Digital Humanitarian Project: Between "Second Class Citizens" and "Entrepreneurial Survivors" ', *Critical Asian Studies*, 53 (2017).

applications, social media and chatbots, for example, continue to prosper, along with internet access and automated data processing, creating a natural engagement between humanitarians and tech companies.[45] This collaboration has led to better, more data-driven decision-making throughout the humanitarian programme cycle and improved communication between humanitarians and beneficiaries, which support earlier, faster humanitarian response as well as a move towards anticipatory action.

Digital and often also mobile applications quickly capture information about incidents and the needs of affected populations so that they can understand and respond to crises better. They facilitate communication with vast numbers of people to crowdsource information and paint a more holistic picture of a crisis as it unfolds. They can expedite the transmission of life-saving messages, even to and from inaccessible areas. Fundamentally, they can serve as a lifeline for those affected by a crisis; enhance community engagement and acceptance; and bring about a more people-centred, coordinated and accountable response. It has been shown that with crowdsourcing, drone mapping and unmanned aerial vehicles, for example, anticipatory action can be built on more holistic data.[46] Real-time crisis data can be recorded by drones and beneficiaries reached with unmanned aerial vehicles. This is time and resource saving and can build community trust. Predictive analytics and emergency preparedness planning also indicate a move towards anticipatory action or anticipatory humanitarianism. Current and historical data is used in forecasting predictions about future humanitarian crises such as floods or famines, facilitated in various countries.[47]

Ong argues that digitalised humanitarianism has the potential to correct past inefficiencies and increase transparency and accountability, since digital technologies facilitate communication among all parties – the business sector, humanitarians and beneficiaries.[48] Sandvik agrees that digitalisation can change the distribution of power among agencies, since it provides beneficiaries with a digital voice that can upend hierarchical power structures.[49]

45 From 2004 to 2015, the world saw a rise of over 50% in smartphone and internet use in Africa, the Middle East and elsewhere. More than 78% of the world's mobile-phone subscriptions are linked to developing countries. See GSMA, 'Mobile Connectivity Charter', www.gsma.com/mobilefordevelopment/mobile-for-humanitarian-innovation/humanitarian-connectivity-charter, accessed 1 May 2022.

46 OCHA facilitates anticipatory action, see project examples since 2020 via www.unocha.org/our-work/humanitarian-financing/anticipatory-action. See also Mark Lowcock, 'A Casement Lecture: Towards a Better System for Humanitarian Financing' UNOCHA (2018), Press release 23 March.

47 Through the World Food Programme, the Food and Agriculture Organisation of the UN, the International Federation of Red Cross and Red Crescent Societies and the Start Network, for example. See Bo Pieter Johannes Andree et al., 'Predicting Food Crises', Policy Research Working Paper, No. 9412. World Bank, Washington, DC (2020).

48 Ong and Combinido (n 44), 4.

49 Sandvik (n 17), 22 and see Róisín Read, Bertrand Taithe and Roger Mac Ginty, 'Data Hubris? Humanitarian Information Systems and the Mirage of Technology', *Third World Quarterly*, 37(8) (2016).

Nowadays, displaced people can speak out and express their opinions on various digital platforms, such as Twitter or Facebook, and complain about suspected fraud, problems with e-transfers or digital registration, mistreatment by or defects in the data processing of the United Nations High Commissioner for Refugees (UNHCR) or digital cash transfers by the World Food Programme (WFP), for example. In this digital environment, efforts to combat corruption, malpractice, incompetence, illegal data handling and digital inclusion boost accountability. Read et al. state that 'systems constructed to move information up and down hierarchies are facing a new reality where information can be generated by anyone, shared with anyone and acted on by anyone'[50] – that is, anyone with an internet connection and access to digital technology.

2.2. Digitalised humanitarianism and digitally included children

This section illustrates digital inclusion of children in humanitarian response to crises by means of a few humanitarian technologies. Innovations range from new products and technologies to novel systems and approaches. In terms of digital inclusion, access to and the affordability of digital technology promote free and secure access, as do policies supporting informed use of digital technologies, not only in educational settings but in communities and homes.[51]

Clearly, both the United Nations International Children's Fund (UNICEF) and UNHCR are highly engaged in digital innovations, whether directly through cash-based interventions integrating e-transfers (UNHCR) or indirectly. Examples of their indirect action are improved internet access and the UNICEF Cryptocurrency Fund, designed to accelerate and grow projects and bring internet connectivity to schools.[52]

Digital platforms that combine information on rights, obligations and service locations with interactive chatbots that reply in real time to questions raised by migrants are becoming more common in the migration context as in others.[53] Because they can rapidly convey critical information to huge numbers of people, the use of chatbots – launched via messaging

50 Ibid., Read et al. 8.

51 CRC/C/GC/25 (n 1), para 28; UNICEF Innovations, '10 Ways UNICEF Innovates', www.unicef.org/innovation/stories/10-ways-unicef-innovates-children, accessed 3 June 2022; #TechForUkraine (techtotherescue.org), accessed 1 May 2022.

52 Linda Raftree and Bachan Keshet, 'Integrating Information and Communication Technologies into Communication for Development Strategies to Support and Empower Marginalized Adolescent Girls', UNICEF, 1 August 2013; ibid. UNICEF Innovations; UNHCR, 'Connectivity for Everyone', www.unhcr.org/innovation/connectivity-for-everyone/ accessed 3 June 2022.

53 UNHCR Turkey, for example, has facilitated this, along with EU humanitarian aid and other donors for refugees and asylum seekers; https://turkey.servicesadvisor.org, accessed 1 May 2022.

platforms like WhatsApp, Facebook and Viber – increased with the pandemic. Chatbot use favours specific user objectives of AI learning from data and interactions, requiring automated data processes and thus user-friendly access to, and digital inclusion in, reliable data interactions.[54] Today, for example, Microsoft, jointly with the Norwegian Refugee Council and University College Dublin, is developing AI-powered chatbots to help educate adolescent refugees to increase digital inclusion. UNICEF is developing a safe guide, with blueprints for vulnerable women and children using chatbots, to combat automated messages that may cause further emotional suffering among, for example, digital users who have been sexually exploited. For correct automated data processing, such blueprints require the digital participation, access and inclusion of vulnerable groups.

Informed and practical guidance on how best to implement child rights in light of the evolving digital society is offered in the General Comment.[55] The issues concerned are complex, often controversial and politically charged, touching on 'sharenting' (when people blog, tweet and post information and pictures about every aspect of their children's lives), exploitation and end-to-end encryption, to name a few topics. Duty bearers are often reminded that the same principles – such as the best interests of the child, the proportionality of responses and the principle of evolving capacities – that apply to child rights in offline space apply equally in online space. Balancing important protection rights and needs against the emphasis on digital inclusion and the urgent need for children to access digital technology accentuates crisis response with the humanitarian child protection aims of enabling rights to privacy, civil and political participation and family and community life. Owing to online safety risks and big data protection, protection responses have resulted in near-neglect of other types of response.[56] Again, a right to expression would emphasise not only children's digital inclusion but their meaningful access.

The General Comment also ably assists in describing how, when there is a conflict between two different rights in the CRC, it conflicts should be resolved with the aim of upholding the highest levels of realisation for both. For example, digitalised health and child protection interventions use several technologies (such as solar power to run mobile telephones, internet and radio) to expand health protection objectives, particularly through

54 WHO and Rakuten, 'Viber Fight COVID-19 Misinformation with Interactive Chatbot', 31 June 2020, www.who.int/news-room/feature-stories/detail/who-and-rakuten-viber-fight-covid-19-misinformation-with-interactive-chatbot.

55 The 25th General Comment is one of the more cognisant of the Committee's general comments, since consultation with children took place; see Third and Moody (n 12), 17, 95. All references to children's views refer to this report, https://5rightsfoundation.com/uploads/OurRIghtsinaDigitalWorld-FullReport.pdf.

56 The Child Rights Committee's 2019 *Guidelines Regarding the Interpretation of the Optional Protocol to the Convention on the Rights of the Child on the Sale of Children, Child Prostitution and Child Pornography* should be read in conjunction with GC/25.

distribution and mapping of antenatal and postnatal data.[57] Lambo suggests that Mwana3, the UNICEF project in Zambia and Malawi, has improved early HIV diagnosis and provided health care via mobile phones.[58]

Reaching remote and vulnerable groups and situations means that births that would otherwise be undocumented can be registered – a first step in securing a child's right to identity and access to services, as discussed by Mattila in the Syrian context.[59] The numerous opportunities that digital identification and birth registration offer for realisation of children's rights to health, education and welfare must be recognised. At the same time, the sensitive data stored in digital birth registration systems must be considered, with emphasis on the need for robust privacy and data protection frameworks.

Children are often aware that digital technology, biometric data and automated data processing can be detrimental to their rights and health, yet their responses indicate that the advantages of technology for their right to health and wellbeing outweigh the drawbacks.[60] Scholars indicate how digitalisation is changing our understanding of humanitarian response and at times serving as an end in itself, in terms of improving crisis preparedness or effective response, through such concepts like digital information-as-aid.[61] E-transfers – digital payments as part of a strategic global shift from distribution of in-kind relief to e-transfers – emerged in many places during the pandemic and should be seen as part of a multifaceted protection response in which no single, standardised response can afford complete protection.[62] E-transfers are associated with biometric identity management systems that include fingerprints and iris scans to facilitate and accelerate system-protected identification for digital payments. This empowers children by enhancing their freedom of expression and giving them agency

57 M Mosoke, 'Some ICTs and Their Effect on Maternal Health in Uganda', in Dorothea Kleine, David Hollow and Sammia Poveda (eds), *Children, ICTs and Development: Capturing the Potential, Meeting the Challenges, Innocenti Insight* (UNICEF Office of Research. Innocenti, 2009).

58 N Lambo et al., 'Using Mobile Phones to Improve Early Infant HIV Diagnostic Services, Post-Natal Follow-up and Care' (2011) in ibid Kleine, Hollow and Poveda (2014).

59 M Mattila, 'Mobile Phones in Child Protection' (2011) in ibid Kleine, Hollow and Poveda (2014).

60 Third and Moody (n 12), 43, 48, 84.

61 Katja Lindskov Jacobsen and Kristin Bergtora Sandvik, 'UNHCR and the Pursuit of International Protection: Accountability through Technology?', *Third World Quarterly*, 39(8) (2018), 1508–1524; Sandvik (n 17); Patrick Vinck (ed), 'World Disasters Report', International Federation of Red Cross and Red Crescent Societies (2013), 20.

62 Gil Loescher, 'UNHCR and the Erosion of Refugee Protection', *Forced Migration Review*, April 2001; UNHCR, *Emergency Handbook: Accountability to Affected Populations* (2022), UNHCR, *Emergency Handbook: Accountability to Affected Populations*, https://emergency.unhcr.org/entry/42554/accountability-to-affected-people-aap, accessed 1 May 2022; ibid., Jacobsen and Sandvik.

to meet their own needs, with greater discretion than non-digital alternatives.[63] Access to e-transfers concerning cash-based interventions[64] and data processing related to arriving refugees' family structure and contact information accelerates mapping, relocation and transfer procedures and reduces waiting time to supplementary protection and health services.[65] Participation and digital inclusion are facilitated by means of additional connectivity programmes, if they are part of the same crisis response, and by the omnipresence of mobile phones.[66] At the same time, e-transfers facilitate a more transparent, traceable, cost-/time-effective and accountable humanitarian response.[67] Moreover, a cultural shift is under way that fosters involvement with the business sector, such as service providers in various countries at a very local level as well.[68]

Restrictions on content may be the only feasible means of protecting children from harmful materials. This kind of control must be balanced against other, conflicting rights, such as freedom of expression and the right to privacy. Stressing the importance of children's right to privacy and the privacy-by-design in the General Comment are seen as reflecting the Committee´s view that privacy rights are as important as protection rights, and this is also reflected in its position on end-to-end encryption.[69]

If end-to-end encryption is considered the appropriate measure, alternative ways of detecting child sexual exploitation and abuse, strictly according to the principles of legality, necessity and proportionality, should be

63 The World Food Programme has taken the lead in cash assets, where the benefits of being able to work from afar in difficult security environments are an additional reason the beneficiaries prefer e-transfers: they afford freedom of choice and lessen insecurities concerning cash and its misuse. World Bank, *Cash for Assets: World Food Programme's Exploration of the In-kind to E-payments Shift for Food Assistance in Kenya* (Washington, DC: CGAP/World Bank, 2013), www.cgap.org/sites/default/files/eG2P_Kenya.pdf, accessed 1 July 2022.

64 Cash-based interventions have increased not only in terms of range. Many organisations are moving from material assistance to digital cash, and this has also identified engagement with the business sector as a requirement for prompt deployment of local payment mechanisms. Jenny Casswell et al., *Navigating the Shift to Digital Humanitarian Assistance: Lessons from the International Rescue Committee's Experience*, Global System for Mobile Communications (GSMA) (December 2019).

65 See UNHCR's 'Policy on Biometrics in Refugee Registration and Verification Processes', 20 December 2010, IOM/083/2010 – FOM/083/2010 (internal). See also the digital app UNHCR Verify Plus on the App Store (apple.com) or UNHCR Verify Plus (apps available on Google Play).

66 UNHCR, 'Connectivity for Everyone', www.unhcr.org/innovation/connectivity-for-everyone/ accessed 3 June 2022; UNICEF, '10 Ways UNICEF Innovates', www.unicef.org/innovation/stories/10-ways-unicef-innovates-children, accessed 3 June 2022.

67 See Belinda Baah, *Mobilising Cash and Voucher Assistance Programmes: The Case for Mobile Money*. Global System for Mobile Communications (GSMA) (March 2019).

68 See Jenny Casswell et al., *Navigating the Shift to Digital Humanitarian Assistance: Lessons from the International Rescue Committee's Experience*. Global System for Mobile Communications (GSMA) (December 2019).

69 CRC/C/GC/25 (n 1), paras 70, 77, 88, 110, 116.

considered. Content control, which is necessary to some extent with big data, requires data protection legislation, regulations and policies that include children and their digital access. Since February 2022, use of the Russian developed application Telegram, which offers end-to-end encryption, has increased by 200%.[70] Prior to 2022, humanitarian information and communication technology had subsisted mainly through mobile applications (such as WhatsApp), social media and e-transfers. Telegram has turned out to be the Ukrainians' chosen mode of communication, and humanitarians and a huge network of volunteers elsewhere have followed suit, reaching the many response channels organised in the application. The founders claim that privacy is a sacred necessity in the complex information-sharing sphere.[71]

Evident from this increased participation is how digital technology enabling two-way communication is also vital in creating trust to enable digital inclusion. This is even more important with cyberwarfare and extensive attempts to control social media under way, as the Russian invasion of Ukraine has highlighted. Individual beneficiaries and communities willingly share knowledge of access when the equipment is trusted, and the information shared is peer to peer or through the local community. Otherwise, children have difficulty in finding appropriate information in their own language.[72]

To make the digital solution fit the context, local partnership in digitalised technology is important and empowers local knowledge and meaningful access. Local partnership is, moreover, a means of avoiding digital colonialism, or at least humanitarian-driven solutions.[73] Negotiating connectivity with telecom companies to provide early-warning messaging, distribution of additional technology, power lines and free internet access points adds value to the primarily used and trusted mobile phones, in locations such as evacuation centres where communication is of the utmost importance. Viewing digital technology as adding value to the beneficiaries' existing preferred channels of communication means that essential knowledge about, and trust in, the technology already exists. This saves valuable time and resources, while furthering accessibility, digital inclusion, local partnership, impact and accountability.

70 NRP, 'Telegram Is the App of Choice in the War in Ukraine Despite Experts' Privacy and Protection Concerns', 14 March 2022, www.npr.org/2022/03/14/1086483703/telegram-ukraine-war-russia?t=1652383321929, accessed 2 July 2022.

71 Using blockchain, cryptocurrency has been allowed for transfers of money into the country, similar to the UNICEF cryptocurrency fund. Daniel Kardefelt-Winther, E Day, G Berman, SK Witting and A Bose, on behalf of UNICEF's cross-divisional task force on child online protection, *Encryption, Privacy and Children's Right to Protection from Harm.* Innocenti Working Paper 2020–14 (Florence: UNICEF Office of Research. Innocenti, 2020).

72 Third and Moody (n 12), 27.

73 Nick Couldry and Ulises Mejias, 'Data Colonialism: Rethinking Big Data's Relation to the Contemporary Subject', *Television & New Media*, 20(4) (2019).

Within days, collective interagency humanitarian response must be in place, engaging with the beneficiaries. When electricity and the internet are available and mobile phones are largely accessible, as in Ukraine, there can be a rapid response that involves the local community; avoids misinformation; and improves crisis mapping, accessibility and digital inclusion. This, in turn, enhances the legitimacy of humanitarian anticipatory action by creating trust in the feedback channels and enhancing big data and early assessments.

3. Technology must do no harm

The 'do no harm' principle was developed for humanitarian assistance by Mary Anderson in the 1990s. Humanitarians must prevent or mitigate any adverse effects of the interventions that can make people more vulnerable to both physical and psychosocial risks.[74] The rapid evolution of digital technology during the past decade has significantly influenced crisis response. Sandvik discusses how, when digital innovations become more dominant in humanitarian crisis response, new risks and failures also arise.[75]

Unlawfully accessed and distributed humanitarian data and surveillance technology increase vulnerability and reduce any meaningful access and digital inclusion. Duty bearers, tech developers and humanitarians alike have increasingly realised that technology innovations are enabling new opportunities whilst necessitating protection of both data and of privacy.[76] Using data for purposes other than those for which they were collected or sharing data with third parties can, for example, put already vulnerable individuals and communities at further risk, especially in places where data-protection laws are underdeveloped or non-existent.

Today's digitalised borders take in an increased amount of personal data through AI, with the associated risk of digital discrimination and increased vulnerability, especially for migrant travellers. Automated decision-making includes algorithmic profiling and also facial recognition (biometric data), which are also used for categorising people and tracking data.[77] Algorithmic profiling should not include sensitive data for risk indicators, but there

74 See Mary B Anderson, *Do No Harm: How Aid Can Support Peace or War* (Boulder, CO: Lynne Rienner Publishers, 1999).

75 Sandvik (n 17), 40.

76 Mark Duffield, 'The Resilience of the Ruins: Towards a Critique of Digital Humanitarianism', *Resilience*, 4(3) (2016), 158; UNCRC article 16 '1. No child shall be subjected to arbitrary or unlawful interference with his or her privacy, family, home or correspondence, nor to unlawful attacks on his or her honour and reputation. 2. The child has the right to the protection of the law against such interference or attacks.'

77 Amended Europol Regulation 2018/1725 of the European Parliament and of the Council of 23 October 2018 on the protection of natural persons with regard to the processing of personal data by the Union institutions, bodies, offices and agencies and on the free movement of such data; see further video lie detector test with iBorderCtrl Case T-158/19,

is a potential for indirect discrimination because of the data profiling systems' difficulties with data concerning complex, fluid and changing migration movements.[78] There is an apparent limitation on the right to privacy in the context of cross-border sharing of the data. This border data grab is usually justified by arguments concerning national security, terrorism, serious crime and illegal movements.

Children's meaningful access to digitalised humanitarian response is not a question of successful ownership of any particular innovation or digital application that is used more frequently than others. Accountability must remain the main goal, with achievement of impact on beneficiaries and coordinated crisis response. Yet digital technology is not necessarily developed with the same approach in the non-profit sector as in the business sector, according to Jim Fruchterman of Tech Matters. Fernanda Baumhardt-Grojean of UN-OCHA agrees that digitalisation, from design to testing, takes place not *with* the beneficiaries (communities) but, rather, *for* them. The innovation market and challenging environment invites actors to test new technologies. There is cause for concern where, in automated data processing, aspects of misrepresentation, or of an absence of representation, lead to erroneous machine learning and data input. Accordingly, a high risk of further vulnerability is caused. Beneficiaries recognise the data-collecting process, and its possibly inadequate digital inclusion of the local partnership, and are affected by such data even if they are given no access.[79]

Similarly, when data collection is associated with incentives – when, for example, participants are given provisions – beneficiaries will lie in order to receive them, again distorting the data. To guarantee any meaningful sense of accountability, engaging not only humanitarians but also beneficiaries is essential. Undeniably, success in humanitarian response to crises is not driven by or measured in rights-holders accessing the digital environment. Moreover, technology does not generate but, rather, supports reform. The required reform is thus driven by successful access by and digital inclusion of children, where rights-holders and developers unite and set aside previous donor-led structures. These joint efforts, with continuous collaborative updating of software or other forms of innovation, have become evident in public health, for example. The power shift is further reinforced when it is endorsed by governments and large organisations that procure the technology, empowering grassroots participation.

Technology can break down. Humanitarians have been actively developing their own digital communication technology, to the extent that they

General Court of the European Union – Order of November, 12, 2019, in the case no T-158/19 (ECLI:EU:T:2019:791, EU-Lisa, Europol and Frontex collaboration.

78 See, for example, pre-vetting (EU REG 2018/1240) in the European Travel Information and Authorisation System (ETIAS) and flagging of potentially risky travellers (EU REG 2021/1134) in the Visa Information System (VIS).

79 Third and Moody (n 12), 108, 124.

appear obsessed with pursuing demand-driven solutions without questioning their own digital expertise. Capacity may be an available resource, but deficiencies in knowledge of how to use these applications or technologies persist. Furthermore, the drive to continue digitalising humanitarianism may favour preparedness for a new cycle of crisis response (AI foresight, anticipatory action) but also spells a risk that the protection window – the crisis response timeline of approximately a few months that may have elapsed during the development of new technology – may be missed.[80] As digital innovations are rapidly adopted and used in various crisis responses as part of digitalised humanitarianism, there is often less transformation of existing humanitarian infrastructure as a whole. Many organisations still use basic software programs to collect, manage and analyse data, for example.

Another essential feature is not 'reinventing the wheel': staying cost effective and learning from experience. In the non-profit sector, humanitarian applications already developed should be assessed jointly with the beneficiaries. In collaborative partnership enhancement, common tech applications can be improved in terms of accessibility and responsibilities. What is necessary, perhaps, is not constant invention of digitalised applications but merging of the most user-friendly ones, combined with a focus on connectivity – the other essential – to ensure that there is access and that no harm is done.

3.1. Digitalised marginalisation

The impact of internet development and digital technologies is well known. Today, the internet reaches most of the globe. From the 1950s, it rapidly became the fastest growing means of communication in history, with some of the world's largest companies in digital technology. The pandemic further accelerated digitalisation. Yet 37% of the global population, 2.9 billion people, have never accessed the internet, and many of them would lack the requisite technology or knowledge for access even if there were connectivity.[81]

The world's unimaginable need to access technology during the pandemic underlined how inequality of access to technology had created wide gaps in access to healthcare, education and earning capacity. This is

80 See, for example, Kristin Bergtora Sandvik, Katja Lindskov Jacobsen and Sean Martin McDonald, 'Do No Harm: A Taxonomy of the Challenges of Humanitarian Experimentation', *International Review of the Red Cross*, 99(904) (2017): Migration and Displacement, 99(1), 319–344; World Humanitarian Summit, 'Approach Paper – WHS Theme 3: Transformation through Innovation' (2014); Ramalingam et al. in Ong and Combinido (n 44); Frank Pasquale, 'Beyond Innovation and Competition: The Need for Qualified Transparency in Internet Intermediaries', *Northwestern University Law Review*, 104 (2010), 105.

81 UN ITU Report, '2.9 Billion People Still Offline', 30 November 2021, via itu.int, accessed 3 June 2022; N Buxton (ed), 'Digital Colonialism. Analysis of Europe's Trade Agenda', *Trade and Investment Policy Briefing*, October 2021.

discussed by Sandvik, who points out that, in relation to beneficiaries and crisis response, the 'digital divide continues to contribute to the power distributions among actors'.[82] In many areas regularly stricken by emergencies, digital inclusion is elusive because of poor infrastructure, a low level of technology and thus relatively little expertise, which impede access to the benefits of digitalised humanitarianism. Children report the costs of equipment and connection as key obstacles, along with lack of electricity and of awareness of technology in dire situations.[83] A UNICEF study found that, during the pandemic, at least 31% of schoolchildren lacked access to remote programmes via the internet, TV or radio, primarily because equipment or remote learning policies were lacking, while as many as two-thirds of school-aged children had no connectivity.[84] More than 70% of these students lived in rural areas, and over 75% came from the poorest 40% of households.[85] Only 47% of low-income countries used internet-based instruction, against 95% of upper-middle-income countries.

The digital divide extends beyond low- and middle-income countries. More than 24 million Americans have no access to broadband internet at home.[86] Increased marginalisation of children of colour was evident in online instruction during the pandemic, Native American children being the most marginalised.[87] The war in Ukraine further highlights marginalisation concerning access to digital technologies and digital know-how. Women have less access to and knowledge of connectivity, and the most vulnerable children have difficulty in accessing connected technology, such as mobile phones.

This is not an argument against a right to internet access – rather the opposite, since it is even more difficult to legislate and regulate around soft law policies. A right to internet access is important globally. Never has this been more apparent than today, after the COVID-19 pandemic. The use, or rather the lack, of digital technologies and connectivity is harming already marginalised groups and exacerbating the digital divide, widening the gaps

82 Sandvik (n 17), 22.

83 Third and Moody (n 12), 18.

84 UNICEF, 'Two Thirds of School Aged Children Have No Internet Access' (August 2020), www.unicef.org/press-releases/two-thirds-worlds-school-age-children-have-no-internet-access-home-new-unicef-itu, accessed 4 July 2022.

85 Carlos Brito, 'Covid-19 Has Intensified the Digital Divide', World Economic Forum, 24 September 2020.

86 G Porumbescu, 'The Digital Divide Leaves Millions at a Disadvantage during the Coronavirus Pandemic', 18 March 2020, https://theconversation.com/the-digital-divide-leaves-millions-at-a-disadvantage-during-the-coronavirus-pandemic-133608, accessed 1 May 2022.

87 Alliance for Excellent Education, 'New Analysis Shows Students of Color Far More Likely to Be Cut off from Online Learning', *COVID Response & Recovery, Data, Digital Divide*, 22 July 2020, https://all4ed.org/publication/homeworkgap/ accessed 3 June 2022; NRP, 'Native Americans on Tribal Land Are the Least Connected to High Speed Internet' (2018), www.npr.org/2018/12/06/673364305/native-americans-on-tribal-land-are-the-least-connected-to-high-speed-internet?t=1633013501045, accessed 1 May 2022.

between those with and without access, and between those who control and those who use the technologies. A right to internet access would facilitate digital inclusion for full realisation of child rights.

Minority languages are underrepresented in online, age-appropriate content. Even the world's fourth-largest language, Arabic, is lacking in content; machine learning and automated data processing have proved difficult to convert into Arabic, for example. Child-friendly content further marginalises many children in need, reducing or eliminating the meaningfulness of these children's internet access, even if they have it.[88]

Present-day digital colonialism sees the Global South in the hands of international corporations and governments that can control big data and internet censorship, where (according to Taylor) unevenly developed data protection laws allow this.[89] Discussed by Hosein and Nyst, the same types of technology that are used in the Global North, where regulations and legal safeguards are in place, are developed or tested in the Global South, where many crises-stricken countries have few and/or very weak data protection regulations and safeguards.[90] These, along with limited and expensive connectivity, also marginalise non-profit organisations with limited resources, knowledge and expertise in accessing information. Better-informed organisations with superior access to information might be able to develop better interventions and, consequently, potentially secure more resources to meet demands. Sandvik considers the political economy aspect of digitalisation a non-neutral factor to reckon with in the potential marginalisation of partnerships.[91] The vastness of the tech industry both attracts and forces new markets, and humanitarian partnerships add legitimacy. It is urgently necessary for transformation through innovation to stay relevant and effective, and scope for non-humanitarian or non-mandated trade-offs may have to be weighed against the prospect of being left behind by new organisations.[92]

In several ways, marginalising influences affect both access to funds and the distribution of power among the actors involved, which in turn affect the value of meaningful access and digital inclusion.

4. Concluding remarks

This section touches on the widespread use of digital technologies in the quest for improved accountability; the recognised shift towards more

88 Third and Moody (n 12), 19.

89 Taylor (2013), cited in Duffield (n 76).

90 Hosein and Nyst (2013), cited in Duffield (n 76).

91 Kristin Bergtora Sandvik, M Gabrielsen Jumbert, J Karlsrud and M Kaufmann, 'Humanitarian Technology: A Critical Research Agenda', *International Review of the Red Cross*, 96(893) (2014), 4.

92 World Humanitarian Summit (n 80); Ramalingam et al. in Ong and Combinido (n 44), 2232–2233.

anticipatory digitalised humanitarianism; and the relevance of the legal framework, in a humanitarian context, to progress in children's access to and inclusion in the digital environment.

Today's digitalised humanitarian response efforts have brought significant changes in how emergencies are recognised and tackled, whereas crisis response previously relied on information received and collected on a more ad hoc basis from random resources available. Modern mobile applications, social media, big-data analytics, e-transfers and chatbots have improved many beneficiaries' chances of accessing humanitarian technologies and taking informed decisions in a crisis, and humanitarians have better situational awareness of how to improve aid delivery.

Yet, while the Committee emphasises the role of the business sector in relation to safeguarding children's digital inclusion, humanitarians and tech developers keep missing the main mark: ensuring that the most essential platforms and technology are impactful and, at the same time, accountable. As long as digital innovation and digital inclusion do not go hand in hand, neither meaningful access nor humanitarian anticipatory action can be achieved.

Digital technology can greatly empower communities to receive the information they need to make the best decisions and sustain communication and trust. If humanitarians genuinely want to use digital technology to be accountable, serve the beneficiaries and respond to the local community, digitalised protection must empower the beneficiaries to actually influence crisis response. It must do so through real communication that includes local partners in developing and testing digital technology. This shift in power may gradually become a reality.

Excessive reliance on the digital environment is accentuating the digital divide, depriving the most vulnerable, marginalised groups in remote, rural areas even more of the information from and communication with frontline humanitarians on which they often depend. Whereas many urban areas today can and do provide access and connectivity, non-technical engagement in rural areas cannot be overlooked. Humanitarians are neither perfect nor always in possession of relevant know-how. Communities frequently communicate with one another, but humanitarians are now also adding digital expertise and knowledge of how and when to deploy such technology. Fundamentally, however, humanitarians are not yet proficient in digital communication nor fully aware of digital literacy in specific contexts. Such awareness is crucial, given the innumerable and changeable crises and beneficiaries, when digital knowledge and connectivity are often lacking.

Technology developers and humanitarians are, moreover, falling short when it comes to understanding the social and behavioural components of not only access to digital technologies but also trust in these applications. Learning to appreciate digital innovation and the humanitarian technology on offer, getting accustomed to them and, more importantly, trusting them take time. So, too, does making the digital application the preferred choice.

Children's agency and evolving childhood, as reflected in the general principles of the CRC, must be understood in light of the similarly evolving digital environment. Digital technologies affect children's lives in a variety of interdependent ways, including their rights and whether they have internet access. The Committee is failing to highlight the importance of child rights concerning connectivity, although it stresses digital inclusion and access. Without digital inclusion, the most vulnerable and often marginalised people lack input, while automated data processing in turn lacks the necessary impact.

Connectivity has a major bearing on realisation of a cross-section of child rights in the digital environment. The fact is that none of these rights alone can guarantee a right to internet access. As argued by Çalı, for example, and supported by various declarations, internet access must be seen as an instrumental legal human right derived simultaneously from existing rights protected under international law. Meaningful access and, indeed, digital inclusion will remain merely an aspiration in many contexts and countries without an express right being recognised internationally.

After more than a decade of humanitarian digital technology and new innovation and connectivity programmes, a new kind of digitalised humanitarianism is perceptible. Its *modus operandi* is not only accessed differently but also reshapes distribution, where and when distribution occurs and what is distributed to whom. This digital progress towards anticipatory action needs to be examined not in isolation but, rather, as a component of crisis response.

Integrated with robust decision support frameworks, these technologies can improve access to information, assistance and livelihoods. They can also facilitate improvements across the enhanced humanitarian programme cycle, including more robust, relevant needs analysis; more prioritised, people-centred response; and more meaningful, systematic monitoring. This facilitation, however, requires digital inclusion, which will continue to lack marginalised groups' impact until free global internet access exists.

Digitalised humanitarianism cannot be regarded as undesirable and must not be ignored. It should be seen as adding value to beneficiaries' preferred channels of communication, especially those of the most vulnerable and marginalised groups where connectivity will remain unrealistic. Digital technology is only as good as we allow it to be, and even if the dilemma of accessibility is unresolved, additional options and solutions that tackle humanitarian problems effectively may indeed be enhanced by digitalised humanitarianism as an essential part of crisis response. Essentially, humanitarians act in response to, rather than in anticipation of, events. They also react to digital innovations, whereas proaction is perhaps key to adding the missing components of digitalising in partnership with beneficiaries, for improved inclusion, access, and accountability.

The author maintains that by continuing to facilitate means of access, digital technologies can improve children's digital inclusion. The General

Comment's comprehensive references to access to and affordability of digital technology in terms of digital inclusion embraces free, safe access and programmes to impart knowledge about using digital technologies – not only in educational settings but in communities and homes. Yet until there is an officially recognised right to internet access, the Committee remains compelled to report a lack of digital inclusion and national and business sector policies 'aimed at providing children with the opportunity to benefit from engaging with the digital environment and ensuring their safe access to it'.[93]

Creating an enabling and participatory environment may require departing from established tools developed by a patriarchal, privileged group – tools that perpetuate or even reinforce injustice, inequality in digital proficiency and unfair distribution. Broader access to and participation in digitalised technologies are vital for achieving the overall aim of accountability and extending the proper protection to designated beneficiaries. Even *if* or *when* technology and data become accountable enough, the ability to use their full potential will remain elusive. Our vantage point must thus represent the beneficiaries and their communities, not the developers or the humanitarians.

List of references

Treaties

Convention on the Rights of the Child, G.A. Res. 44/25, Annex, 44 UN *General Assembly Official Records* (GAOR) Supplement (No. 49) 167, entered into force 2 September 1990 (1980).

International Covenant on Civil and Political Rights, 660 *United Nations Treaty Collection* (UNTC) 171, entered into force 23 March 1976 (1966).

Case law

General Court of the European Union – Order of November, 12 2019 in the case no T-158/19 (ECLI:EU:T:2019:791).

Literature

Anderson, MB, *Do No Harm: How Aid Can Support Peace or War*. Boulder, CO: Lynne Rienner. 1999.

Andree, BPJ et al., 'Predicting Food Crises', Policy Research Working Paper, No. 9412. Washington, DC: World Bank. 2020.

Baah, B, 'Mobilising Cash and Voucher Assistance Programmes: The Case for Mobile Money', *Global System for Mobile Communications GSMA*, March 2019.

Brito, C, 'Covid-19 Has Intensified the Digital Divide', *World Economic Forum*, 24 September 2020.

Buxton, N (ed), 'Digital Colonialism. Analysis of Europe's Trade Agenda', *Trade and Investment Policy Briefing*, October 2021.

93 CRC/C/GC/25 (n 1), Chapter V: General Measures of Implementation by States Parties A–F.

Çali, B, 'The Case for the Right to Meaningful Access to the Internet as a Human Right in International Law', in Von Arnauld, A, Von Der Decken, K and Susi, M (eds), *The Cambridge Handbook of New Human Rights: Recognition, Novelty, Rhetoric*. Cambridge: Cambridge University Press. 2020.

Casswell, J et al., 'Navigating the Shift to Digital Humanitarian Assistance: Lessons from the International Rescue Committee's Experience', *Global System for Mobile Communications GSMA*, December 2019.

Cerf, V, 'Internet Is Not a Human Right', *New York Times*, 5 January 2012. www.nytimes.com/2012/01/05/opinion/internet-access-is-not-a-human-right.html?_r=1, accessed 1 June 2022.

Couldry, N and Mejias, UA, 'Data Colonialism: Rethinking Big Data's Relation to the Contemporary Subject', *Television & New Media*, 20(4), 2019.

Council of Europe Committee of Ministers to the member states, Guidelines to Respect, Protect, and Fulfil the Rights of the Child in the Digital environment, 101818GBR, CM/REC(2018)7.

Duffield, M, 'The Resilience of the Ruins: Towards a Critique of Digital Humanitarianism', *Resilience*, 4(3), 2016.

Hamelink, CJ, 'Human Rights in Cyberspace', in *Cyberidentities: Canadian and European Presence in Cyberspace*. Ottawa: Les Presses de l'Université d'Ottawa | University of Ottawa Press. 1999.

Jacobsen Lindskov, K and Sandvik, KB, 'UNHCR and the Pursuit of International Protection: Accountability through Technology?', *Third World Quarterly*, 39(8), 2018.

Kardefelt-Winther, D, Day, E, Berman, G, Witting, SK and Bose, A on behalf of UNICEF's crossdivisional task force on child online protection, 'Encryption, Privacy and Children's Right to Protection from Harm', Innocenti Working Paper. Florence: UNICEF Office of Research – Innocenti. 2020. www.unicef-irc.org/publications/pdf/Encryption_privacy_and_children%E2%80%99s_right_to_protection_from_harm.pdf

Karp, DJ, 'What Is the Responsibility to Respect Human Rights? Reconsidering the "Respect, Protect, and Fulfill" Framework', *International Theory*, 12, 2019.

Klein, D, Hollow, DH and Poveda, S, *Children, ICTs and Development: Capturing the Potential, Meeting the Challenges*. Florence. Innocenti Insight, United Nations Children's Fund UNICEF Office of Research Innocenti. 2014.

La Rue, F, 'Report of the Special Rapporteur on the Promotion and Protection of the Right to Freedom of Opinion and Expression', Human Rights Council, U.N. Doc. A/HRC/17/27, 16 May 2011.

Land, M, 'Toward an International Law of the Internet', *Harvard International Law Journal*, 54(2), 2013.

Liddicoat, J, 'Internet Access and Human Rights', APC Wellington, 29 May 2017.

Loescher, G, 'UNHCR and the Erosion of Refugee Protection', *Forced Migration Review*, April 2001.

Lowcock, M, 'A Casement Lecture: Towards a Better System for Humanitarian Financing', UNOCHA Press release 23 March 2018.

Lowcock, M, 'Response to Humanitarian Crises', Speech delivered at the London School of Economics. London, 2 December 2019. Under-Secretary-General for Humanitarian Affairs and Emergency Relief Coordinator – Anticipation saves lives: How data and innovative financing can help improve the world's response to humanitarian crises – World | ReliefWeb accessed 2 May 2022.

Ong, JC and Combinido, P, 'Local Aid Workers in the Digital Humanitarian Project: Between "Second Class Citizens" and "Entrepreneurial Survivors" ', *Critical Asian Studies*, 53, 2017.
Pasquale F, 'Beyond Innovation and Competition: The Need for Qualified Transparency', *Internet Intermediaries, Northwestern University Law Review*, 104, 105, 2010.
Pettrachin, A, 'Towards a Universal Declaration on Internet Rights and Freedoms?', *International Communication Gazette*, 80(4), 2018.
Porumbescu, G, 'The Digital Divide Leaves Millions at a Disadvantage during the Coronavirus Pandemic', https://theconversation.com/the-digital-divide-leaves-millions-at-a-disadvantage-during-the-coronavirus-pandemic-133608, accessed 18 March 2020.
Raftree, L and Keshet B, 'Integrating Information and Communication Technologies into Communication for Development Strategies to Support and Empower Marginalized Adolescent Girls', UNICEF, 1 August 2013.
Read, R, Taithe, B and Mac Ginty R, 'Data Hubris? Humanitarian Information Systems and the Mirage of Technology', *Third World Quarterly*, 37(8), 2016.
Regulation (EU) 2018/1240 of the European Parliament and of the Council of 12 September 2018 establishing a European Travel Information and Authorisation System (ETIAS).
Regulation (EU) 2018/1725 of the European Parliament and of the Council of 23 October 2018 on the protection of natural persons with regard to the processing of personal data by the Union institutions, bodies, offices and agencies and on the free movement of such data.
Regulation (EU) 2021/1134 of the European Parliament and of the Council of 7 July 2021 for the purpose of reforming the Visa Information System.
Sandvik, KB, 'The Humanitarian Cyberspace: Shrinking Space or an Expanding Frontier?', *Third World Quarterly*, 37(1), 2016.
Sandvik, KB, Jumbert, MG, Karlsrud, J and Kaufmann, M, 'Humanitarian Technology: A Critical Research Agenda', *International Review of the Red Cross*, 96(893), 2014.
Sandvik, KB, Lindskov Jacobsen, K and McDonald SM, 'Do No Harm: A Taxonomy of the Challenges of Humanitarian Experimentation Migration and Displacement', *International Review of the Red Cross*, 99(1), 2017.
Stephenson, R and Anderson, PS, 'Disasters and the Information Technology Revolution', *Disasters*, 21(4), 1997.
Third, A, Livingstone, S and Lansdowne, G, 'Recognising Children's Rights in Relation to Digital Technologies: Challenges of Voice and Evidence, Principle and Practice', in Wagner, B, Kettemann, MC and Vieth, K (eds), *Research Handbook on Human Rights and Digital Technology: Global Politics, Law and International Relations.* Cheltenham, United Kingdom: Edward Elgar Publishing. 2019.
Third, A and Moody, L, *Our Rights in the Digital World: A Report on the Children's Consultations to Inform UNCRC General Comment 25.* London and Sydney: 5Rights Foundation and Western Sydney University. 2021.
Tully, S, 'A Human Right to Access the Internet? Problems and Prospects', *Human Rights Law Review*, 14(2), June 2014.
UN Committee on the Rights of the Child (CRC) General Comment No. 9 (2006): The rights of children with disabilities, 27 February 2007, CRC/C/GC/9.
UN Committee on the Rights of the Child (CRC) General Comment No. 14 (2013) on the right of the child to have his or her best interests taken as a primary consideration (art. 3, para. 1), 29 May 2013, CRC/C/GC/14.

UN Committee on the Rights of the Child (CRC) General Comment No. 21 (2017) on children in street situations CRC/C/GC/21.
UN Committee on the Rights of the Child (CRC) General Comment No. 25 (2021) on children's rights in relation to the digital environment CRC/C/GC/25.
UN Committee on the Rights of the Child, 2019 Guidelines regarding the interpretation of the Optional Protocol to the Convention on the Rights of the Child on the Sale of Children, Child Prostitution and Child Pornography.
UN High Commissioner for Refugees, *Emergency Handbook Accountability to Affected Populations.* AAP Operational Guidance, September 2020. UNHCR/OG/2020/02. Geneva. UNHCR.
UN High Commissioner for Refugees', 'Policy on Biometrics in Refugee Registration and Verification Processes', IOM/083/2010 – FOM/083/2010 (internal). 20 December 2010.
UN Human Rights Committee General Comment No. 34 on Article 19 Freedoms of Opinion and Expression, 15, U.N. Doc. CCPR/C/GC/34, September 12, 2011.
UN Human Rights Council, The promotion, protection and enjoyment of human rights on the Internet: Resolution/adopted by the Human Rights Council, 18 July 2016, A/HRC/RES/32/13.
UN Human Rights Council, The promotion, protection and enjoyment of human rights on the Internet: resolution/adopted by the Human Rights Council on 13 July 2021 (Draft A/HRC/47/L.22) A/HRC/RES/47/16.
UN Report of the Secretary-General, 'Secretary-General's Roadmap for Digital Cooperation', A/74/821, 11 June 2020.
United Nations Office for the Coordination of Humanitarian Affairs, 'What Is Communications with Communities?', OCHA on Message (humanitarian principles), 19 November 2013.
Vinck, P (ed), *World Disasters Report.* Geneva. International Federation of Red Cross and Red Crescent Societies. 2013.
World Bank, 'Cash for Assets: World Food Programme's Exploration of the In-kind to E-payments Shift for Food Assistance in Kenya', Washington, DC: CGAP/World Bank. 2013. www.cgap.org/sites/default/files/eG2P_Kenya.pdf.
World Humanitarian Summit, 'Approach Paper – WHS Theme 3: Transformation through Innovation', 25 September 2014.
World Summit on the Information Society, 'Plan of Action para 9(e)', WSIS-03/GENEVA/DOC/5-E, 2003.

Other sources

Alliance for Excellent Education, 'New Analysis Shows Students of Color Far More Likely to Be Cut off from Online Learning', COVID Response & Recovery, Data, Digital Divide. 22 July 2020. https://all4ed.org/publication/homeworkgap/ accessed 3 June 2022.
BBC News, 'Internet Poll', 2010. http://news.bbc.co.uk/2/shared/bsp/hi/pdfs/08_03_10_BBC_internet_poll.pdf, accessed 1 May 2022.
Department for International Development, 'The Use of Mobile Technology for Humanitarian Programming in Syria: Potential and Constraints', 29 March 2017. https://reliefweb.int/sites/reliefweb.int/files/resources/20170324%20SIM%20O3%20Research%20Report%201_Mobile%20Technology%20%281%29.pdf, accessed 1 May 2022.

GSMA, 'Mobile Connectivity Charter', www.gsma.com/mobilefordevelopment/mobile-for-humanitarian-innovation/humanitarian-connectivity-charter, accessed 1 May 2022.

NRP, 'Native Americans on Tribal Land Are the Least Connected to High Speed Internet', 6 December 2018. www.npr.org/2018/12/06/673364305/native-americans-on-tribal-land-are-the-least-connected-to-high-speed-internet?t=1633013501045, accessed 1 May 2022.

NRP, 'Telegram Is the App of Choice in the War in Ukraine Despite Experts' Privacy and Protection Concerns', 14 March 2022. www.npr.org/2022/03/14/1086483703/telegram-ukraine-war-russia?t=1652383321929, accessed 2 July 2022.

Offshore Technology, 'I'm Not Planning to Die, Ukraine's Besieged Tech Workers and the Response from Their Colleagues around the World'. www.offshore-technology.com/special-focus/Im-not-planning-to-die-Ukraines-besieged-tech-workers-and-the-response-from-their-colleagues-around-the-world/ accessed 29 May 2022.

UN ITU Report, '2.9 Billion People Still Offline', 30 November 2021. www.itu.int, accessed 3 June 2022.

UNHCR, 'Connectivity for Everyone'. www.unhcr.org/innovation/connectivity-for-everyone/ accessed 3 June 2022.

UNHCR Service Advisor, https://turkey.servicesadvisor.org, accessed 3 June 2022.

UNICEF Innovations, '10 Ways UNICEF Innovates'. www.unicef.org/innovation/stories/10-ways-unicef-innovates-children, accessed 3 June 2022.

UNICEF Press Releases, 'Two Thirds of School Aged Children Have No Internet Access', August 2020. www.unicef.org/press-releases/two-thirds-worlds-school-age-children-have-no-internet-access-home-new-unicef-itu, accessed 4 July 2022.

United Nations Treaty Collection, https://treaties.un.org/Pages/ViewDetails.aspx?src=TREATY&mtdsg_no=IV-11&chapter=4&clang=_en

WHO and Rakuten, 'Viber Fight COVID-19 Misinformation with Interactive Chatbot'. www.who.int/news-room/feature-stories/detail/who-and-rakuten-viber-fight-covid-19-misinformation-with-interactive-chatbot, accessed 31 June 2020.

5 Strengthening the right to education in emergencies

Normative change in humanitarian responses to children

*Sonja Hövelmann**

1. Introduction

Since the 1990s, there has been a fundamental change regarding the way the role of education in humanitarian responses is perceived. While, prior to the 1990s, education in armed conflict played hardly any role at all in international development policy,[1] during the mid-1990s, a global policy shift occurred that placed education at the core of humanitarian responses. Since then, the provision of education activities in times of disasters or crises has seen a significant rise in interest, acceptance and funding. As a result, a new institutional practice called education in emergencies (EiE) has taken shape and become increasingly adopted, applied and institutionalised. The establishment of a global education cluster, the formulation of minimum standards of education in emergencies and the increased share of funding from humanitarian donors such as the European Commission earmarked for EiE are indicative of this trend. The chapter analyses how this shift in humanitarian policy was achieved by analysing the strategic rhetoric of actors supporting EiE.

In times of disaster and emergencies, humanitarian action is provided to save and sustain lives, alleviate suffering and maintain human dignity.[2] It encompasses mainly short-term interventions such as food assistance, emergency shelter or medical services guided by the humanitarian principles of humanity, impartiality, neutrality and independence.[3] In contrast,

* Sonja Hövelmann is a research fellow with the Centre for Humanitarian Action in Berlin.

1 Rebecca Winthrop and Elena Matsui, 'A New Agenda for Education in Fragile States' (The Brookings Institution, 2013) Working Paper; Sarah Dryden-Peterson, 'Policies for Education in Conflict and Post-Conflict Reconstruction', in Karen Mundy et al. (eds), *The Handbook of Global Education Policy* (Dryden-Peterson: Chichester, John Wiley & Sons, 2016).

2 Development Initiatives, 'Global Humanitarian Assistance Report 2019' (Development Initiatives, 2019), http://devinit.org/wp-content/uploads/2019/09/GHA-report-2019.pdf, accessed 1 October 2019.

3 Zeynep Sezgin and Dennis Dijkzeul (eds), *The New Humanitarians in International Practice: Emerging Actors and Contested Principles* (Sezgin and Dijkzeul: New York, 2015).

DOI: 10.4324/9781003187493-5

development cooperation refers to medium to long-term processes of societal transformation targeting social and economic development.[4] These are typically closely linked to state actors. The provision or continuation of education in times of crisis falls between those two types of intervention. Although populations affected by disasters place a high value on the continuation of their children's education,[5] EiE is frequently sidelined by humanitarian actors, as they often do not consider it a core humanitarian intervention but rather a more long-term development intervention.

1.1. Legal and policy frameworks

The right to education is a powerful global norm enshrined in several treaties and conventions of international law, including the Universal Declaration of Human Rights (1945), the ICESCR (1966), the Convention on the Rights of the Child (CRC) (1989) and the Convention Relating to the Status of Refugees (1951).[6] In particular, Article 39 of the CRC stresses the importance of psychosocial support for children affected by conflict. Many humanitarian organisations support or justify the provision of EiE based on this article within the rights-based approach that they apply. Although its scope is universal, because every country in the world has ratified at least one of the relevant treaties, the realisation of the right to education in times of emergency is often neglected.[7] To elevate the importance of providing EiE, the United National General Assembly adopted Resolution 64/290 in 2010, which urged states to ensure the right to and provision of education activities as an integral part of humanitarian assistance. Even though these legal frameworks provide powerful arguments as to why the provision of EiE is critical, the international community seldom feels obliged to intervene in cases where the right to education is impaired.

Despite the strong legal basis, EiE was barely registered in global policy frameworks until 1996.[8] Even the 1990 World Declaration on Education for All (EFA), a key global policy, paid little attention to children in conflict or disaster zones. The period from the mid-1990s onwards saw a significant increase in policy developments relating to EiE. A new study, for instance, brought children living in armed conflicts to the centre of the international communities' attention, while increased collaboration between key

4 Annalisa Addis, 'Linking Humanitarian and Development Action in Ethiopia', Ruhr-Universität Bochum and University of Cagliari, 2015. https://iris.unica.it/retrieve/handle/11584/266840/345239/PhD_Thesis_Addis.pdf.

5 Susan Nicolai, Sébastien Hine and Joseph Wales, 'Education in Emergencies and Protracted Crises', ODI, 2015, www.odi.org/sites/odi.org.uk/files/odi-assets/publications-opinion-files/9714.pdf.

6 Allison Anderson, Jennifer Hofmann and Peter Hyll-Larsen, 'The Right to Education for Children in Emergencies', *Journal of International Humanitarian Legal Studies*, 2 (2011), 84.

7 Nicolai, Hine and Wales (n 5).

8 Dryden-Peterson (n 1).

humanitarian actors also played a role. In the literature, it is concurrently argued that the publication of Graça Machel's study on *Children and Armed Conflict* in 1996 marked the starting point for institutional developments and policy space that followed and shaped the practice that is now called EiE.[9] While there were educational activities for refugees or internally displaced persons (IDPs), mostly in camps prior to 1996, Machel was the first to call for an "educational activity to be established as a priority component of all humanitarian assistance".[10] She furthermore appealed to donors to extend the boundaries of emergency funding and to stop viewing education purely as a long-term development activity (ibid., 55, 59). It can thus be argued that her report "paved the way for a policy space for education within humanitarian response".[11] At the same time, several global actors, such as the United Nations High Commissioner for Refugees (UNHCR), the United Nations Educational, Scientific and Cultural Organization (UNESCO) and the United Nations International Children's Emergency Fund (UNICEF) recognised the importance of EiE and founded multi-stakeholder collaboration fora such as the Inter-Agency Network for Education in Emergencies (INEE) to tackle the issue more comprehensively.[12]

Most of the early literature analyses the reasons the provision of education in times of crises is critical.[13] Although there is research that looks into the historic developments or policy analysis of EiE as a sector,[14] there is to

9 Winthrop and Matsui (n 1); Nicolai, Hine and Wales (n 5); Dryden-Peterson (n 1).

10 Graça Machel, 'Impact of Armed Conflict on Children', 55, www.unicef.org/graca/.

11 Dryden-Peterson (n 1), 196.

12 Dryden-Peterson (n 1); Kacem Bensalah et al., 'Education in Situations of Emergency and Crisis: Challenges for the New Century', UNESCO, 1999, https://unesdoc.unesco.org/ark:/48223/pf0000123484.

13 Bensalah et al. (n 12); Kenneth D Bush and Diana Saltarelli, *The Two Faces of Education in Ethnic Conflict* (United Nations Publications, 2000), www.unicef-irc.org/publications/pdf/insight4.pdf; Mary Joy Pigozzi, 'Education in Emergencies and for Reconstruction: A Developmental Approach', https://healtheducationresources.unesco.org/sites/default/files/resources/EducEmerg.pdf; Gonzalo Retamal and Ruth Aedo-Richmond, *Education as a Humanitarian Response* (Retamal and Aedo: London, Cassell, 1998); Margaret Sinclair, 'Planning Education in and after Emergencies', https://www.researchgate.net/publication/44829669_Planning_education_in_and_after_emergencies; Laura Brannelly, Susy Ndaruhutse and Carole Rigaud, 'Donor's Engagement: Supporting Education in Fragile and Conflict-Affected States' (IIEP, UNESCO, 2009), Research Report.

14 Dana Burde, *Schools for Conflict or for Peace in Afghanistan* (Burde: New York, Columbia University Press, 2014); Dana Burde et al., 'Education in Emergencies: A Review of Theory and Research', *Review of Educational Research*, 20(19) (2016), 1; Kevin M Cahill, *Even in Chaos* (New York: Fordham University Press, 2010); Mario Novelli and Susan L Robertson, 'The Politiziation of Development Aid to Education after September 11', in Kenneth J Saltman (ed), *Schooling and the Politics of Disaster* (Novelli and Robertson: New York, Taylor and Francis, 2007); Francine Menashy and Sarah Dryden-Peterson, 'The Global Partnership for Education's Evolving Support to Fragile and Conflict-Affected States', *International Journal of Educational Development*, 44 (2015), 82; Karen Mundy and Sarah Dryden-Peterson, *Educating Children in Conflict Zones* (Mundy and Dryden-Peterson: New York, Teacher's College, Colombia University, 2011); Winthrop and Matsui (n 1).

date no specific analysis of the discourse used to evoke this change. Therefore, this chapter looks at actions and practices that were used strategically to ensure EiE's positionality in humanitarian action through a discursive analysis.

1.2. Changing normative pressures in the humanitarian enterprise

The rise of EiE has been flanked by a change in the nature of crises and the way actors respond to them. First, not only does the severity and frequency of environmental, health and political crises lead to a yearly increase in requests for humanitarian action,[15] emergencies are also becoming increasingly complex and protracted. A recent study estimated the average time of displacement at 26 years.[16] This puts pressure on humanitarian actors to reconsider what affected populations need in a prolonged situation of distress and fragility, which includes ensuring sustainable futures for children and young people. Second, the humanitarian mandate has been extended over time.[17] Traditional or Dunantist humanitarians consider their aid politically neutral and to rest firmly on humanitarian principles, and thus they try to separate development and relief activities.[18] New humanitarians, in contrast, believe that assistance must be broader in scope than solely addressing urgent physical needs,[19] which has led to support for an expansion of the humanitarian agenda to connect to and include activities such as post-conflict recovery, human rights work and peace-building (ibid.).[20]

Third, humanitarian actors themselves have come under pressure to legitimise their actions, increase transparency and ensure more accountability to the populations they serve. In particular in the complex crisis in Syria and its neighbouring region, the affected populations voiced their support for the prioritisation of education openly.

These developments create an alternative environment that allows new practices and a normative understanding of humanitarianism. These

15 OCHA, 'Global Humanitarian Overview 2021', OCHA (2020), www.unocha.org/sites/unocha/files/GHO-2021-Abridged-EN.pdf.

16 UNHCR, 'Contribution to the Fifteenth Coordination Meeting on International Migration', UNHCR, 2017 UN/POP/MIG-15CM/2017/14, www.un.org/en/development/desa/population/migration/events/coordination/15/documents/papers/14_UNHCR_nd.pdf, accessed 9 March 2020.

17 Michael N Barnett, *Empire of Humanity: A History of Humanitarianism* (Barnett: New York, Cornell University Press, 2011).

18 Dana Burde, 'Response Paper: Empower or Control? Education in Emergencies and Global Governance', *Current Issues in Comparative Education*, 9(2) (2007), 55.

19 Sezgin and Dijkzeul (n 3); Dorothea Hilhorst, 'Classical Humanitarianism and Resilience Humanitarianism: Making Sense of Two Brands of Humanitarian Action', *Journal of International Humanitarian Action*, 3 (2018), 15.

20 This is a very broad conceptualisation of organisational mandate, as humanitarian actors have different rationales regarding what humanitarian action entails based on their own specialisation Hilhorst (n 19).

changes have also given education its position within the field of humanitarian response. It is important to take them into account, as these global pressures have had an impact on the humanitarian enterprise as such and rendered the norm-setting process successful.

With these external factors in mind, this chapter discusses how EiE has increasingly been institutionalised as a sector of humanitarian action. It analyses how humanitarian practitioners who are in favour of EiE used discursive practices or framing to evoke the mainstreaming of education into core humanitarian responses. Thus, they challenged the norm of what is considered part of traditional humanitarian interventions by invoking a norm change.

As this chapter points to a case of normative change, theories and concepts of norm diffusion are introduced. Taking a constructivist approach to language, frame analysis is used both as a theoretical understanding of how norms can be altered, as well as a methodological approach to examine a norm change. In the second section, the methodological approach outlines data collection and analytical approaches. The findings are presented in Section 3. The study shows how EiE advocates made use of a specific kind of rhetoric to open up a space for education in humanitarian discourse. Thereafter, I turn to three empirical cases which are illustrative for the discursive strategies used by advocates to evoke a norm change in humanitarian action. Taken together, the findings offer a rather dynamic character of EiE as a normative concept and an increasingly institutionalised practice.

2. Theoretical frameworks and concepts

This chapter traces normative and institutional changes within EiE by systematically analysing when and how international organisations have altered their policy positions and operational practices. It does so by following a constructivist understanding and is in line with sociological institutionalism, meaning that humanitarian actors did not adopt educational programmes because they are the most functional but because of a change in the understanding of the contents of humanitarian action promulgated by the international regime.[21] Norms and institutional rules are especially important in the context of humanitarian action and human rights work because their practices are often determined by codes of ethics or conduct which are fundamentally based on morals or values. Which norms are considered appropriate changes over time and is often determined by norm entrepreneurs. These are agents (individuals or organisations) with a strong

21 John W Meyer and Brian Rowan, 'Institutionalized Organizations: Formal Structure as Myth and Ceremony', *American Journal of Sociology*, 83 (1977), 340; Paul J DiMaggio and Walter W Powell, 'The Iron Cage Revisited: Institutional Isomorphism and Collective Rationality in Organizational Fields', *American Sociological Review*, 48 (1983), 147.

notion about an appropriate or desirable type of behaviour.[22] These agents or norm entrepreneurs may promote an issue through the use of *framing*. Framing refers to the process by which people develop a particular conceptualisation or adapt their thinking of an issue.[23] In other words, the framing of norms is a highly strategic process where agents recast something in a new light to highlight certain aspects. Entrepreneurs define norms in ways that they anticipate will resonate well with audiences by using a language that names, interprets and dramatises.[24] Through the use of framing, agents seek to demonstrate either how a current norm violates acceptable behaviour or defines new appropriate behaviour to advance a new norm. Norms are successful when they resonate with a wider audience.

Scholars have identified different means by which new norms emerge, gain recognition and diffuse. Two prevailing models are the norm cascade by Finnemore and Sikkink[25] and transnational advocacy networks by Keck and Sikkink.[26] While both models highlight the importance of norm entrepreneurs in elevating the importance of a certain issue, they differ in their explanation of the diffusion process. The first model theorises norm diffusion as a cascade, where agreement among a critical mass of actors on an emergent norm can create a tipping point, which results in a "bandwagoning" effect.[27] The second model focuses on the formation of transnational advocacy networks across national borders to enlarge their power for change.

Theoretical models of norm emergence have been criticised for their linear assumptions of norm emergence, communication and institutionalisation and thus seen as being too static or ignorant of how transnational norms merge or counter with local norms.[28] In contrast, Krook and True[29] show through a case on gender norms that they are subject to a different dynamism. They demonstrate that the "evasive nature of norms"[30] allows for greater leverage. Norms diffuse because they can encompass different meanings and are subject to framing by different actors. The authors show

22 Martha Finnemore and Kathryn Sikkink, 'International Norm Dynamics and Political Change', *International Organization*, 52 (Keck and Sikking: Ithaca, 1998), 887; Margaret Keck and Kathryn Sikkink, *Activists beyond Borders* (Cornell University Press, 1998).

23 Dennis Chong and James N Druckman, 'Framing Theory', *Annual Review of Political Science*, 10 (Schön and Rein: New York, 2007), 103; Donald Schön and Martin Rein, *Frame Reflection* (Basic Books, 1994).

24 Finnemore and Sikkink (n 22).

25 Ibid.

26 (n 22).

27 Finnemore and Sikkink (n 22), 839.

28 Amitav Acharya, 'How Ideas Spread: Whose Norms Matter? Norm Localization and Institutional Change in Asian Regionalism', *International Organization*, 58 (2004), 239; Mona Lena Krook and Jacqui True, 'Rethinking the Life Cycles of International Norms: The United Nations and the Global Promotion of Gender Equality', *European Journal of International Relations*, 18(1) (2010), 103.

29 (n 28).

30 Ibid., 105.

that norms are mediated by agents who give them varied contents, which seek to link or de-link them from other actors.[31] At the same time, this dynamism is a double-edged sword because it promotes new norms but may increase the possibility to lose control over meaning. The following analysis will show examples of both dynamics. Their model of understanding norms as processes is used to theorise the norm emergence of EiE.[32] This means that norms are subject to ongoing attempts to reconstitute their meanings even as they exert effects on social behaviour.

To understand the norm emergence and norm institutionalisation process in EiE, the chapter uses a discursive approach. It combines strategic framing and frame alignment strategies with frameworks that analyse discourse institutionalisation.

Framing is central to an actor's political strategy, designed to persuade key interlocutors of the moral necessity of certain political or social changes.[33] Thus, this research investigates how strategic framing was used by norm entrepreneurs to "sell" the idea of including education in humanitarian action. Framing or frame analysis has identified several techniques for how norm entrepreneurs achieve their goals. Snow et al.[34] have coined the term *frame alignment*, which describes different strategies that link frames strategically with prospective members, allies or resource providers.

Hajer[35] argues that different types of discourse, like frames, are a collection of ideas, concepts and categories through which meaning is given to phenomena. He states that norm entrepreneurs – although he calls them discourse coalitions – elevate a certain conceptualisation of an issue by distinguishing certain aspects of a situation from others. If many people use this discourse to conceptualise the world, it will grow into an institution, an organisational practice or a traditional way of reasoning.[36] This understanding of discourse institutionalisation is used to analyse how the norm entrepreneurs elevated their understanding of EiE as a practice of humanitarian action. Eventually, their conceptualisation was taken over by other actors and became a shared definition of that practice.

In order to analyse what strategies norm entrepreneurs employed to frame EiE, a model by Philips et al.[37] helps us to understand how actors via means

31 Ibid.

32 Ibid., 108.

33 Bronwen Magrath, 'Global Norms, Organisational Change: Framing the Rights-Based Approach at ActionAid', *Third World Quarterly*, 35(7) (2014), 1273.

34 Snow, D et al., 'Frame Alignment Processes, Micromobilization, and Movement Participation', *American Sociological Review*, 51 (1986), 464.

35 'Discourse Coalitions and the Institutionalization of Practice: The Case of Acid Rain in Britain', in Frank Fischer and John Forester (eds), *The Argumentative Turn in Policy Analysis and Planning* (Hajer: Durham, Duke University Press, 1993).

36 Ibid.

37 N Phillips, TB Lawrence and C Hardy, 'Discourse and Institutions', *Academy of Management Review*, 29 (2004), 635.

of communication come to accept a shared definition of reality. According to the model, norm entrepreneurs adopt three strategies to ensure that their social construction is successful: First, they may draw on discourse from other fields or society to produce new institutions or to de-legitimise existing ones. Second, they may ensure that their construction is accessible and understandable to maximise diffusion. Third, they may increase legitimacy, formal authority and centrality to ensure acknowledgement. The discursive approach views norms as anchored in language. By deciphering framing strategies applied by different actors, this study traces how EiE as a normative concept emerged and became increasingly institutionalised.

3. Data collection and method

For this study, policy documents and interview data were analysed using a discursive approach to trace normative changes within EiE. In international relations research, discursive approaches have been used before to explain norm-setting processes in global governance.[38] In order to trace how practitioners and organisations have helped the field to adapt, their rhetoric is explored through a discourse analysis of policy documents. The shift in policies of international organisations (IOs) is taken as a basis to determine how actions may lead to the development of a field in practice.

In order to elucidate how and why actors have altered their policy stances, a document analysis and process tracing analysis is applied to the data. By investigating key past events and documents within the EiE architecture, the chapter traces how the issue has been put on the agenda of humanitarian organisations. Documents selected for this study have been chosen on the basis of their relevance. Based on these findings, publications and reports by the organisations listed in Table 5.1 are included for detailed, in-depth document analysis. A second criterion for the inclusion of texts is that they were frequently quoted and function as a "node" within the larger debate on EiE. Within each organisation, documents were selected that specifically addressed EiE (criterion sampling) and/or if they were considered important documents by the interviewees. This encompassed education strategies, policy statements and thematic reports on education. The documents were selected if they made frequent reference to the phrase *education in emergencies* or EiE, contained certain keywords and were published between 1996 and 2017. 1996 was chosen as a starting date because the Machel Report (1996) can be seen as an instance of *frame transformation*[39] within EiE. In total, 44 resolutions by UN agencies and 35 documents by the other actors were analysed via qualitative content analysis using MaxQDA.

38 See, for example, Anna Holzscheiter, *Children's Rights in International Politics* (Holzscheiter: Basingstoke, Palgrave/Macmillan, 2010); Katja Freistein, *Institutioneller Wandel Im (Kon) Text* (Freistein: Baden, Nomos, 2012); Lene Hansen, *Security as Practice* (Hansen: New York, Routledge, 2006).

39 Snow et al. (n 34).

Table 5.1 Organisations chosen for document analysis

Type of Actor	*Organisation*
UN agencies	Security Council, General Assembly, ECOSOC, UNICEF, UNESCO
INGOs	Norwegian Refugee Council, Save the Children
Networks	INEE, Global Partnership for Education
Donors	Government of Norway, ECHO

With regard to data collection, the documents selected are all in English and mostly publicly available on the relevant organisation's website. Some documents are internal documents made available for this research by the interviewees. It should be noted that the documents are *not neutral*, but political statements, written with a certain agenda.[40]

The findings gathered from the document analysis are supplemented and cross-checked by means of interviews with experts. Seven semi-structured qualitative expert interviews were conducted with representatives from different IOs active in the field of EiE. Most interviewees are high-ranking officials with several years of experience working in the humanitarian sector and all hold posts related to EiE. The interviews are presented anonymously throughout the study. Five interviews were transcribed verbatim. Two interviewees did not wish to be recorded and transcribed for reasons of confidentiality. The sample covers representatives from three international nongovernmental organisations (INGOs), a donor, two networks and a field practitioner working for a government-implementing organisation.[41] Interviewees were selected due to their expert knowledge of the development of the EiE sector. Furthermore, the experts interviewed represent leading actors that influence EiE policy or practice. All interviews were conducted via telephone and took place between June and September 2017.

There are several limitations that might impact the results. First, it was only possible to analyse a restricted number of documents and conduct a limited number of interviews, which means that there are important institutional or organisational perspectives missing. It was possible to include most relevant actors in the analysis but access to an interview with UN representatives was difficult to obtain. Additionally, due to resource and time constraints, the documents were not examined with regard to potential readership, context or political motivation. While the findings from the document analysis are validated through the interviews, the second level or document reality was not at the forefront of the study.[42]

40 Alan Bryman, *Social Research Methods* (Oxford: Oxford University Press, 2016).

41 It should be noted that all interviewees who participated in the study were extremely cooperative and hold an interest in the findings of this study. I cordially thank all interviewees for their time and insights.

42 Bryman (n 40).

4. Results

The findings of the document and interview analyses are divided into three parts. The first part investigates the framing strategies that were used to make room for education in humanitarian discourse. The chapter discusses the fact that framing was a strategic activity deployed by practitioners to achieve the inclusion of education in humanitarian action. Framing was central to the political strategy, designed to persuade key targets (e.g., donors, other humanitarian organisations) of the moral necessity of certain political or social changes and their role in fostering that change.[43] The second part examines the dynamic nature of the emergent norm and how actors have struggled to flesh out the content of the new norm. The third part builds on the findings from the discursive analysis. Here, the process of norm institutionalisation is traced.[44] Based on the analysis, it is argued that EiE is an emergent norm that has become increasingly institutionalised in the past few years.

4.1. Norm emergence: opening space for humanitarian reasoning

The objective of the analysis was to investigate the use of language and *framing* of the inclusion of education in humanitarian action. It thus examines the framing strategies that were necessary to lobby for EiE. The analysis of policy documents reveals three sets of arguments relating to the function of education in international development. The first set revolves around the role of education in fostering economic growth (development frame). The second set calls for education as a means to save and protect lives (humanitarian frame). The third set relates to the contribution of education to state and peace-building (security frame). Each frame highlights or emphasises only a few salient arguments regarding why the provision of education is critical. Taken together they establish the discourse on education in international cooperation and how it is discussed.

Each frame is applied by different actors and represents a different conceptualisation or *framing*. The development frame takes institution-building and state-building as a starting point. It recognises that education is an investment in both individuals and society as a whole.[45] The humanitarian frame views education as a component of rapid emergency response. This is by necessity emergency driven and short term, which means a minimal provision of education.[46] Within the security frame, education is viewed as a

43 Magrath (n 33).

44 Hajer (n 35); Phillips, Lawrence and Hardy (n 37).

45 Dryden-Peterson (n 1); Clive Harber, *Education and International Development* (Harber: Oxford, Symposium Books, 2014); Caroline Marks, 'A Critical Analysis of Donor Education Strategies for International Development', University of Ulster, 2014.

46 Burde (n 18); Dryden-Peterson (n 1).

political instrument to contribute to the stabilisation of states. The approach draws from a wider discourse in humanitarian and security studies concerning the merging of humanitarian aid and stabilisation measures.[47]

The analysis of the documents and interviews shows that in order for education to become a prioritised component of humanitarian assistance, norm entrepreneurs did not emphasise the contribution of education to economic development (development frame). Rather, they employed a new rhetoric, by framing education as a *life-saving* and *life-sustaining* intervention. This contrast is striking as education is seldom associated with saving lives. Norm entrepreneurs made use of these terms in order to anchor education in the short term in humanitarian actions – constructing the humanitarian frame.

The analysis indicates that establishing the narrative of education as a life-saving and life-sustaining intervention was fundamental for the inclusion of education in humanitarian action. Several cases demonstrate this. One example that highlights this change is how the Directorate-General for European Civil Protection and Humanitarian Aid Operations (ECHO) included education in their funding guidelines. Two statements from 2009 and 2016, respectively, serve to illustrate how framing education as life-saving has enabled a normative shift within the sector. In 2009, an ECHO policy officer stated:

> [t]he main obstacle to promoting education in emergencies is that for some it does not fall within a narrow humanitarian mandate to save lives. Taking a narrow survival view, we come easily to the conclusion that education does not save lives.[48]

In 2016, an evaluation of ECHO's involvement in EiE indicates that: "ECHO's increased support to EiE . . . also represented a paradigm shift to recognising that EiE was life-saving, in light of the growing body of evidence on the life sustaining and protective role of education in emergencies" (ICF 2016, 84). Meanwhile, ECHO has shifted its funding guidelines, formulating an explicit EiE policy and has become the largest EiE donor.[49] This example is evidence of a shift among donors regarding the recognition of EiE as important because of its life-saving features. It also shows that the issue at stake is the role of education as a life-saving intervention.

47 Dryden-Peterson (n 1); Novelli and Robertson (n 14); Mario Novelli, 'The New Geopolitics of Educational Aid: From Cold Wars to Holy Wars?', *International Journal of Educational Development*, 30 (2010), 453.

48 UNESCO, 'The Hidden Crisis: Armed Conflict and Education', 200, http://unesdoc.unesco.org/images/0019/001907/190743e.pdf.

49 European Commission, 'Education in Emergencies in EU-Funded Humanitarian Aid Operations' (European Civil Protection and Humanitarian Aid Operations, 2019), https://ec.europa.eu/echo/files/news/eie_in_humanitarian_assistance.pdf, accessed 28 August 2021.

Interviewees confirmed that life-saving and life-sustaining arguments had indeed played a role in justifying the provision of EiE. They emphasised that it had involved a great deal of work for the community to find convincing arguments and that this was the only argument humanitarians listened to.[50] At the same time, interviewees also noted that there are many challenges linked to this concept of education being a life-saving intervention. They stated that there was little acceptance among traditional humanitarian actors and that it was "often a fight" to ensure the recognition of EiE.[51] In addition, the life-saving aspect seems to be a contested subject among the promoters of EiE. One interviewee noted that "it's a trap that education in emergencies has fallen into"[52] or "personally, I feel that we might have shot ourselves a bit in the foot by insisting on the life-saving. I'm not necessarily sure that insisting on the life-saving . . . is the best argument to use. We are going back and forth. I don't know why."[53] These perceptions appear to come from the realisation that the life-saving argument is also limiting. Only certain educational activities fall under the narrow conceptualisation of life-saving, such as mine risk education, health education and similar activities. Hence, more encompassing educational activities such as accelerated education or psycho-social support fall outside this framework.

These accounts show how norm entrepreneurs used strategic framing to draw on the existing discourse in the humanitarian sector. In line with Philips et al.'s[54] framework, advocates demonstrated the compatibility with humanitarian norms in order to make room for EiE within the traditional conceptualisation of humanitarianism. The analysis demonstrated that norm entrepreneurs used deliberate framing strategies – a language that interprets and dramatises – in order to argue for the inclusion of education in humanitarian action. It was stressed that EiE formed a category separate from development activities to facilitate incorporation into mainstream humanitarian assistance. The following section analyses at a micro level how strategic framing by different actors enabled access to core humanitarian institutions.

4.2. Norm dynamism: room to expand but losing control over meaning

The analysis revealed that over time there was more scope to move beyond the narrow conceptualisation of education as a life-saving intervention. The data gathered demonstrate that advocates were able to build on the achievements made – using arguments beyond the live-saving rhetoric – and to

50 Interview with representatives from a donor, INGO, network.
51 Interview with INGO representative.
52 Interview with network representative.
53 Interview with INGO representative.
54 (n 37).

build an evolved EiE framing strategy.[55] The evolved strategy entails not only adjusting to core humanitarian values but being recognised for the unique strengths that education provides. One interviewee described it as: "something that I think has been recognised more and more by the humanitarian community and less and less do we have to try and fit ourselves into this very narrow category of life-saving in the same way as other sectors."[56] The evolved strategy seems to aim at expanding the narrative: instead of tailoring education to fit humanitarian action, humanitarian action should adapt in order to make education fit.

While building on the achievements gained, the research also revealed examples of the dynamic nature of emergent norms. As Krook and True[57] argue, emergent norms are subject to an ongoing reconstitution of meaning. More specifically, they suggest that during their emergence, norms may inspire alternative interpretations as supporters and opponents struggle to flesh out the content of a given norm. The discursive analysis demonstrated that over the course of time, rhetoric departing from the life-saving humanitarian argumentation was detected. It refers to education being a stabilising feature and a key instrument for nation and peace-building. Taken together they form the security frame. This frame was mainly driven by donors and represents an opposing, politicised understanding as to why the provision of EiE is critical.

The discursive analysis showed that the security frame is often used in documents by donors, but the interviewees were aware of it too. The data show that recent developments, such as the increased refugee and migrant movements to Europe, as well as a new interest in education as a tool to countering violence and extremism (CVE), have led to an increase in rhetoric relating to the security frame. For example, an interviewee noted that it can be argued that funding EiE might be related to the aim of reducing refugee movements to Europe.[58] This is connected with the general recognition that a lack of educational options is often a reason for migration. Other interviewees mentioned that donors have become more interested in children and adolescents and that education is seen as an element to counter extremism. They noted, however, that donor interest in education due to CVE is putting a lot of pressure on humanitarian organisations which have an interest in remaining neutral. One interviewee noted that

> there's this big discussion within *[name of organisation]* how do we deal with that. I think it's partly on the countering violence/extremism discussion and partly about stabilisation discussion. Those two come up regularly. But as it is also UNESCO who is heavily involved in the CVE

55 Interview with network representative.
56 Interview with INGO representative.
57 (n 28).
58 Interview with network representative.

> discussion . . ., which doesn't necessarily help, for an organisation like ours that doesn't want to look at it that way.[59]

The notion that education has potential "security benefits"[60] in order to pursue political interests is called into question particularly by humanitarian and education actors alike. For example, the Norwegian Refugee Council (NRC) distanced itself from the CVE frame in a written position statement.[61]

The pressure of linking education with CVE demonstrates the dynamic nature of emergent norms. Through the publication of texts, organisations are working to positively influence the discourse by using terms and phrases that view the young as a "positive resource". This demonstrates how norm leaders "lose control over their meanings" when new norms take shape[62] and again how they use framing to affect discourse as a means to regain control.

4.3. Norm institutionalisation

4.3.1. Norm institutionalisation: maximising diffusion

The second part of the findings focus on how, based on their framing strategies, norm entrepreneurs lobbied for the inclusion of education in humanitarian assistance to evoke a norm change within the humanitarian sector. The objective is to show how EiE as a normative concept has been adopted by different actors and how these actors actively shape the meaning of it. This is done by applying the frameworks of discourse institutionalisation developed by Hajer[63] and Philips et al.[64] to uncover how and why EiE as a normative concept has become institutionalised over the past few years.[65]

The formulation of Minimum Standards for Education in Emergencies (MSEE) is a case in point concerning how EiE advocates adopted strategies to demonstrate the compatibility of education with other forms of

59 Interview with INGO representative.

60 Mario Novelli and Mieke Lopes Cardozo, 'Globalizing Educational Interventions in Zones of Conflict: The Role of Dutch Aid to Education and Conflict', in Antoni Verger, Mario Novelli and Hülya Kosar Altinyelken (eds), *Global Education Policy and International Development* (Novelli and Cardozo: London, Bloomsbury Academic, 2012), 225.

61 NRC, 'Countering Violent Extremism and Humanitarian Action', NRC Position Papers, June 2017.

62 Krook and True (n 28), 109.

63 (n 35).

64 (n 37).

65 While it is beyond the scope of this chapter to investigate each of the actors sampled individually, three selected case studies are presented here to demonstrate recent advocacy and policy successes in EiE. For a full review of each actor, please refer to Sonja Hövelmann, 'Education in Emergencies. Tracing an Evolving Concept', Unpublished Master Thesis, Ruhr-University Bochum (2017).

humanitarian goods and services. The humanitarian community has developed several guidelines and standards to hold themselves accountable. One of these guidelines is the Sphere Handbook,[66] which was first published in 2000.[67] The Handbook includes chapters on food, nutrition, water, health and shelter. In the process of establishing consensus on these sectors, education was discussed as well, especially by the UNHCR, UNICEF and Save the Children. Their argument was that education is an essential protection and conflict prevention measure and could thus be considered a life-saving provision. This opinion was not shared by the Sphere Project Management Committee, which argued against including education on the grounds that it is not an "essential sector of relief assistance".[68] It was noted, however, that "other sector programmes such as education and training, which may take place during relief operations may be examined in later stages of this project".[69] Shortly after the launch of the first handbook in 2000 and second version in 2002, the Management Committee was asked to clarify its position on education regarding whether education would be considered, again resulting in an inconclusive answer.

Yet education advocates were aware of the importance of the Sphere Projects: "Spurred on by the need to make education a priority for humanitarian response, [INEE] approached the SPHERE [sic] Project because it seemed to be an ideal solution to legitimise standards for EiE."[70] What becomes clear from this statement is the power and hegemonic status that is given to the Sphere Project. The group perceived that it has the power to *legitimise* educational standards, to serve the ultimate goal of having education recognised as a priority in humanitarian action. Meanwhile, the group agreed to work outside the framework of Sphere while at the same time building on Sphere formats and processes.[71] The rejection by Sphere remained a concern within the group of experts because in the report, an important concern for drafting minimum standards was "[h]ow to overcome the life-saving argument? Is education life saving?"[72]

For the revised edition in 2011, the Board concluded that due to the size of the handbook, no further sectors would be included (INEE 2009). However, recognising the changes within the humanitarian context, the

66 In 1997, a group of humanitarian actors set to work on the so-called Sphere Project to develop standards to improve the quality and accountability of humanitarian action across sectors (e.g., health, water and shelter) (Jürgen Lieser and Dennis Dijkzeul, *Handbuch Humanitäre Hilfe* (Berlin, Heidelberg: Springer, 2013), 278).

67 Sphere Project (ed), 'What Is Sphere?', www.spherehandbook.org/en/what-is-sphere/.

68 INEE, 'Integrating Quality Education with Humanitarian Response for Humanitarian Accountability: The Sphere-INEE Companionship', 6, http://s3.amazonaws.com/inee-assets/resources/Sphere_INEE_paper_FINAL.pdf.

69 Ibid.

70 INEE 2002, 2.

71 Ibid., 3.

72 Ibid., 5.

Sphere Project and INEE signed a Companionship Agreement in 2008, stating that "the Sphere Project recognises the INEE Minimum Standards . . . as Companion Standards to the Sphere Project Humanitarian Charter and Minimums Standards in Disaster Response."[73] In 2012, this agreement was renewed on the terms that

> both Parties recognise that education in emergencies is a necessity that can be both life-sustaining and life-saving, providing physical, psychosocial and cognitive protection. Education in emergencies is an integral component of humanitarian aid alongside assistance in water and sanitation, health, nutrition, shelter and protection.[74]

Through successful lobbying, the Sphere Project revised its original position, ultimately recognising education as among the life-saving sectors and an integral part of humanitarian action.

This case study shows how norm entrepreneurs recognised the hegemonic status of the Sphere Project within the humanitarian community. In order to maximise the diffusion of their idea of EiE, a working group led by the INEE formulated minimum standards for education in emergencies. Within 24 months they composed a handbook which mirrored the layout and approach of the Sphere Handbook. It can be argued that the formulation of MSEE is in line with Philipps et al.[75] and their second strategy to maximise the diffusion because many humanitarian practitioners rely on the Sphere handbooks in their operations. As a diffusion agent, INEE not only contributed to the norm emergence but significantly advanced the process of norm institutionalisation by increasing standardisation and professionalisation of EiE as a practice.

At the same time, the analysis also revealed that emergent norms are a subject of contestation, even as they become embedded in institutional practices. As, for example, Carpenter[76] has shown, actors may not necessarily adopt a new norm because of a conviction but instead it may be down to opportunism.[77] The establishment of the Global Education Cluster within the Inter-Agency Standing Committee (IASC)[78] Cluster Approach is a case in point.

During the formation of the IASC Cluster Approach, education was identified as a key sector in the review process. However, it did not appear

73 INEE, 'Sphere-INEE Companionship Agreement', 4, http://s3.amazonaws.com/inee-assets/resources/Sphere-INEE_Companionship_Agreement_(signed)_(23_10_2008).pdf.

74 INEE, 'Sphere-INEE Companionship Agreement', 1, www.ineesite.org/en/partnerships/sphere-companion.

75 (n 37).

76 C Carpenter, 'Setting the Advocacy Agenda: Theorizing Issue Emergence and Nonemergence in Transnational Advocacy Networks', *International Studies Quarterly*, 51 (2007), 99.

77 Ibid; Krook and True (n 28).

78 The IASC is an important humanitarian actor for the inter-organisational coordination of UN and non-UN agencies.

in the final recommendation of the working group.[79] Based on these recommendations, the IASC principals designated global cluster lead agencies in nine critical programme and operational areas – education was not among them.[80] The omission of education was based on two arguments. First, UNICEF was considered the *de facto* lead, thus removing the need to designate a lead agency; second, and more importantly, the perceived hierarchy of humanitarian needs led to education not being seen as a priority and part of the life-saving sector.[81] Education practitioners challenged these arguments pointing to the life-saving and life-sustaining role of education in emergencies, as well as the powerful argument that communities themselves very frequently identify education as a priority (Anderson and Hodgkin 2010; Save the Children 2008). These arguments were used by the INEE and NGOs to advocate for an Education Cluster within the humanitarian reform approach. Based on these arguments, UNICEF submitted another proposal, which was again rejected on the basis of the same arguments. Advocates of EiE were concerned by this setback, as they feared this sent an implicit message that EiE was not important.[82]

Through continuous joint lobbying and advocacy efforts, norm leaders such as Save the Children, UNICEF and INEE were able to convince the IASC principals of a joint cluster lead[83] between Save the Children and UNICEF, which catered to IASC's wish of a closer UN and non-UN collaboration. In December 2006, after two rejections, the IASC adopted the proposal and endorsed an Education Cluster within the Cluster Approach. The endorsement of education as part of the Cluster Approach represents a significant achievement because it recognises the importance of education by the humanitarian community and their support of its provision. It also demonstrates a willingness to strengthen the response capacity, leadership, accountability and partnership in the education sector.[84]

The process serves as an example to understand how new norms galvanise attention. It highlights power as integral to the processes of social construction of norms, determining what can and cannot be said – and, as a result, who can and cannot speak.[85] First, it demonstrates how norm

79 Allison Anderson and Marian Hodgkin, 'The Creation and Development of the Global IASC Education Cluster' (UNESCO, 2010) Background paper for the Global Monitoring Report 2011.

80 The initial clusters included logistics, telecommunication, shelter, health, nutrition, water and sanitation, early recovery, camp coordination and protection.

81 Anderson and Hodgkin (n 79); Adele Harmer and Joanna Macrae, 'Beyond the Continuum. The Changing Role of Aid Policy in Protracted Crises', https://odi.org/en/publications/beyond-the-continuum-the-changing-role-of-aid-policy-in-protracted-crises-2/.

82 Anderson and Hodgkin (n 79).

83 The Education Cluster is the only cluster co-led by a UN agency and an NGO (UNICEF and Save the Children) (Anderson and Hodgkin (n 79), 10).

84 Anderson and Hodgkin (n 79).

85 Hansen (n 38).

entrepreneurs were able to affect the decision by joining forces. Second, it shows that the framing strategy – to establish education as life-saving – did not work in this case. Instead, the IASC only agreed to give education a cluster because it served their purpose of closer UN and non-UN collaboration. This reveals that emergent norms are subject to contestation. In this case, the adopter endorsed the norm without necessarily being persuaded of its advantages but because it served its own purposes.

4.3.2. Norm institutionalisation: increasing legitimacy

The adoption of the ICRC's *Framework for Access to Education* is illustrative of the third strategy of norm entrepreneurs to increase the legitimacy by ensuring that their conceptualisation of EiE is adopted by other actors. INEE, as a norm leader, has significantly supported this process.[86]

Since May 2016, the International Committee of the Red Cross (ICRC) has decided to consider education-related activities in their humanitarian response. Although the Red Cross/Red Crescent Movement (IFRC) has been involved in education-related activities in the past, its measure to formalise efforts into a coherent framework can be considered a change of paradigm.[87] The Framework as such was an important signal for the EiE community because of the ICRC's strong interest in remaining neutral and independent. Critics have argued that by supporting EiE, humanitarian organisations are encroaching on development work and venturing into highly political terrain. Given its special role in the humanitarian system as a subject of international law and custodian of the Geneva Conventions and the humanitarian principles of humanity, neutrality, impartiality and independence,[88] the ICRC's positioning as a supporter of EiE represents a paradigm shift. The ICRC's commitment to engage in EiE is an important step which supports the empirical findings that EiE is an emergent norm. It shows that a conservative albeit important humanitarian actor has adopted the norm. It can be argued that the strategies employed by norm entrepreneurs to increase the legitimacy of their conceptualisation were successful. These achievements symbolise the growing recognition and increasing institutionalisation of education as a sector of emergency relief work.

86 Interview with a network representative; interview with an INGO representative.

87 Filipa Schmitz-Guinote, 'Three Reasons Why Education Needs the Support of Humanitarian Actors in Conflict Zones', *Humanitarian Law & Policy Blog*, 12 December 2019, https://blogs.icrc.org/law-and-policy/2019/12/12/three-reasons-education-humanitarian-conflict/ accessed 29 August 2021.

88 Christina Bennett, Matthew Foley and Sara Pantuliano, 'Time to Let Go. Remaking Humanitarian Action for the Modern Era' (ODI, 2016), www.odi.org/sites/odi.org.uk/files/resource-documents/10422.pdf, accessed 6 May 2020; Peter Walker and Daniel G Maxwell, *Shaping the Humanitarian World* (Walker and Maxwell: Oxford, Routledge, 2009).

The case studies and arguments presented here indicate that EiE has been strategically framed in certain ways to achieve various interests. Snow's[89] frame alignment strategies allow for an analytical division of strategies. It can thus be concluded that norm entrepreneurs used these strategies to open up a closed space for an EiE discourse. The studies describe how advocates *amplified* their messages by using language that named, dramatised, and interpreted. The most prominent examples, establishing education as a life-saving intervention but also coining the term *education in emergencies* as such, are captivating. Thereby, norm entrepreneurs strategically triggered certain values or beliefs that are associated with these concepts. They also *bridged* different frames by linking the discourses on protection, humanitarian action, peace-building and stability.[90] Furthermore, they *extended* the boundaries of the frame to incorporate the interests of other target groups. An example for this strategy is the successful application of the Cluster Approach.

4.3.3. Acceptance and adoption of a new norm

The growing prominence of EiE is also demonstrated by a timeline which plots influential events and frameworks in the field from 1989 onwards (see Figure 5.1). This shows the increase in actions in the field since the UN Convention on the Rights of the Child came into effect. Figure 5.1 plots important humanitarian frameworks as well as the annual humanitarian funding of education on a timeline, showing that, especially after the establishment of the Global Education Cluster and the founding of INEE, crises received more funding for education. However, the funding received depends heavily on the geographical context. It confirms the findings from the document analysis, which suggest that the Machel Report from 1996, as the first instance education was framed as a sector for emergency response, triggered a large number of important changes in the field, especially around the year 2000. Likewise, the precedent-setting UNGA resolution on education in emergency situations also induced a number of significant events.[91]

What has been established so far is that international actors can become diffusion agents by using communicative powers. They actively and passively impact on the meaning and content of norms through their discursive outputs (e.g., the production and communication of texts). According to Krook and True,[92] it is the evasive nature of norms, which offers greater

89 (n 34).

90 Ian Macpherson, 'An Analysis of Power in Transnational Advocacy Networks in Education', in Karen Mundy et al. (eds), *The Handbook of Global Education Policy* (Macpherson: Malden, John Wiley & Sons, 2016), 413.

91 However, it should be noted that the pooling of events in the years 2000 and 2015 is due to the fact that these were important UN years which saw the launch of the Millennium Development Goals (MDGs) and the Sustainable Development Goals (SDGs), respectively.

92 Krook and True (n 28).

analytical leverage, that makes the norm diffusion process successful. Just as the authors did, empirical data showed two sources of dynamism – internal and external. With regard to internal dynamism, the analysis demonstrates that the dynamic nature of norms is a double-edged sword, promoting the creation of norms but also increasing the possibility of losing control over their meaning. This dynamism could be observed empirically with the success of the security frame, and it is currently happening with framing education as a means to counter violence and extremism. As established in the previous sections, this frame has emerged very strongly in the last few years, and actors feel compelled to position themselves against this rhetoric.[93] The analysis has demonstrated a conquering of meaning – a strategic use of framing – to adopt the concept of EiE to the organisation's overall political strategy. With regard to external dynamism, Krook and True[94] suggest that certain norms gain a foothold when they are associated with other, widely accepted ideas. The deliberative framing of EiE as a life-saving and life-sustaining intervention, as well as the strategic use of keywords that are frequently associated with humanitarian discourse, demonstrates how advocates have explicitly drawn these connections.

Yet the empirical findings not only underpin theoretical assumptions about the norm diffusion process, how they are created, why they spread and what accounts for their variation in meaning, they also suggest an increasing institutionalisation of EiE as a norm. The analysis suggests that IOs have significantly altered their policy positions and operational practices over a relatively short period of time. It is argued here that the institutionalisation of EiE as a normative concept manifests itself via growth in three areas: *prominence*, *formality* and *contents*. First, it can be ascertained from the document and interview transcript analysis that EiE has gained more *prominence*, especially since the UN resolution 290/64 on *Education in Situations of Emergency* from 2010, which calls for all UN member states to establish EiE as a key priority for the international community.[95]

Second, the formation of the MSEE, Education Cluster and Sphere Companionship, as established in the empirical case studies, indicates an increased *formality* within the field. Not only do they contribute to a more standardised and formalised education response, they also denote and institutionalise the role of education as a core humanitarian sector. Especially through the MSEE Handbook but also with the Education Cluster, INEE has significantly engaged in frames of professionalisation in order to actively create and shape the discourse around EiE.[96]

93 NRC (n 61).
94 Krook and True (n 28).
95 UNGA, 'The Right to Education in Emergency Situations. Resolution A/64/290', www.unesco.org/education/postconflict/educationinemergencies.pdf.
96 Macpherson (n 91).

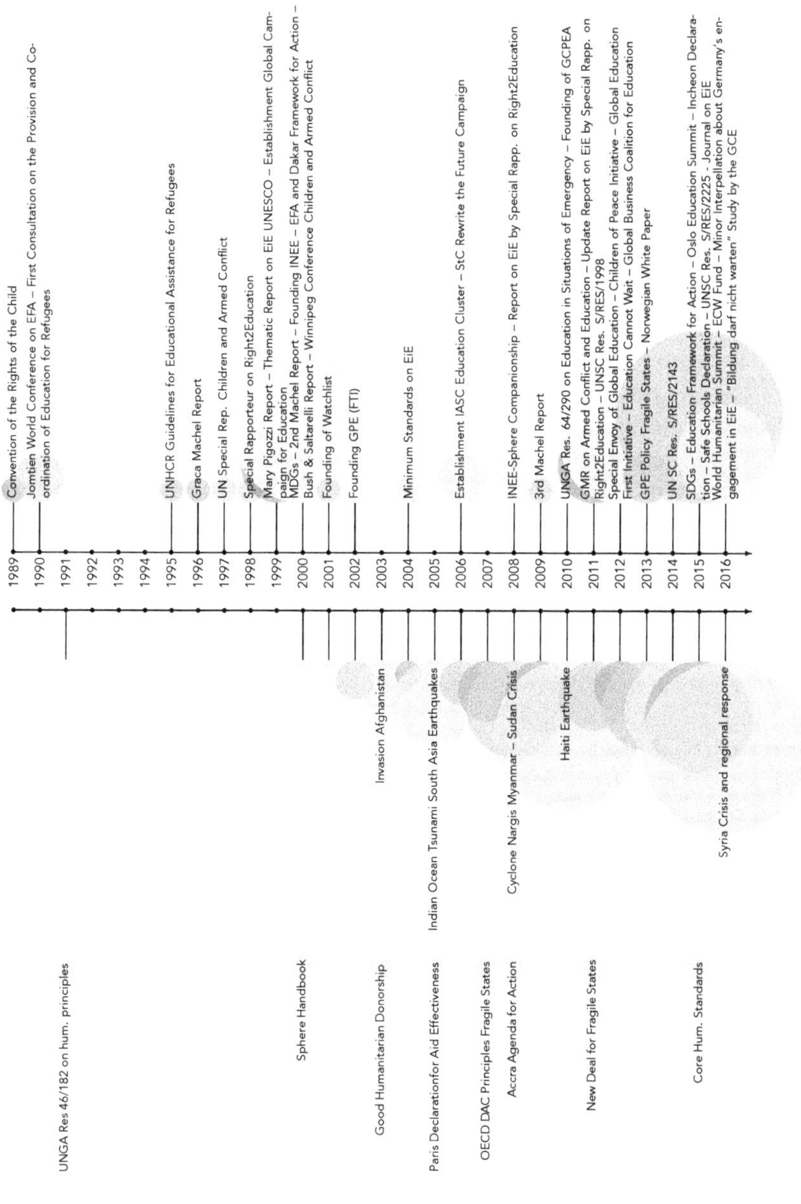

Figure 5.1 Timeline of important EiE frameworks. The size of the bubble is relative to the number of frameworks/events/funding that happened in each year. Left column: Humanitarian frameworks. Middle column: Total humanitarian funding for education per year (OCHA 2016). Right column: Important EiE frameworks, policy and events

Third, an analysis of the *contents* of EiE reveals that the field is currently seeking to move beyond a narrow conceptualisation internally. Instead of purely focusing on access, the field is witnessing a shift towards good-quality programming. At the same time, EiE is experiencing room to manoeuvre out of a very narrow definition. It seems that recent advocacy and policy successes allow for a wider conceptualisation of the emergent norm.

5. Discussion and conclusion

This chapter provides an analysis of the question of how and why EiE as a sector of emergency response experienced a surge in attention, resources and policy changes. The research endeavour sought to trace shifting global ideas and narratives about the role of education in humanitarian action by looking at the evolution of EiE. The framing analysis applied to document and interview data revealed that language was an important tool in this process. By framing education as a life-saving and life-sustaining intervention, advocates sought to demonstrate its compatibility with humanitarian norms. Education is framed by drawing from global norms and reflecting global dynamics such as the rights-based approach, humanitarian protection and education as a service. At the same time, the dynamic nature of the emergent norm allows for different actors to gain control over its meaning. The emergence and rise of the security frame and its associated concept of CVE is an example of how some actors have lost control over the norm and how it is implemented. The case study thereby offers insight into the practices of diffusion agents, who actively and passively impact meaning and content through their discursive outputs. Thus, the analysis traced advocates' framing strategies and demonstrated how they opened up a space within humanitarian discourse and maximised the diffusion of their conceptualisation by making a connection with hegemonic institutions such as the Sphere standards or the Cluster Approach. Last, the legitimacy of their conceptualisation was increased through the adoption of EiE by other actors. The findings furthermore unveil an increasing institutionalisation within the field. Several IOs have changed their institutional practices and operational procedures, allowing for an increase in prominence, formality and contents.

By examining the practice of EiE, this research endeavour has contributed to a theoretical understanding of how new norms emerge, develop and are communicated. It showed how alignment with other humanitarian norms and processes facilitated the adoption of the new norm. At the same time, the dynamic nature of norm emergence accounts for a variation and inspired alternative interpretations as supporters and opponents struggle to define the content of the new norm.

While this research identifies framing as an important factor, it simultaneously acknowledges that shifting global pressures – such as increasingly protracted conflicts, the expansion of the humanitarian mandate into developmental work in fragile and protracted contexts (mission creep) and changing demands from target populations – led to an altering environment, which rendered them successful.

Similarly, framing is not the only possible explanation for the success of EiE activities. Alongside the reasons given, other potential factors to explain the recent rise in interest – and opening up avenues for further research – include the discourse surrounding: the globalisation of education policy, the protection of children during armed conflicts, conflict-sensitive education, peace education, resilience and social cohesion. Meanwhile, the chapter paid little attention to the Western construction of global norms and how they serve as a means of promoting cultural ideals elsewhere. The EiE sector, like other sectors, has been criticised for promoting Western values and an erasure of racism being deeply entrenched in education and international development.[97] Further research on EiE should examine these trends with respect to the global emergence, diffusion and institutionalisation of norms.

List of references

Literature

Acharya, A, 'How Ideas Spread: Whose Norms Matter? Norm Localization and Institutional Change in Asian Regionalism', *International Organization*, 58, 239, 2004.

Addis, A, 'Linking Humanitarian and Development Action in Ethiopia', Ruhr-Universität Bochum and University of Cagliari. 2015. https://iris.unica.it/retrieve/handle/11584/266840/345239/PhD_Thesis_Addis.pdf

Anderson, A and Hodgkin, M, 'The Creation and Development of the Global IASC Education Cluster', Background paper for the Global Monitoring Report, UNESCO. 2010.

Anderson, A, Hofmann, J and Hyll-Larsen, P, 'The Right to Education for Children in Emergencies', *Journal of International Humanitarian Legal Studies*, 2, 84, 2011.

Barnett, MN, *Empire of Humanity: A History of Humanitarianism*. Barnett: New York, Cornell University Press. 2011.

Bennett, C, Foley, M and Pantuliano, S, 'Time to Let Go. Remaking Humanitarian Action for the Modern Era', ODI. 2016. www.odi.org/sites/odi.org.uk/files/resource-documents/10422.pdf, accessed 6 May 2020

Bensalah, K et al., 'Education in Situations of Emergency and Crisis: Challenges for the New Century', UNESCO. 1999. https://unesdoc.unesco.org/ark:/48223/pf0000123484

97 Arathi Sriprakash, Leon Tikly and Sharon Walker, 'The Erasures of Racism in Education and International Development: Re-Reading the "Global Learning Crisis"', *Compare: A Journal of Comparative and International Education*, 50 (2020), 676; Jess Oddy, 'We Need to Start Talking about Race, Power, and Privilege in the Education in Emergencies Sector', *Medium*, 20 November 2020, https://medium.com/rethinking-education/we-need-to-start-talking-about-race-power-and-privilege-in-the-education-in-emergencies-sector-51cf06ac202a, accessed 24 November 2020; Julia C Lerch, 'INGO Memberships Revisited: Local Variation of Receptor Sites in the Education Sector', *International Journal of Comparative Sociology*, 60 (2019), 117.

Brannelly, L, Ndaruhutse, S and Rigaud, C, 'Donor's Engagement: Supporting Education in Fragile and Conflict-Affected States', *Research Report*, IIEP, UNESCO. 2009.

Bryman, A, *Social Research Methods*. Bryman: Oxford, Oxford University Press. 2016.

Burde, D, 'Response Paper: Empower or Control? Education in Emergencies and Global Governance', *Current Issues in Comparative Education*, 9(2), 55, 2007.

Burde, D, *Schools for Conflict or for Peace in Afghanistan*. Columbia University Press. 2014.

Burde, D, 'Education in Emergencies: A Review of Theory and Research', *Review of Educational Research*, 20(19), 1, Burde: New York, 2016.

Bush, KD and Saltarelli, D, *The Two Faces of Education in Ethnic Conflict*. United Nations Publications. 2000. www.unicef-irc.org/publications/pdf/insight4.pdf

Cahill, KM, *Even in Chaos*. Cahill: Fordham, Fordham University Press. 2010.

Carpenter, C, 'Setting the Advocacy Agenda: Theorizing Issue Emergence and Nonemergence in Transnational Advocacy Networks', *International Studies Quarterly*, 51, 99, 2007.

Chong, D and Druckman, JN, 'Framing Theory', *Annual Review of Political Science*, 10, 103, 2007.

DiMaggio, PJ and Powell, WW, 'The Iron Cage Revisited: Institutional Isomorphism and Collective Rationality in Organizational Fields', *American Sociological Review*, 48, 147, 1983.

Dryden-Peterson, S, 'Policies for Education in Conflict and Post-Conflict Reconstruction', in Karen Mundy et al. (eds), *The Handbook of Global Education Policy*. Dryden-Peterson: Chichester, John Wiley & Sons. 2016.

Finnemore, M and Sikkink, K, 'International Norm Dynamics and Political Change', *International Organization*, 52, 887, 1998.

Freistein, K, *Institutioneller Wandel Im (Kon)Text*. Baden-Baden: Nomos. 2012.

Hajer, M, 'Discourse Coalitions and the Institutionalization of Practice: The Case of Acid Rain in Britain', in Fischer F and Forester J (eds), *The Argumentative Turn in Policy Analysis and Planning*. Durham: Duke University Press. 1993.

Hansen, L, *Security as Practice*, New York: Routledge. 2006.

Harber, C, *Education and International Development*. Oxford: Symposium Books. 2014.

Harmer, A and Macrae, J, 'Beyond the Continuum. The Changing Role of Aid Policy in Protracted Crises'. https://odi.org/en/publications/beyond-the-continuum-the-changing-role-of-aid-policy-in-protracted-crises-2/

Hilhorst, D, 'Classical Humanitarianism and Resilience Humanitarianism: Making Sense of Two Brands of Humanitarian Action', *Journal of International Humanitarian Action*, 3, 15, 2018.

Holzscheiter, A, *Children's Rights in International Politics*. Basingstroke: Palgrave Macmillan. 2010.

Keck, M and Sikkink, K, *Activists Beyond Borders*. Ithaca: Cornell University Press. 1998.

Krook, ML and True, J, 'Rethinking the Life Cycles of International Norms: The United Nations and the Global Promotion of Gender Equality', *European Journal of International Relations*, 18(1), 103, 2010.

Lerch, JC, 'INGO Memberships Revisited: Local Variation of Receptor Sites in the Education Sector', *International Journal of Comparative Sociology*, 60, 117, 2019.

Lieser, J and Dijkzeul, D, *Handbuch Humanitäre Hilfe*. Berlin, Heidelberg: Springer. 2013.

Macpherson, I, 'An Analysis of Power in Transnational Advocacy Networks in Education', in Mundy, K et al. (eds), *The Handbook of Global Education Policy*. Malden: John Wiley & Sons. 2016.

Magrath, B, 'Global Norms, Organisational Change: Framing the Rights-Based Approach at ActionAid', *Third World Quarterly*, 35(7), 1273, 2014.

Marks, C, 'A Critical Analysis of Donor Education Strategies for International Development', University of Ulster. 2014.
Menashy, F and Dryden-Peterson, S, 'The Global Partnership for Education's Evolving Support to Fragile and Conflict-Affected States', *International Journal of Educational Development*, 44, 82, 2015.
Meyer, JW and Rowan, B, 'Institutionalized Organizations: Formal Structure as Myth and Ceremony', *American Journal of Sociology*, 83, 340, 1977.
Mundy, K and Dryden-Peterson, S, *Educating Children in Conflict Zones.* New York: Teacher's College, Colombia University. 2011.
Nicolai, S, Hine, S and Wales, J, 'Education in Emergencies and Protracted Crises', ODI. 2015. www.odi.org/sites/odi.org.uk/files/odi-assets/publications-opinion-files/9714.pdf
Novelli, M, 'The New Geopolitics of Educational Aid: From Cold Wars to Holy Wars?', *International Journal of Educational Development*, 30, 453, 2010.
Novelli, M and Lopes Cardozo, M, 'Globalizing Educational Interventions in Zones of Conflict: The Role of Dutch Aid to Education and Conflict', in Verger, A, Novelli, M and Altinyelken, HK (eds), *Global Education Policy and International Development.* London: Bloomsbury Academic. 2012.
Novelli, M and Robertson, SL, 'The Politicization of Development Aid to Education after September 11', in Saltman, KJ (ed), *Schooling and the Politics of Disaster.* New York: Taylor and Francis. 2007.
NRC, 'Countering Violent Extremism and Humanitarian Action', NRC Position Papers, June 2017.
Oddy, J, 'We Need to Start Talking about Race, Power, and Privilege in the Education in Emergencies Sector', *Medium*, 20 November 2020. https://medium.com/rethinking-education/we-need-to-start-talking-about-race-power-and-privilege-in-the-education-in-emergencies-sector-51cf06ac202a, accessed 24 November 2020.
Phillips, N, Lawrence, TB and Hardy, C, 'Discourse and Institutions', *Academy of Management Review*, 29, 635, 2004.
Pigozzi, MJ, 'Education in Emergencies and for Reconstruction: A Developmental Approach'. https://healtheducationresources.unesco.org/sites/default/files/resources/EducEmerg.pdf
Retamal, G and Aedo-Richmond, R, *Education as a Humanitarian Response.* London: Cassell. 1998.
Schmitz-Guinote, F, 'Three Reasons Why Education Needs the Support of Humanitarian Actors in Conflict Zones' (*Humanitarian Law & Policy Blog*, 12 December 2019. https://blogs.icrc.org/law-and-policy/2019/12/12/three-reasons-education-humanitarian-conflict/ accessed 29 August 2021.
Schön, D and Rein, M, *Frame Reflection.* New York: Basic Books. 1994.
Sezgin, Z and Dijkzeul, D (eds), *The New Humanitarians in International Practice: Emerging Actors and Contested Principles.* Routledge. 2015. www.taylorfrancis.com/books/9781317570622, accessed 11 May 2020.
Sinclair, M, 'Planning Education in and after Emergencies'. https://www.researchgate.net/publication/44829669_Planning_education_in_and_after_emergencies
Snow, D et al., 'Frame Alignment Processes, Micromobilization, And Movement Participation', *American Sociological Review*, 51, 464, 1986.
Sriprakash, A, Tikly, L and Walker, S, 'The Erasures of Racism in Education and International Development: Re-Reading the "Global Learning Crisis"', *Compare: A Journal of Comparative and International Education*, 50, 676, 2020.

Walker, P and Maxwell, DG, *Shaping the Humanitarian World*. Oxford: Routledge. 2009.
Winthrop, R and Matsui, E, 'A New Agenda for Education in Fragile States', Working Paper, The Brookings Institution. 2013.

Other sources

Development Initiatives, 'Global Humanitarian Assistance Report 2019', Development Initiatives. 2019. http://devinit.org/wp-content/uploads/2019/09/GHA-report-2019.pdf, accessed 1 October 2019.
European Commission, 'Education in Emergencies in EU-Funded Humanitarian Aid Operations', European Civil Protection and Humanitarian Aid Operations. 2019. https://ec.europa.eu/echo/files/news/eie_in_humanitarian_assistance.pdf, accessed 28 August 2021.
INEE, 'Integrating Quality Education With Humanitarian Response For Humanitarian Accountability: The Sphere-INEE Companionship'. http://s3.amazonaws.com/inee-assets/resources/Sphere_INEE_paper_FINAL.pdf
INEE, 'Sphere-INEE Companionship Agreement'. http://s3.amazonaws.com/inee-assets/resources/Sphere-INEE_Companionship_Agreement_(signed)_(23_10_2008).pdf
INEE, 'Sphere-INEE Companionship Agreement'. www.ineesite.org/en/partnerships/sphere-companion
Machel, G, 'Impact of Armed Conflict on Children'. www.unicef.org/graca/
OCHA, 'Global Humanitarian Overview 2021', OCHA. 2020. www.unocha.org/sites/unocha/files/GHO-2021-Abridged-EN.pdf
Sphere Project (ed), 'What Is Sphere?' www.spherehandbook.org/en/what-is-sphere/
UNESCO, 'The Hidden Crisis: Armed Conflict and Education'. http://unesdoc.unesco.org/images/0019/001907/190743e.pdf
UNGA, The Right to Education in Emergency Situations. Resolution A/64/290. www.unesco.org/education/postconflict/educationinemergencies.pdf
UNHCR, 'Contribution to the Fifteenth Coordination Meeting On International Migration', UNHCR 2017. UN/POP/MIG-15CM/2017/14. www.un.org/en/development/desa/population/migration/events/coordination/15/documents/papers/14_UNHCR_nd.pdf, accessed 9 March 2020.

6 The right to self-determination and participation for refugee children with disabilities

*Jamie Bolling**

Introduction

Invisible, forgotten and overlooked, people with disabilities are most marginalised in a crisis response.[1] The United Nations Children's Fund (UNICEF) raises the issue of children paying the highest price in the humanitarian crisis of armed conflict, natural disasters and other emergencies exposing millions of children to unthinkable forms of violence, exploitation, abuse and neglect.[2] Refugee children with disabilities are even more marginalised due to disability, dependence and support needs.[3]

There are assumptions that children and disabled persons are not among those coming ashore in Europe,[4] but according to the Human Rights Watch, there are an estimated 9.7 million disabled persons[5] among the 82.4 million forcibly displaced persons in the world, and they estimate that 42% of that group are children.[6] The disabled children among the 42% have needs that children without disabilities do not have. They are dependent on their family, if they have one, and, depending on the type of disability, they may not even be able to make their voice heard.

* Jamie Bolling is the Director of the Independent Living Institute and co-chair of the European Network on Independent Living.

1 Woman's Committee for Refugee Women and Children, *Disabilities Among Refugees and Conflict Affected Populations: Resource Kit for Fieldworkers* (Woman's Committee for Refugee Women and Children, 2008), 1, https://cms.emergency.unhcr.org/documents/11982/43580/Women's+Commission+for+Refugee+Women+and+Children%2C+Resource+Kit+for+Field+Workers%2C+2008/8b368bc0-6ecb-44db-81e7-c60e46630717, accessed 26 October 2021.

2 UNICEF, *Protecting Children in Humanitarian Action* (UNICEF, 2021), 1, www.unicef.org/protection/protecting-children-in-humanitarian-action, accessed 17 October 2021.

3 D Mitchell and V Karr, *Crises, Conflict and Disability – Ensuring Equality* (Routledge London and New York, 2014) xvii.

4 Mary Crock, Laura Smith-Khan, Ron McCallum and Ben Saul, *The Legal Protection of Refugees with Disabilities – Forgotten and Invisible?* (Edward Elgar Publishing Limited, Cheltenham Glos and Northampton, 2017), 4.

5 www.hrw.org/news/2020/06/09/un-strengthen-humanitarian-aid-people-disabilities#, accessed 26 October 2021.

6 UNHCR, Figures at a glance (UNHCR 2021), 1, www.unhcr.org/figures-at-a-glance.html, accessed 26 October 2021.

DOI: 10.4324/9781003187493-6

In 2015, the Independent Living Institute (ILI) met Julius Ntobuah, a refugee with disabilities fleeing from Cameroon, and learned of his experience and his meeting with the Swedish Migration Agency. His stories were of maltreatment, inaccessibility and poor attitudes. Together with the founder of the ILI, Adolf Ratzka, himself also a refugee with disabilities, the two discussed the issues of migration and disability and applied for and received funding through the ILI for the project Disabled Refugees Welcome (DRW), upon which this chapter is based.[7]

The chapter highlights the area of crisis response for refugee children with disabilities and of integration based on work that has been carried out in Sweden through the DRW project. Considering that Sweden is a high-income country, you might think that this work was not necessary, but through meetings with refugees with disabilities who came to Sweden during the refugee influx of 2015, the ILI learned that the opposite was true. Refugee children with disabilities are met with inaccessibility, poor treatment, prejudice, lack of support and more, where they should instead see their rights of self-determination and participation fulfilled, as well as their best interests taken into consideration. Some of the DRW findings should be of interest not only for Swedish stakeholders but for stakeholders in other receiving countries, as well as in the sending countries, to safeguard the protection of refugee children with disabilities along the whole route.

Refugee children with disabilities lack information that may lead to a lack of agency and empowerment, with their voices not being heard.[8] The DRW project, carried out from 2017 to 2020, met about 100 refugees with disabilities. In the group of 100 individuals, there were 8 children between the ages of 6 and 12. DRW heard what they had to say through their parents or a contact person if they were not able to express themselves. Authorities, organisations and volunteers, a total of 16, contacted DRW looking for support for refugee children with disabilities. These organisations were five municipalities, two migration offices, four non-governmental organisations and five volunteers.

DRW gave both support and information and referred people to relevant actors in the areas of migration and disability, such as the Swedish authorities and/or civil society organisations. Support sought by families, the authorities, organisations and volunteers pertained to different areas such as: the asylum process, family reunification, access to social services, access to inclusive education, access to medical care, access to technical assistive aids, access to incontinence supplies and access to family support. DRW referred families to, for example, the Swedish Red Cross, where there

7 Sooz Romero, Ola Linder, Riitta Leena Karlsson and Jamie Bolling, *The Road to Reciprocal Integration* (Vägar mot ömsesidigt integration), (Excellent Print, Stockholm, 2020), 3–7.

8 Lori Peek and Laura M Stough, 'Children with Disabilities in the Context of Disaster: A Social Vulnerability Perspective', *Society for Research in Child Development, Inc.*, 81(4) (July/August 2010), 1260–1270, 1263.

were medical volunteers who could ensure that refugees without the right to medical care were still able to get the care they needed. Other organisations were the Swedish Church, which carries out many activities for refugees, and organisations for people with different disabilities, including organisations for children and for people with seeing impairments, hearing impairments, mobility impairments and autism. FARR (the Swedish Network of Refugee Support Groups) and the Swedish Refugee National Council, working with refugee rights, were contacted for family reunification.

When promoting rights for children with disabilities, DRW found it key to use the social model of disability, which reframes disability in terms of the right to participation and accessibility.[9] The right to participation is also promoted in the United Nations Convention on the Rights of the Child from 1989 (CRC), being the first convention to include disability.[10] General Comment (GC) No. 12 (2009) elaborates on Article 12 of the CRC, which ensures the right of children to express their views freely in all matters.[11] The United Nations Convention on the Rights of Persons with Disabilities (CRPD) was also indispensable, with DRW giving special consideration to the guiding principles of individual autonomy, including freedom to make your own choices (or what will be referred to as self-determination), along with full and effective participation and inclusion in society and that of accessibility.[12]

Some of the conclusions drawn from the DRW project are that there is a gap and need for actors within the area of disability and migration to have what DRW calls dual competence, or knowledge and experience, on both issues – migration and disability – in order to have a broad knowledge of the two areas. The disability perspective, intersectional perspective, health perspective and rights perspective need to be applied when working in the field of crisis management concerning migration and integration, as the perspectives provide for a wider knowledge and understanding of the situation of people to find the appropriate solutions to meet their needs. Families and individuals with disabilities should be given timely and accessible information on how the Swedish national social system works, as well as empowerment, so that they themselves are able to go through the process of finding the support they need and so that they are able to become included in Swedish society. Inaccessibility proved one of the greatest obstacles for the families of children with disabilities, showing that there is a need to remove obstacles and increase accessibility for better integration. This should be done for the implementation of Article 9 of the CRPD.[13]

9 Peter Beresford and Suzy Croft, 'Service Users' Knowledges and the Social Construction of Social Work', *Journal of Social Work*, 1(3) (Sage Publications, 2001), 295–316, 304.

10 1989 Convention on the Rights of the Child (entered into force 2 September 1990) 1577 UNTS 3.

11 2009 General Comment No. 12 *The right of the child to be heard* CRC/C/GC12.

12 2006 The Convention on the Rights of Persons with Disabilities A Res/61/106/.

13 2006. Ibid.

In addition to remedying the lack of knowledge on disability and including people with disabilities in humanitarian work, there is also a need for research on refugee children with disabilities in order to better understand their situation.[14]

Another conclusion is that non-governmental organisations (NGOs) should contribute to a paradigm shift in the humanitarian response, going from paternalism to empowerment and the right to participation. Actors in the fields of migration and disability not allowing the voices of the children concerned to be heard, assuming they know what children need and acting as protectors hinder participation and prevent the best solutions from being found. This is not respecting the CRPD and Article 4(3) that oblige states to actively involve people with disabilities themselves or the UN Special Rapporteur's emphasis on citizen control.[15] The voices of refugee children and their inclusion in decision-making processes are of importance for their inclusion in society and their integration, as supported by the CRC and as further explained in paragraphs 123 and 127 of General Comment No. 12.[16]

This chapter looks more closely at the important terms of participation, empowerment and reciprocal integration. It also includes background on the Swedish migration influx of 2015. There is a brief analysis of the relevant international law and policies on disabilities, children and migration, including those that focus on the right to self-determination and participation. The scene is set for the DRW project, with a background in the independent living (IL) philosophy and the ILI. Methods, results and conclusions from the DRW project regarding refugee children with disabilities in humanitarian crises are presented.

The aim of the chapter is to spread the lessons learned through DRW from the 2015 migration influx and to avoid unpreparedness in the response to the situation of refugee children with disabilities. It is also hoped that it will soon facilitate the safeguarding of the protection of refugee children with disabilities through participation and empowerment.

DRW terminology

The choice of words is always important, as they carry power in themselves.[17] In order to pursue the key principles of IL used in the project, it was essential to understand participation and empowerment, both defined

14 Crock, Smith-Khan, McCallum and Saul (n 4), 4.

15 Colin Caughey, 'Government Human Rights Focal Points; Lessons Learned from Focal Points under the Convention on the Rights of Persons with Disabilities', *Netherlands Quarterly of Human Rights*, 39(2) (2021), I, 19–139, 130, SAGE, sagepub.com/journals-permissions, https://doi.org/10.1177/0924051921101557journasl.sagepub.com/home/nqh.

16 2009 General Comment No. 12 *The right of the child to be heard* CRC/C/GC12.

17 Niclas Sennerteg, *Ord som dödar-om Folkmord och Propaganda* (Natur och Kultur, Stockholm, 2010), 9.

here in greater depth. Another term important for DRW, briefly defined here, is that of reciprocal integration. These terms can be considered from a general perspective, but important for this piece of work is to consider the terms from the disability and child perspectives.

Participation is a civil and political right. The principle of participation is enshrined in both the CRC and the CRPD. IL is based on the principle of equal opportunities and the participation of people with disabilities in society and dates back to as early as the 1980s.[18] General Comment No. 12 of the CRC concerns the right of the child to be heard.[19] Article 23 of the CRC protects the right to the fullest possible social integration of children.[20] General Comment No. 7 of the CRPD elaborates on participation.[21] DRW informed people of their right to participation and to be included in decisions that concern them.

The participation of people with disabilities is hindered by inaccessibility and by being seen as a homogenous group, instead of each person being unique with different capabilities and needs. Support needs are to be taken into consideration if someone with a disability is to be able to participate. A refugee with disabilities will need to access information on available support. For refugee children with disabilities, it is important that the parent(s) or guardian access the information and that each child be seen as unique with different capabilities and needs. DRW found that it was important for refugees with disabilities to overcome the language barrier to enable their participation, and thus interpretation and translation services were provided.

Empowerment – The CRC obliges states to act for the empowerment of children. The protection and encouraged development of the child can be found in, among others, the following articles:[22]

Article 5 – evolving capacities
Article 23 – abilities
Article 3 – the best interests of the child
Article 2 – without discrimination
Articles 28 and 29 – access to education
Article 12 – the expression of views
Article 13 – the freedom of expression of views
Article 17 – access to information

18 https://enil.eu/wp-content/uploads/2022/06/Principles-of-Independent-Living.pdf, accessed 9 March 2023.

19 2009 General Comment No. 12 *The right of the child to be heard* CRC/C/GC12.

20 The Convention on the Rights of the Child (entered into force on 2 September 1990) 1577 UNTS 3.

21 2018 General Comment No. 7 *On the participation of persons with disabilities, including children with disabilities, through their representative organizations, in the implementation and monitoring of the Convention* CRPD/C/GC7.

22 United Nations Committee on the Rights of the Child, Day of General Discussion (DGD) 2018, *Protecting and Empowering Children as Human Rights Defenders*, Paragraph 2.2.

The concept of empowerment, developed in the United States in the 1920s, consists of three ingredients: strength, power and force. People want to be strong and forceful; they want to have a say and to have power and control over their lives. Empowerment has developed into a collective and political standpoint where people are to be given support but not seen as passive, unknowledgeable and needing to be steered.[23] Empowerment is a tool for independent living and for the DRW project.

People with disabilities are often seen as dependent and as objects of overprotection, viewed as having limited expectations, and children with disabilities even more so. To be empowered, they need access to self-determination. Appropriate measures need to be taken to ensure full development, advancement and empowerment for the purpose of the exercising and the enjoyment of human rights and for having control over your own life.

Reciprocal integration – DRW strove for reciprocal integration, finding it important to acknowledge that integration requires mutual responsibility. Society needs to ensure certain conditions so that everyone can live a life of self-determination, and individuals need to assume responsibility to meet the requirements of society. This is expressed differently by various scholars, where there are those who argue that integration is dependent on the progress immigrants make in their new country but also on the structure of the receiving society and its openness. Where integration policies and the rhetoric of the migration area are "one-way", the responsibility is put on the people migrating, and there is little or no focus on the role of the countries receiving people.[24]

Reciprocal integration is based on equality and participation but obstructed, as refugees with disabilities meet obstacles such as environmental inaccessibility, a lack of accessible information and a lack of the disability perspective. Without accessibility of the required information regarding what is expected of you and concerning available support services, refugees and refugee children with disabilities will not enjoy equal opportunities or have access to participation. DRW found that the reception was poor due to the inaccessible environment, inaccessible services and lack of accessible information. People were not met with respect and expectations.

The refugee influx of 2015 and Sweden

Many people were displaced in 2015, with Sweden experiencing a substantial increase in the number of refugees seeking asylum. In 2015 and 2016, the figure was 191,816. The Swedish Agency for Participation (Myndigheten

23 Ole Petter Askheim and Bengt Starrin, 'Empowerment – A Buzz Word?' ('Empowerment – ett modeord?'), in Ole Petter Askheim and Bengt Starrin (eds), *Empowerment in Theory and Practice* (Empowerment i Teori och Praktik) (Gleerups Utbildning AB, Malmö, 2007), 9–12.

24 Lea M Klarenbeek, 'Reconceptualising "Integration as a Two-Way Process"', *Migration Studies*, 0(0), (2019), 1–20, 1.

för Delaktighet – MFD) is the authority responsible for issues concerning people with disabilities and for ensuring that the Swedish authorities work towards the inclusion of people with disabilities. MFD conducted a study in 2017 about people with disabilities in the asylum process, showing that there was little knowledge about their situation and needs.[25]

Reports from the World Health Organisation and the World Bank have identified about 15% of the world's population as having a disability. The MFD report thus claims that it is reasonable to believe that there are people with disabilities among the refugees who come to Sweden but that too little has been done in this area to know more exactly. The few studies and reports that do exist show that this group is especially exposed to the effects of conflict and refugee situations.[26]

The MFD study covers access to accommodation, healthcare, support services, education and employment. A survey was sent to authorities and organisations that in some way work with migration. The results confirm that there is little knowledge about this group in Sweden, but what is known is that disabled refugees are in a difficult situation. Those understood to be in the most difficult situation are unaccompanied children with disabilities, women with disabilities and children not living in housing provided for refugees and migrants. Changes to the Swedish legislation on migration from 2016 have entailed negative consequences for disabled refugees, especially regarding obtaining a temporary permit to stay in Sweden and for family reunification. The requirement of having a job affects refugees with disabilities to a greater extent than other refugees. Before the legislative changes were introduced, there was the possibility of acquiring a permit to live in Sweden on the grounds of distressing circumstances, which allowed children with disabilities to stay in Sweden.[27]

Some of the areas identified for development and the recommendations put forward in the study were:

- Studies and reports about disabilities and seeking asylum need to have a disability perspective.
- The existing process of health controls needs to be developed so that a disability can be identified as quickly as possible.
- Information targeting the group needs to be in the relevant languages and in an accessible format according to disability requirements, both for adults and children.
- Accommodation and offices need to be accessible for disabled people.
- The right to technical aids and care that is needed must be reviewed.

25 The Swedish Agency for Participation (Myndigheten för delaktighet), *People with a Disability in the Asylum Seeking and Establishment Processes* (*Personer med funktionsnedsättning i asyl-och etableringsprocessen)* (Myndigheten för delaktighet, Sundbyberg, 2017), 6.
26 Ibid., 15.
27 Ibid., 7.

- The legislation needs to be reviewed concerning the access to social services for people in the asylum process.
- Knowledge needs to be provided to the authorities but also to unaccompanied children so that they have the right knowledge and know which rights they can access.
- An analysis of the municipalities' provision of Swedish for Immigrants language courses needs to be carried out, bearing in mind the perspectives of accessibility and disability.
- Support during the establishment period, as well as in accessing employment, and the need to include better ways to identify disabilities to ensure that people can access the support they need faster and to facilitate the processes.[28]

Youth hostels, camping facilities and gymnasiums became full in 2015 when they housed refugees until they could be moved to Swedish migration facilities. Many organisations from Swedish civil society mobilised to meet the needs of the people arriving in Sweden. The Swedish Church, for example, increased its existing involvement in refugees and mobilised new services within days of the refugee influx.[29]

International law and policies supporting the rights of refugee children with disabilities

DRW ran activities for the rights of refugees with disabilities, especially for the right to self-determination, participation and being included in the community. DRW based its actions and demands on relevant steering documents in the fields of disability, children and migration. As previously stated, the CRPD from 2006 is the main document for the case of self-determination and the right to participation in society.[30] CRPD GC No. 5 on the right to live independently and being included in the community from 2017 includes important definitions supporting life in the community for integration.[31] The CRC was important, with its focus on children, and was the first convention to include disability.[32] As stated in the third paragraph of the introduction to GC No. 12 of the CRC, and although the term participation is not used in the convention, a widespread practice has led to the

28 Ibid., 7–10.

29 Kristina Hellqvist and Andreas Sandberg, *A Time of Meetings – Working with Refugees and New Arrivals in Swedish Parishes* (*En tid av möten – arbetet med asylsökande och nyanlända i Svenska kyrkans församlingar 2015–2016*) (The Church of Sweden – *Svenska kyrkan*, Uppsala, 2017), 9.

30 2006 The Convention on the Rights of Persons with Disabilities A Res/61/106/.

31 2017 General Comment on Article 19: Living Independently and Being Included in the Community CRPD/C/18/1.

32 1989 Convention on the Rights of the Child (entered into force on 2 September 1990) 1577 UNTS 3.

recognition of participation as key for the processes of children. Both participation and the consideration of the child's best interests in paragraph two of the introduction are principles to be considered in the interpretation and implementation of all other rights.[33]

The role of the family is protected through Article 16 paragraph 3 of the Universal Declaration of Human Rights (UDHR), which states that: "The family is the natural and fundamental group unit of society and is entitled to protection by society and the State".[34] In GC No 12. of the CRC, it is pointed out in paragraph 90 how a family which allows the freedom of expression of its children is a model that supports the child's socialisation but also that families are to be supported for such parenting through educational programmes.[35]

The UN Convention and the Protocol relating to the status of refugees was essential for the migration perspective.[36] GC No. 12 of the CRC points out in paragraph 123 that children who are refugees are particularly vulnerable and that children need to be heard on their educational expectations and health conditions in order to integrate.[37]

The legal provisions feed into one another and are important for the promotion of the rights of refugee children with disabilities. The CRC and the CRPD are arguably the most significant of the nine human rights conventions, based as they are on the construction of people as rights-bearers rather than recipients of charity, which is especially important for the prosperity of children with disabilities in humanitarian crises.[38] Charity has been promoted and still plays a strong role in societies to raise money for disability issues, using pictures of children with disabilities to spark pity, leading to people reaching into their pockets to donate money for disability causes. The problem with that is that the attitude of people is that of pity, where people with disabilities are not seen as our equals and as people with rights.[39]

In the earlier conventions, the needs of children were expressed as the right to the provision of special care and protection, which are covered in Article 25 of the UDHR from 1948 and even as early as in 1924 in the Declaration on the Rights of the Child and its updated version in 1959.[40] The provisions in these documents reflected a welfare approach for the provision of assistance to children in need rather than on real rights, including the empowerment of children. With the adoption of the CRC, only the

33 2009 General Comment No. 12 The right of the child to be heard CRC/C/GC12.
34 1948 Declaration of Human Rights/A/RES/21217 (III).
35 2009 General Comment No. 12 The right of the child to be heard CRC/C/GC12.
36 1950 UNHCR Convention and Protocol Relating to the Status of Refugees Res/429/5/.
37 2009 General Comment No. 12 The right of the child to be heard CRC/C/GC12.
38 Crock, Smith-Khan, McCallum and Saul (n 4), 19.
39 Joseph Shapiro, *No Pity – People with Disabilities Forging a New Civil Rights Movement* (Times Books Random House, New York, 1994), 22.
40 1948 Declaration of Human Rights/A/RES/21217 (III).

minimum standards have been agreed.[41] However, they have led to a paradigm shift with the rights-based approach and also with the view of the child as having evolving capacities, expertise and agency.[42] In the CRC, the right to empowerment is emphasised, but still a great deal depends on the interpretation of the convention.[43] Disabled children are covered in Article 23 of the Convention on the Rights of the Child.[44]

The CRPD was a revolution for disabilities, demanding that disabled people be treated as rights-bearers rather than objects of charity, identified as medical cases and being in need of protection. The CRPD, with its paradigm shift based on the social model of disability, states that disability is created by the lack of accessibility and obstacles/hindrances to participation.[45] The convention highlights the challenges people with disabilities face and the fact that children with disabilities are at greater risk. The risks faced by children with disabilities are stated as violence, abuse, neglect, maltreatment and exploitation, and through Article 7 of the CRPD, states are to ensure the full enjoyment by children with disabilities of all human rights and fundamental freedoms on an equal basis with other children. Article 11 covers protection in the migration process –

> States Parties shall take, in accordance with their obligations under international law, including international humanitarian law and international human rights law, all necessary measures to ensure the protection and safety of persons with disabilities in situations of risk, including situations of armed conflict, humanitarian emergencies and the occurrence of natural disasters.[46]

Having raised awareness of the risks, the CRPD then obliges states to take measures to prevent the risks and to promote the rights of, in this case, refugee children with disabilities.[47]

Children in a humanitarian crisis are, in general, marginalised, with no attention being paid to context, cultural differences, religious differences, their gender or whether they are disabled. It is important to have an intersectional perspective to understand the situation of an individual child and to understand the discrimination to which that child may be subjected.[48] Intersectionality takes into consideration the different factors that may lead

41 John Tobin, *The UN Convention on the Rights of the Child* (Oxford: Oxford University Press, 2019) [Hereafter: Tobin] Chapter I *The Adoption of the Convention* I C.
42 Tobin, Chapter *Introduction*.
43 Tobin, Chapter *Conclusion*.
44 1989 Convention on the Rights of the Child (entered into force 2 September 1990) 1577 UNTS 3.
45 Crock, Smith-Khan, McCallum and Saul (n 4), 19–22, 21.
46 2006 The Convention on the Rights of Persons with Disabilities A/Res/61/106.
47 Ibid.
48 Edvina Bešic, Lisa Paleczek and Barbara Gasteiger-Klicpera, "Don't Forget about Us: Attitudes towards the Inclusion of Refugee Children with(out) Disabilities", *International*

to discrimination and that someone may experience multiple discrimination. Multiple discrimination means, for example, that someone with a minority background and a disability could be discriminated against on both grounds or be a victim of simultaneous oppression.[49] Through power structures in humanitarianism, children are met with paternalism; people speak on their behalf and of them as victims. Governments want to send the children back to where they came from, while non-governmental organisations work for the integration of the children into societies.[50]

Accessibility is a principle of the CRPD, with state obligations given in Article 9. To exercise full participation, accessibility is a prerequisite. Measures are to be taken for the accessibility of the physical environment, but also in transportation, communication and services.[51] Accessible information is an important criterion of successful integration, allowing people to understand and access the systems.

Despite all the policies that promote the rights of children, of refugee children and of refugee children with disabilities, their situation remains difficult. Negative attitudes towards disabled refugee children lead to challenges in integration and probable discrimination.[52] The CRC promotes the empowerment of the child. Kyle Vella, an expert on humanitarian affairs, promotes considering the child the best of agents to gather information about the children themselves to find the best solutions for their lives. NGOs should contribute to a paradigm shift in the humanitarian response from paternalism to one on the right to participation to change the situation of children. Listening to the child at hand allows for the participation of the child, a tool for finding the best solutions.[53]

The CRC was incorporated into Swedish national law on January 1, 2020. The legislation enacted by the Swedish Parliament includes only one provision outlining that Articles 1–42 of the CRC are to be enforced as part of Swedish law, precisely the way these provisions are formulated in the original text. This means that, within the Swedish legal system, the CRC is to be enforced in the same way as any other law enacted by the Parliament. This is a significant step towards promoting the rights of children in Sweden, even though, just like with any other piece of legislation, the enforcement of the CRC as a national law is likely to pose its own challenges in practice.[54]

Journal of Inclusive Education, 24(2) (2020), 202–217, 213, Routledge, https://doi.org/10.1080/13603115.2018.1455113.

49 John Swain, Sally French and Colin Cameron, *Controversial Issues in a Disabling Society* (Open University Press, Buckingham, 2003), 57.

50 Kyle Vella, 'Power, Paternalism and Children on the Move', *Journal of Humanitarian Action*, 1(3) (Springer 2016), 7, http://doi.org/10.1186/s41018-016-0003-y.

51 2006 The Convention on the Rights of Persons with Disabilities A/Res/61/106.

52 Bešic, Paleczek and Gasteiger-Klicpera (n 48), 203.

53 Vella (n 50), 9.

54 Lag (2018:1197) om Förenta nationernas konvention om barnets rättigheter, www.riksdagen.se/sv/dokument-lagar/dokument/svensk-forfattningssamling/lag-20181197-om-forenta-nationernas-konvention_sfs-2018-1197, accessed on 26 October 2021.

Setting the scene for DRW in a social context

DRW was based on the principles of empowerment, participation and IL philosophy. The goal of the project was to facilitate the integration process of disabled refugees by mapping out needs, but also by mapping out what is working and not working in the Swedish reception and integration processes. This section of the chapter elaborates on the social context for DRW by introducing IL, ILI and DRW.

Independent living

Independent living is a philosophy and a movement for people with disabilities started in the United States in the 1960s.[55] The fundamental principles of IL are self-determination, equal opportunities, self-respect, full participation and empowerment.[56] It is on these principles that the work of DRW was based and upon which all activity with the refugees with disabilities was organised.

IL has been based on advocacy of those in need of services and support themselves and for the right to live a life with IL. DRW has raised the awareness of this right among the project participants and the importance of being empowered to be the subject in your own integration process. Advocacy is about the right to live with self-determination and to access services when needed according to Article 19 of the CRPD.[57] It is important to note that self-determination and access to services was already included in the IL principles from 1990 in the right to participate equally in society and to exercise self-determination.[58] Adolf Ratzka, the founder of the ILI and of DRW, defines IL in the following way: "Independent Living means that people with disabilities demand the same choices and control in their every-day lives that non-disabled brothers and sisters, neighbours and friends take for granted".[59] People with disabilities want to grow up and have families, go to their neighbourhood school, use the same bus as their neighbours and have a job that is in line with their acquired education and interests.[60]

Within the IL philosophy, people with disabilities themselves are the best experts concerning their lives and their needs. They must have access to full participation and self-determination and be able to determine their own lives.

55 Michael Oliver and Colin Barnes, *Disabled People and Social Policy – From Exclusion to Inclusion* (Pearson Education Limited, Essex, 1998), 83.

56 https://enil.eu/wp-content/uploads/2019/02/Principles-of-Independent-Living.pdf, accessed 26 October 2021.

57 2006 The Convention on the Rights of Persons with Disabilities A/Res/61/106.

58 https://enil.eu/wp-content/uploads/2019/02/Principles-of-Independent-Living.pdf, accessed 26 October 2021.

59 Adolf Ratzka, *Self-Determination for Persons with Extensive Disabilities through Direct Payments for Personal Assistance* (Independent Living Institute, Stockholm, 2017) Section – *What Is Independent Living*, www.independentliving.org/docs7/Self-determination-direct-payments.html, accessed 30 October 2021.

60 Ibid.

Peer support is one of the main methods used for empowerment. Through an exchange of experience, individuals enhance their self-confidence and learn about social expectations and strategies to navigate in society.[61] The DRW team, sharing the experiences of migration and disability, were able to share strategies to counter pity, shame and being considered useless.

You can find the definition of IL in General Comment No. 5 in Article 19 of the CRPD:

> Individuals with disabilities are to be **provided with all necessary means** to enable them to **exercise choice and control** over their lives and **make all decisions** concerning their lives. **Personal autonomy and self-determination** are fundamental to independent living, including **access to transport, information, communication and personal assistance, place of residence, daily routine, habits, decent employment, personal relationships, clothing, nutrition, hygiene and health care, religious activities, cultural activities, and sexual and reproductive rights.** These activities are linked to the **development of a person's identity and personality**: **where we live and with whom**, **what we eat, whether we like to sleep in or go to bed late at night, be inside or outdoors, have a tablecloth and candles on the table, have pets or listen to music.** Such actions and decisions constitute who we are. Independent living is an essential part of the **individual's autonomy and freedom** and does not necessarily mean living alone. It should also not be interpreted solely as the ability to carry out daily activities by oneself. Rather, it should be regarded as the freedom to choose and control, in line with the respect for inherent dignity and individual autonomy as enshrined in article 3 (a) of the Convention. Independence as a form of personal autonomy means that the person with disabilities is not deprived of the opportunity of choice and control regarding personal lifestyle and daily activities.[62]

When working with refugee children with disabilities, DRW was approached with the needs of children that would allow them to gain access to everyday activities. The support that was sought was essential if the children were to be able to exercise their right to choice, control and self-determination and to live lives with IL. In the children's cases, there were obstacles to everyday activities due to the gaps in the provision of support. The needs and the support provided by DRW can be found in the chart in the section of the chapter on results.

It was important for the DRW team to have direct contact with the children to allow genuine participation. Needs were considered based on a

61 Ritva Gough, *Personal Assistance – A Social Coping Strategy* (*Personlig Assistans – en social bemästringsstrategi*) (Ritva Gough & GIL-förlaget, Gothenburg, 1994), 33–37.

62 The Committee on the Rights of Persons with Disabilities, General Comment No. 5 (2017) on Living Independently and Being Included in the Community CRPD/C/GC/5.

rights perspective and the fulfilment of Article 19 of the CRPD, with self-determination and participation in focus. Individuals made their complaints to DRW, which then offered advice and information on where to turn for support. People were referred to municipalities, other authorities and in one case even to the police. DRW contacted schools, social services and organisations for disabled people to sort out issues and support the children involved.

People with disabilities in the IL movement fought against segregation, oppression, exclusion and discrimination.[63] They were joined by Europeans and people from the rest of the world with disabilities promoting de-institutionalisation, empowerment and taking control over their own lives.[64] Independent living activists wanted to change the world so that children with disabilities like themselves would not have to face the same barriers, exclusion in general and more specifically not have to live in institutions or not be able to go to school, be considered sick when they were not or be subject to the medical model and how it blocked them from participation. They fought against the inaccessibility of society and transport systems. They sought access to services. The ideological programme was based on the radical demands of the 1960s and the social change that followed.[65]

Personal assistance, an important concept within IL, was promoted in Sweden in the 1980s by the IL movement. The Stockholm cooperative on Independent Living (STIL), also founded by Adolf Ratzka, ran the Stockholm Project on personal assistance. The project proved successful and led to personal assistance being included in the Swedish Disability Reform legislation – LSS, *Lag (1993:387) om stöd och service till vissa funktionshindrade* (The Act Concerning Support and Service for Persons with Certain Functional Impairments).[66] This legislation was the first of its kind, with personal assistance becoming a right for some Swedish people with disabilities. Personal assistance is also considered essential as a service fulfilling Article 19 of the CRPD.[67]

The project design

The objective of DRW was to improve the reception and integration of refugees with disabilities.[68] The goal of the project was to create new and effective methods that could improve the reception and integration of disabled

63 Judith Heumann with Kristen Joiner, *Being Heumann – An Unrepentant Memoir of a Disability Rights Activist* (Beacon Press, Boston, 2020), 69–70.
64 Oliver and Barnes (n 55), 83.
65 Shapiro (n 39), 41–73.
66 Gough (n 61), 5.
67 The Committee on the Rights of Persons with Disabilities, General Comment No. 5 (2017) on Living Independently and Being Included in the Community CRPD/C/GC/5.
68 Romero, Linder, Karlsson and Bolling (n 7), 4–7.

migrants.[69] The activities in DRW were guided by the IL principles, with the aim of ensuring that refugees and refugee children with disabilities should prosper, be empowered to access self-determination and access services they need for their everyday activities.

DRW wanted to make a difference for individuals, but also politically, by raising awareness of the life situation of the project participants, on the effects of legislation and on power structures faced by refugees with disabilities. To ensure a wide view of the issues at hand, DRW chose to work with four perspectives: the human rights perspective, the disability perspective, the intersectionality perspective and the health perspective. Founded on the IL principles of empowerment and participation, the approach chosen for integration was that of "reciprocal accessible integration", chosen as one of the key messages for DRW advocacy. Reciprocal integration was considered essential as the goal for migration to ensure self-determination, participation and equal opportunity. An accessible reception is also essential if refugees with disabilities are to succeed in the integration process.

Methods and DRW

The methods chosen for the improvement of the reception and integration of refugees with disabilities were also designed to enhance self-determination, empowerment and the participation of the DRW participants according to the IL principles. The methods enabling and facilitating self-determination and empowerment were interviews, counselling, peer support, photovoice, focus groups and theme days. The methods for participation were the same, along with outreach activities, which included the spreading of posters and brochures on DRW in key localities or at relevant conferences, written in Swedish, English, Arabic, Amharic and Tigrinya; this was key to reaching both possible participants and stakeholders that could contribute to the project.

Round tables, seminars, conferences, social media and articles were used to widen the network of actors working in the areas of migration and disability. This would allow DRW to reach the target group and to spread the results of DRW.

Interviews were the main method for gathering data on the target group and allowing the DRW team to support those seeking support. A total of 74 interviews were conducted. The interview form included questions on the background of the interviewee, where they came from and why they had travelled to Sweden. There were questions on support and services they had received to give an indication of the services people were accessing and those they were not. Together, the questions gave an idea of what works and what does not in the integration process, as the services are essential for

69 Ibid., 4.

people to be able to live their lives with IL and have access to society according to Article 19 of the CRPD.

Peer support and photovoice were used as methods of empowerment, with peer support constituting a situation where people with disabilities and migration experience meet to have an exchange of challenges and strategies and photovoice is a method using pictures to express experiences and to spread the messages from the group. The main experience expressed was that the participants felt that many people did not really listen to what they had to say and that people called their experience into question. Inaccessibility meant that they were isolated in homes because there were stairs and heavy doors preventing them from going out. They became dependent on social networks, which most of them did not have. DRW was key, with its support for contacts with the authorities and access to better living conditions.

Results

This section presents the results of DRW in general and regarding the refugee children with disabilities. DRW was successful in meeting the target group, having communicated with over 100 refugees with disabilities and holding interviews with 74 people. The interviewees were of all ages, from the youngest at 6 years of age and the oldest over 60. Men dominated the interviews, with 55 men and 19 women. They were living in the whole of the country, from Malmö to Boden and Borås to Stockholm. Most of the participants were living in Stockholm.

Individuals received support varying from having a roof over their head to support for looking after a new-born baby, despite the municipality threatening to remove the baby. Among other issues, support was provided for access to medical care, access to transport, from being forced out of a housing arrangement, for moving from inaccessible accommodation to accessible accommodation, for access to technical aids and residential permits and for reunification with family members. People took contact with DRW to understand the system and to find out where they could turn to gain the support that they needed. The provision of relevant and timely information is a positive obligation on the part of the authorities under human rights law, included in paragraph 23 of the Convention on the Rights of the Child.[70] The fact that DRW was approached shows that people are not getting this support from the authorities first hand.

Personal stories were a testimony to the deterioration in health of the children and the parents due to, for example, the difficult journey to Sweden, stress and depression, for many reasons, including not making headway in the process of family reunification, the lack of a social network, lack

70 1989 Convention on the Rights of the Child (entered into force 2 September 1990) 1577 UNTS 3 Paragraph 23.4.

of employment, inaccessible accommodation, isolation and segregation. There was inaccessibility in accommodation, in the environment around the accommodation and in the access to social services. Inaccessibility included physical inaccessibility, such as the lack of elevators and steps to an entrance; it included inaccessible information, both with regard to the languages offered and the lack of accessible versions such as easy-to-read versions, braille versions or information in sign language. The experiences of inaccessibility despite the CRPD and its Article 9 on the obligations of accessibility show that there are gaps in the system.[71]

Inaccessibility influenced the right to participation and to empowerment. It caused isolation, which then led to depression. When living in physically inaccessible accommodation, impairments are strained and can worsen. One blind man fell several times on the stairs up to a flat on the fourth floor, as there was no elevator. Children must be carried by parents when living in inaccessible housing. Access to timely information and information in a format that was understood was often a problem. Interpretation was problematic in that a person's situation was not always understood. This led, for example, to people missing out on family reunification due to the time limit of three months; it also led to shortcomings in services that subsequently led to a deterioration in health.

The DRW activities providing strategies for empowerment were appreciated. Learning about rights, Swedish legislation and the Swedish social system empowered the participants leaving them feeling stronger. Participating in activities with other people in the same situation eased feelings of isolation. Some lasting social networks developed between people having connected through DRW.

The cases concerning refugee children with disabilities were limited to eight cases. DRW did not have a stipulated focus on children; the results would surely have been different if that had been the given focus.

The following table gives an overview of the eight cases regarding children.

DRW was also contacted with questions regarding refugee children with disabilities by 16 stakeholders, including five municipalities, two migration offices, four non-governmental organisations and five engaged social workers. Questions were on access to technical aids, services and adapting housing. One municipality wondered whether summer sport activities for refugee children with disabilities were available.

Discussion

The contact taken by authorities and organisations showed that the obligation of timely information had not been sufficiently fulfilled. Arguably, the

71 2006 The Convention on the Rights of Persons with Disabilities A/Res/61/106.

Table 6.1 Refugee children with disabilities

Age	*Country*	*Disability*	*Support sought*	*Support acquired*
4	Ethiopia	Physical	Personal assistance, accessible housing, support and service	Guidance and advice
6	Syria	Autism, Asperger's syndrome	Support and service	Guidance and advice
7	Ethiopia	ADHD	Support and service	Guidance and advice
7	Ethiopia	Autism	Fear the child will be institutionalised	Guidance and advice
8	Mongolia	Intellectual, autism	Housing	Information on housing
9	Syria	Intellectual	Support and service, no residence permit	Referral to the Red Cross, Caritas and the Asylum Rights Centre
12	Syria	Intellectual	Support and service, no residence permit	Referral to the Red Cross, Caritas and the Asylum Rights Centre
12	Eritrea	Physical, intellectual	Personal assistance, accessible housing, legal support	Information on Swedish legislation, guidance to contact the police

support sought could be interpreted to mean that authorities were trying to outsource their legal responsibilities. DRW concluded that it was a sign indicating that authorities and organisations had been unprepared for the influx, that they lacked knowledge and training and that it was still possible that they were avoiding providing the support people needed.

In addition, it is also the case that most people wrongly assume that children and people with disabilities are not displaced, and therefore they are not prepared to receive them.[72] DRW's reputation also seems to result in many thinking that it has more resources than it does, not only for sharing information about the system and referring people to those actors who are equipped to answer questions but also to actually provide support. Swedish civil society has a heavy burden to carry to meet individuals in need and see that they receive the appropriate support. This reveals a gap in the system, with those working in migration knowing little or nothing about disability issues and those working in social services knowing little or nothing about migration.

The personal stories, often told with tears and expressing depression, isolation, segregation and deteriorating health, showed how stakeholders are lacking in their provision of much-needed support that is essential for

72 Crock, Smith-Khan, McCallum and Saul (n 4), 4.

the integration process of refugees with disabilities. In June 2019, a study carried out by the Swedish government highlighted the effects of the migration process on people and how they develop poor health during the migration process.[73] The stories conveyed to DRW confirmed these findings: stories of stress and insecurity, as well as long procedures, contributing to poor health but also stories of how inaccessible housing accentuated these difficulties, leading to a deterioration of physical and mental health, thus exacerbating disabilities.

Allowing those affected to make their voices heard is not a simple task. For children and wives/mothers, it may depend not only on whether they can actually speak but also on the will of the father or the husband. In some cultures, the man dominates and may assume a position of authority, not permitting the voice of his wife or child to be heard. Two of the children who were able to speak were not asked to express their needs. DRW interpreted this to be due to the authoritarian role of the father. This can also be seen even in Swedish culture, with over-protective parents and parents who lack expectations with regard to their children and who have no respect for family democracy. Respect for children with disabilities is even more absent, with people showing that they do not consider that their children with disabilities are like other children and that they are children with rights. Instead, they express guilt and shame. There was a child with autism who could be very loud and unruly, so the parents, in shame and feeling guilt, did not want to bring the child to the interviews.

Reciprocal integration requires that people be met with respect and sensitivity and an understanding of human rights and how rights are to be secured for all. Decisions and procedures should facilitate the participation of those seeking support. The voices of all involved need to be heard and even more so those of children. Stakeholders need resources for training and health and awareness-raising efforts. All services need to take the perspective of the individual, a perspective based on the unique needs of each and every person. Efforts to understand cultural differences and cultural variabilities should be central.[74]

At conferences, DRW heard how many of the problems faced by the refugees with disabilities in Sweden are also faced by displaced persons in developing recipient countries. There is a lack of information, a lack of access to

73 The Public Health Agency of Sweden (Folkhälsomyndigheten), *The Health of People Born Abroad – Differences in Health Based on Country of Birth – A Knowledge Base on Health, Living Conditions and Lifestyle/Way of Life Among People Living in Sweden Who Were Born Abroad* (Hälsa hos personer som är utrikes födda – skillnader i hälsa utifrån födelseland – Ett kunskapsunderlag om hälsa, livsvillkor och levnadsvanor bland utrikes födda personer boende i Sverige) (Folkhälsomyndigheten, Position Papers, 2019), 5.

74 Sooz Romero, Riitta-Leena Karlsson and Jamie Bolling, *Welcome Whoever You Are – DRW's Handbook for Accessible Reception and Establishment of Migrants with a Disability* (*Välkommen vem du än är – DRW:s metodhanbok for ett tillgängligt mottagande och etablering av mirgranter med normbrytande funktionalitet*) (Excellent Print & Design, Stockholm, 2020), 10–11.

social services and a lack of access to technical equipment, with people facing a deterioration in their health and extreme poverty. The ILI concluded that it could be beneficial to have initiatives like DRW, with social workers that have a dual competence, that is, knowledge of migration and disability, so that they are able to support refugees with disabilities at all stages of the migration process.

Conclusions – limitations of the study and recommendations

DRW did not have a specific focus on refugee children with disabilities at the outset of the refugee influx to Sweden in 2015. To gain a better idea of the situation for these children, there is a need for a broader knowledge base through the mapping out of needs and access to existing rights and studies with a specific focus on children at an early stage. This would provide a clearer picture and a more in-depth understanding of the situations faced by the children and their families. It is necessary for the development of more effective strategies to meet the needs and to access rights that could subsequently be developed to provide better support for the children and their families so that they can integrate better.

Empowerment and participation are key for the support of refugee children with disabilities to implement the constructive solutions in the conventions with the children's best interests at heart.[75] But first and foremost, it is important to remember that these constitute rights of the child and hence all children, including those with disabilities. It is only the voice of the refugee child with a disability that is able to provide an expert view of what is really happening, what barriers these children face, what works and also what could work better.

A diversity of perspectives, with those of the children and the dual competence of the actors working in the area of migration and disability at the centre, are vital to gain children's trust and to promote participation. Capturing all perspectives allows for a more complete picture and better solutions.

What lessons can be learned in order to improve the current situation or the situation for future influxes of migrants?

- Be prepared, because people with disabilities, including children, will be amongst the displaced people.
- Base your response to displaced people on the social model, reframing disability in terms of participation and accessibility.
- Close the gap so that the actors in charge have the knowledge and experience of both migration and disability issues that they need.

75 Vella (n 50), 9.

- Apply the perspectives of disability, intersectionality, health and rights to enhance knowledge and ensure a broader understanding of refugee children with disabilities.
- Ensure that the necessary information is accessible and that the environment in which these people live is also accessible. This would allow the removal of the barriers of inaccessibility regarding both the environment and information. It is necessary to ensure that the environment and information are accessible in a format that can be understood if the integration process is to be successful.
- Most importantly, it is vital to pursue a paradigm shift from paternalism to empowerment, as well as to access to participation and rights for refugee children with disabilities.

List of references

Treaties

Convention on the Rights of Persons with Disabilities, 2006, A Res/61/106/.

Convention on the Rights of the Child, G.A. Res. 44/25, Annex, 44 UN Gaor Supp. (No. 49), 167, entered into force on 2 September 1990, (1980).

Lag (2018:1197) om Förenta nationernas konvention om barnets rättigheter. www.riksdagen.se/sv/dokument-lagar/dokument/svensk-forfattningssamling/lag-20181197-om-forenta-nationernas-konvention_sfs-2018-1197, accessed 26 October 2021.

UNHCR Convention and Protocol Relating to the Status of Refugees, 1950, Res/429/5/

Universal Declaration of Human Rights, G.A. res. 217A (III), U.N. Doc A/810 at 71 (1948).

Literature

Askheim, OP and Starrin, B, 'Empowerment – A Buzz Word?' ('Empowerment – ett modeord?') in Askheim and Starrin (eds), *Empowerment in Theory and Practice* (Empowerment i Teori och Praktik). Gleerups Utbildning AB. Malmö, 2007, 9–12.

Beresford, P and Croft, S, 'Service Users' Knowledges and the Social Construction of Social Work', *Journal of Social Work,* 1(3), 295–316, 2001.

Bešic, E, Paleczek, L and Gasteiger-Klicpera, B, 'Don't Forget about Us: Attitudes towards the Inclusion of Refugee Children with(out) Disabilities', *International Journal of Inclusive Education*, 24(2), 202–217, 2020.

Caughey, C, 'Government Human Rights Focal Points: Lessons Learned from Focal Points under the Convention on the Rights of Persons with Disabilities', *Netherlands Quarterly of Human Rights*, 39(2), 19–139, 2021.

Committee on the Rights of the Child, General Comment No. 12, *The Right of the Child to be Heard*, 2009, CRC/C/GC12.

Committee on the Rights of Persons with Disabilities, General Comment No. 5 (2017) on Living Independently and Being Included in the Community CRPD/C/GC/5.

Committee on the Rights of Persons with Disabilities, General Comment No. 7, *On the Participation of Persons with Disabilities, Including Children with Disabilities, through Their Representative Organizations, in the Implementation and Monitoring of the Convention* – 2118, CRPD/C/GC7.

Committee on the Rights of Persons with Disabilities, General Comment on Article 19: Living Independently and Being Included in the Community, 2017, CRPD/C/18/1.

Crock M, Smith-Khan L, McCallum R and Saul B, *The Legal Protection of Refugees with Disabilities – Forgotten and Invisible?* Edward Elgar Publishing Limited. Cheltenham Glos and Northampton, 2017.

Gough, R, *Personal Assistance – A Social Coping Strategy* (Personlig Assistans – en social bemästringsstrategi). Ritva Gough & GIL-förlaget. Gothenburg, 1994.

Hellqvist, K and Sandberg, A, *A Time of Meetings – Working with Refugees and New Arrivals in Swedish Parishes* (En tid av möten – arbetet med asylsökande och nyanlända i Svenska kyrkans församlingar 2015–2016). The Church of Sweden – *Svenska kyrkan.* Uppsala, 2017.

Heumann, J with Joiner, K, *Being Heumann – An Unrepentant Memoir of a Disability Rights Activist.* Beacon Press. Boston, 2020.

Klarenbeek, LM, 'Reconceptualising 'Integration as a Two-Way Process', *Migration Studies,* 1–20, 2019.

Mitchell, D and Karr, V, *Crises, Conflict and Disability – Ensuring Equality.* Routledge. London and New York, 2014.

Oliver, M and Barnes, C, *Disabled People and Social Policy – From Exclusion to Inclusion.* Pearson Education Limited. Essex, 1998.

Peek, L and Stough, LM, *Children with Disabilities in the Context of Disaster: A Social Vulnerability Perspective,* Society for Research in Child Development, Inc., 81(4), 1260–1270, July/August 2010.

Ratzka, A, *Self-Determination for Persons with Extensive Disabilities through Direct Payments for Personal Assistance* (Independent Living Institute, Stockholm, 2017) Section – *What Is Independent Living.* www.independentliving.org/docs7/Self-determination-direct-payments.html, accessed 30 October 2021.

Romero, S, Karlsson, RL and Bolling, J, *Welcome Whoever You Are – DRW's Handbook for Accessible Reception and Establishment of Migrants with a Disability* (Välkommen vem du än är – DRW:s metodhanbok for ett tillgängligt mottagande och etablering av mirgranter med normbrytande funktionalitet). Excellent Print & Design. Stockholm, 2020.

Romero, S, Linder, O, Karlsson R L and Bolling, J, *The Road to Reciprocal Integration* (Vägar mot ömsesidigt integration). Excellent Print. Stockholm, 2020.

Sennerteg, N, *Ord som dödar-om Folkmord och Propaganda.* Natur och Kultur. Stockholm, 2010.

Shapiro, J, *No Pity – People with Disabilities Forging a New Civil Rights Movement.* Times Books Random House. New York, 1994.

Swain, J, French, S and Cameron, C, *Controversial Issues in a Disabling Society.* Open University Press. Buckingham, 2003.

The Public Health Agency of Sweden (Folkhälsomyndigheten), *The Health of People Born Abroad – Differences in Health Based on Country of Birth – A Knowledge Base on Health, Living Conditions and Lifestyle/Way of Life Among People Living in Sweden Who Were Born Abroad* (Hälsa hos personer som är utrikes födda – skillnader i hälsa utifrån födelseland – Ett kunskapsunderlag om hälsa, livsvillkor och levnadsvanor bland utrikes födda personer boende i Sverige). Folkhälsomyndigheten. Position Papers, 2019.

The Swedish Agency for Participation (Myndigheten för delaktighet), *People with a Disability in the Asylum Seeking and Establishment Processes* (Personer med funktionsnedsättning i asyl-och etableringsprocessen). Sundbyberg, Myndigheten för delaktighet, 2017.

Tobin, J, *The UN Convention on the Rights of the Child.* Oxford: Oxford University Press. 2019.

UNHCR, Figures at a glance (UNHCR 2021) 1. www.unhcr.org/figures-at-a-glance.html, accessed 26 October 2021.

UNICEF, *Protecting Children in Humanitarian Action.* UNICEF. 2021, 1. www.unicef.org/protection/protecting-children-in-humanitarian-action, accessed 17 October 2021.

United Nations Committee on the Rights of the Child, Day of General Discussion (DGD) 2018, *Protecting and Empowering Children as Human Rights Defenders.*

Vella, K, 'Power, Paternalism and Children on the Move', *Journal of Humanitarian Action,* 1(3), 2016.

Other

Women's Committee for Refugee Women and Children. 'Disabilities Among Refugees and Conflict Affected Populations: Resource Kit for Fieldworkers' (Woman's Committee for Refugee Women and Children, 2008), 1, https://cms.emergency.unhcr.org/documents/11982/43580/Women's+Commission+for+Refugee+Women+and+Children%2C+Resource+Kit+for+Field+Workers%2C+2008/8b368bc0-6ecb-44db-81e7-c60e46630717, accessed 26 October_2021.

Principles of Independent Living, https://enil.eu/wp-content/uploads/2022/06/Principles-of-Independent-Living.pdf , accessed 9 March 2023.

Strengthen Humanitarian Aid, www.hrw.org/news/2020/06/09/un-strengthen-humanitarian-aid-people-disabilities#, accessed 26 October 2021.

7 The child right's perspective in response to the humanitarian crisis at the Belarus-Lithuania border

*Laima Vaigė**

1. Introduction

This chapter takes a rather narrow approach. It focuses on a recent crisis at the Lithuania–Belarus border during 2021, when thousands of migrants and asylum seekers arrived at the border of Lithuania. Their goal was to reach safety in the European Union. Lithuania and other "Eastern route States" (Latvia and Poland) claimed that flows of migrants are used in the "hybrid war" against them.[1] National and international organisations reported various human rights violations in the border area and in temporary detention centres. For instance, there were reports of pushbacks against families with children at the border and of unsuitable treatment of minors at accommodation (detention) centres.

The materials used in this chapter are primarily legal sources, with some recourse to media articles where necessary for illustration. The chapter does not examine Lithuanian asylum procedures in depth but analyses legal changes in response to this particular crisis and human rights violations. The focus is on the decisions of independent experts for human rights within Lithuania, such as the ombudsperson for child rights.

All translations of the citations are provided by the author, except where otherwise indicated. For the sake of clarity, certain deviations from State-offered translations are made, for instance, the Lithuanian legislative enactments are called *Acts* in this text, rather than *Laws*. This is because the word "law" has a broader meaning than a legislative enactment. The word "foreigners" is used with respect to foreign nationals rather than "aliens" in order to avoid alienation and othering of migrants. None of the available translations of legal acts to English can be called "official", and only the text in original language has a legally constitutive meaning.

* Laima Vaige is a senior lecturer in law, Uppsala University, Sweden.

1 Hybrid war is a phenomenon that entails a variety of measures used to exploit vulnerabilities of states without meeting the threshold of a conventional war. Conventional war, by contrast, usually includes a "lethal or kinetic force". See, for instance, Arsanal Bilal, 'Hybrid Warfare – New Threats, Complexity, and "Trust" as the Antidote' *NATO,* 30 November 2021, www.nato.int/docu/review/articles/2021/11/30/hybrid-warfare-new-threats-complexity-and-trust-as-the-antidote/index.html, accessed 2 March 2022.

DOI: 10.4324/9781003187493-7

This chapter uses the dogmatic legal method with elements of discourse analysis (see Section 3.2) and intersectional theory (Section 5.2). The dogmatic legal method focuses on positive law, and it is used only as a starting point of the analysis, in particular of the amendments by the Parliament in 2021. Discourse analysis is used to challenge the formulations in these amendments, which the author considers a linguistic strategy to mask the likely violations of human rights. "Intersectionality"[2] is understood as unique vulnerability of persons at intersections of vulnerabilities based on their race, gender, sexual orientation, religion or age. In this text, the particularly vulnerable groups are children in migration. In the Lithuanian Act on the Legal Status of Foreigners,[3] children and single parents raising children are among those who are considered "vulnerable persons". Special needs of vulnerable persons should be taken into consideration; hence vulnerability is important whether at the border, in transit or in "accommodation" centres.

On February 24, 2022, a historical date for Europe, Russia attacked Ukraine. Ukraine is a sovereign state of over 44 million people, heavily devastated by the ongoing war. The chapter excludes the response in Lithuania with regard to Russia's aggression against Ukraine, which resulted in an even greater number of asylum seekers. People discussed in this chapter were called "illegal migrants" in official legislation, statistical data and media in Lithuania, whereas the Ukrainian asylum seekers are "war refugees" and receive great sympathy and support from Lithuanian society. In reality, the people coming from Belarus are difficult to categorise, and this could be claimed to be a case of mixed migration. Some comparisons might be fragmentally included for the purpose of illustrating the problematic treatment of migrants and asylum seekers coming from the territory of Belarus.

This text has been mainly written at the time of the most acute humanitarian crisis and prior to Russia's full-scale attack on Ukraine in 2022. It must be highlighted that the European Court of Justice (the ECJ) adopted a judgment on 30 June 2022 in case C-72/22 PPU that confirmed a suggestion in this text that "accommodation" of migrants in Lithuania without a possibility to leave is in fact detention, and held it constitutes an infringement of EU law. After the ECJ's judgment, migrants who had been "accommodated" in the said centres (note that it means they entered the country prior to August 2021, see sections 3.2 and 3.3), have been released. The biggest problem remains, that of collective removal of people, including children, without an individual analysis of their situation. Regarding pushbacks to Belarus, the European Court of Human Rights (the ECtHR) already had analysed, prior to 2021, the situation of a family from Chechnya with five very young children, removed repeatedly back to Belarus, when they tried to cross the border to Lithuania and Poland. In the case of *M.A. v*

2 Kimberlé Crenshaw, 'Demarginalizing the Intersection of Race and Sex: A Black Feminist Critique of Antidiscrimination Doctrine, Feminist Theory and Antiracist Politics', *University of Chicago Legal Forum*, 1(8) (1989), 139–167.

3 Act on Legal Status of Foreigners, 29 April 2004, No. IX-2206 Article 2 (18)^2.

Lithuania, app. no. 59793/17, the ECtHR found an infringement of Article 3 (prohibition of torture and inhuman or degrading treatment) as well as Article 13 (right to legal remedy) of the Convention. Poland also infringed the Convention, the ECtHR held in 2020, in the key case of *M.K. v Poland*, app.nos 40503/17, 42902/17 and 43643/17. Nevertheless, the Eastern-route pushback policy has only became stricter, as this text illustrates.

2. The state and people in crisis

2.1. Geopolitical situation and prior events

This chapter focuses on the legal situation of migrants coming from the side of Belarus to Lithuania. Most readers are not familiar with the recent history of the events; hence a short insight of the geopolitical situation of these states is considered necessary. Lithuania is a state with approximately 2.8 million inhabitants. The state has a border with Belarus measuring nearly 700 kilometres, the longest border with the European Union (EU) in the east. By comparison, the Poland–Belarus border is approximately 400 kilometres, and the border between Latvia and Belarus is about 170 kilometres. Vilnius, the capital of Lithuania, is about a 30-minute drive from the border with Belarus – which is often called the last dictatorship in Europe. On the Lithuanian side, the border had not been well guarded until the summer of 2021 and is mostly an area of forest with hills and ditches.

Belarus is a state with approximately 9.4 million inhabitants and has been controlled by Alexander Lukashenko since 1994. This candidate, previously a Communist and currently “independent” (no party affiliation), has been “elected” as president of the state six times in a row with an alleged 80% support of votes. No election observers have ever been admitted, and the elections cannot be evaluated as free and fair. Additionally, Belarus is not a party to the European Convention of Human Rights (the ECHR) and is not a member of the Council of Europe. In contrast, Lithuania is a member of the EU and a member of the Council of Europe, and it is a party to the ECHR.

Lithuania and Belarus are parties to the UN Convention on the Rights of the Child (the CRC), the UN Convention on Elimination of All Forms of Discrimination against Women (the CEDAW) and the UN Convention on the Elimination of All Forms of Racial Discrimination (the CERD). However, in Belarus, the human rights situation is evaluated as very problematic and has deteriorated sharply since 2020. For instance, the UN High Commissioner for Human Rights reported that 13,500 people were arbitrarily arrested and detained for protesting against the regime in Belarus during a period of only five days between 9 and 14 August 2020. At least 700 of the people arbitrarily arrested and detained over these few days were children.[4] It is considered an important fact, because when the Lithuanian

4 UN High Commissioner for Human Rights, ‘Situation of Human Rights in Belarus in the Run-up to the 2020 Presidential Election and in Its Aftermath’ (4 March 2022) A/HRC/49/71 para 36.

state uses pushbacks to Belarus, the presumption is that Belarus is a sufficiently safe state for migrants. However, until the current migration crisis, Lithuania consistently expressed concern that the Lukashenko regime does not respect human rights[5] (also see Sections 4 and 5.5).

A chain of political events in 2020 contributed to a quick deterioration of the diplomatic relationships between Lithuania, the EU as a whole and Belarus. In the presidential elections of 2020 in Belarus, Svetlana G. Tikhanovskaya had been widely supported by the population and reported as winning the elections – which Alexander Lukashenko denies. Mass protests and their repression began; Svetlana G. Tikhanovskaya was forced to flee for her safety after threats that her children would be forcibly removed.[6] She is currently living in Vilnius. In 2021, a plane flying from Athens to Vilnius was intercepted by Belarus authorities and forced to land in Minsk. Two Vilnius inhabitants – a couple originally from Belarus – were arrested. The man was a journalist critical of Alexander Lukashenko, and the woman was a student at the European Humanities University, an exiled Belarussian university re-established in Vilnius. They remain in Belarus as political prisoners.

Strong EU sanctions followed. As a response, Alexander Lukashenko promised to flood Europe with "drugs and migrants".[7] In the summer of 2021, Belarus started to issue visas to persons interested in coming to Europe and promised open borders to the EU. Flight connections from the Middle East to Belarus were increased, and state-controlled tourist firms started to promote the route. By August 2021, more than 4000 migrants arrived at the Lithuanian border, compared to fewer than 100 migrants in previous years. Overall, more than 8000 migrants arrived via an Eastern route in 2021.

It must be stressed that after Lithuania and other Eastern-route states allowed pushbacks, it became difficult to estimate the extent of migration. For instance, the European Commission noted in December 2021 that "42,741 attempts to cross have been prevented by the three Member States" (Lithuania, Latvia and Poland), and, in addition, around 10,000 more people were stranded at the borders at that time.[8] Since August 2021, the statistical data shows smaller numbers of asylum requests, because these are often impossible to make (see Section 3.3).

5 See, for instance, 'Lithuanians Form "Freedom Way" Human Chain in Solidarity with Belarus Opposition', *Radio Free Europe,* Prague, 23 August 2020, www.rferl.org/a/30798715.html, accessed 24 March 2022.

6 Threats against children of political rivals has been used with respect to Vitalia Navumik and Svetlana Tikhanovskaya, see n 4, 'Situation of Human Rights in Belarus' para 17.

7 Marc Bennets, 'Lukashenko Willing to Flood EU with Drugs and Migrants to Stop New Sanctions', *The Times* (London, 28 May 2021).

8 Commission, 'Proposal on Council Decision for Provisional Emergency Measures for the Benefit of Latvia, Lithuania and Poland' COM(2021) 752 final, Explanatory Memorandum, Context of the Proposal.

2.2. Profiles of people in crisis: mixed migration

This crisis could be evaluated as a situation of mixed migration. People and families who experience pushbacks include migrants who are searching for better economic conditions and asylum seekers in need of legal protection. Human realities and decisions to leave the state of origin might contain intertwined nuances that can be difficult to categorise into either of two statuses, that is, as a migrant or a refugee – which are two distinct legal categories under international and national law.[9] These distinct statuses (the refugee and the migrant) are the two "pigeon-hole boxes" that state officials have in mind, but it can be very hard to categorise people at the Belarussian border, considering that there is a shortage of time and often a lack of documents.

In the Lithuanian popular media and in the official statistics and documents in Lithuania, the people who arrive from the side of Belarus to Lithuania are called "illegal migrants". According to the Department of Statistics, the "illegal migrants" (further – simply migrants) are citizens of over 20 states (Iraq, Syria, Democratic Republic of Congo, Cameroon, Senegal, Mali, Afghanistan and other states).[10] Among these citizens of various states, Iraqi citizens are overrepresented. The statistics also show that 28% of the migrants were women and 25% were children.

Many migrants speak about their experiences at the border as extremely challenging and life-threatening:

> Soldiers in Belarus tell you they will take you to Poland, but they take you to Lithuania. They take your phone card away, leave you in the forest and tell you to go. It is your problem whether you live or die. They took our water and left us in the forest.[11]

There have not been deaths at the Lithuanian border with Belarus. Nevertheless, after state authorities received the discretion to push people back and winter came, the situation has deteriorated. For humanitarian reasons, such as the threat to life from sickness, dehydration and hypothermia, the state authorities admitted a small number of migrants.[12]

9 See, for instance, 'Mixed Migration' (*Migrationsdatenportal*, 21 February 2022), www.migrationdataportal.org/de/node/3152, accessed 14 March 2022.

10 'Monitoring of Illegal Migration from January 1, 2021' (Department of Statistics, Official Statistics Portal, updated daily), https://osp.stat.gov.lt/gyventoju-migracija, accessed 4 March 2021.

11 'Į Iraką Sugrįžę Migrantai Papasakojo, Ką iš Tikrųjų Patyrė Baltarusijoje' ('Migrants Who Returned to Iraq Told of What They Had Really Experienced in Belarus') *Delfi* (Vilnius, 19 November 2021), www.delfi.lt/news/daily/world/i-iraka-sugrize-migrantai-papasakojo-ka-is-tikruju-patyre-baltarusijoje.d?id=88724767, accessed 12 January 2022.

12 According to Article 7[1] of the Act on the Legal Status of Foreigners, humanitarian reasons include "an illness, other acute health impairment or condition, personal reasons which a foreigner could not foresee and avoid, *force majeure* due to which the foreigner is unable to leave".

The legal status of refugee was granted in only a small number of cases; for instance, according to data from December 2021, only 54 people received the status of refugee, while 3272 were ordered to return to their states of origin.[13] Of the 610 decisions of the Migration Department that were appealed to court, none were satisfied. In most cases, the application was dismissed, and in some cases, it was left without a court analysis – likely for procedural reasons. Those who were granted refugee status were from Syria, Afghanistan, Eritrea, Yemen and Iraq.[14] At the time of writing, there was no data on the age or gender of the people who received refugee status in the available statistical data.[15]

Due to the acute situation, immediate funding and support were mobilised by the EU. For instance, the European Commission funded the repatriation costs of those migrants who agreed to return to their states of origin. Overall, Lithuania received €36.7 million in emergency aid from the EU. In December 2021, the European Commission announced a proposal for a Council Decision on provisional emergency measures for the benefit of Latvia, Lithuania and Poland, which is currently (March 2022) at the stage of negotiations.[16] This legislative measure at the EU level provides for "longer registration deadlines and the possibility to decide at the border or at transit zone on the admissibility or substance of all applications, except where specific vulnerabilities cannot be catered for".[17] If adopted, the Council Decision is an "emergency" measure that can only work temporarily and with safeguards. Furthermore, it is questionable whether such restrictions of rights can be justified from the perspective of a broader human rights framework. The EU might allow derogations and restrictions on rights arising from EU law, but that cannot affect rights under CoE or global instruments.

3. Response in Lithuania: in law and in practice

3.1. Hybrid aggression

On July 2, 2021, the government of Lithuania announced a national emergency[18] due to the influx of migrants. It must be stressed that this national emergency is *not* the same as "war" or "time of emergency", as defined

13 'Savanoriškas Migrantų Grįžimas į Kilmės Šalis Bus Skatinamas Triskart Didesne Pinigų Suma' ('Voluntary Return of Migrants to States of Origin Shall Be Fostered by Three Times Higher a Sum'), *Migris Electronic Migration Services*, 8 December 2021, www.migracija.lt/-/savanori%C5%A1kas-migrant%C5%B3-gr%C4%AF%C5%BEimas-%C4%AF-kilm%C4%97s-%C5%A1alis-bus-skatinamas-triskart-didesne-pinig%C5%B3-suma, accessed 20 March 2022.

14 Ibid.

15 The national systems MIGRIS and MIPAS. The Statistical database for "illegal migrants" includes age and gender, but that does not show how many women and children received the status of refugee.

16 COM(2021) 752 final.

17 COM(2021) 752 final Explanatory memorandum.

18 Resolution of the Government no. 517 of July 2, 2021, TAR, published July 3, 2021, No. 15235.

in Article 15 of the European Convention of Human Rights.[19] The article allows derogations from the Convention rights, provided that these derogations are taken at the time of war or public emergency. Furthermore, there can never be derogations from certain human rights, such as Article 2: Right to life or Article 3: Prohibition of torture or inhuman or degrading treatment or punishment.[20] In any case, the national emergency in Lithuania did not meet the threshold for derogations from the rights under the ECHR or other human rights treaties. The Lithuanian authorities never asked for derogations from the ECHR.

On July 13, 2021, the Parliament passed a resolution on "countering hybrid aggression". The resolution allowed, among other things, to use "detention, protection and accommodation" of "third country nationals" without reliable identity documents, in order "to address threats to the constitutional order and public peace of the Republic of Lithuania".[21] As mentioned, legally this is not a situation covered by Article 15 of the ECHR, and neither did the government inform the CoE about any intended derogations from the Convention. Articles 142 and 144 in the Constitution of Lithuania, which are reserved for situations of public emergency and war, were not used either. Thus, the use of the term "hybrid war" or "hybrid aggression" is a political statement or national contextualisation rather than a legal reality from the perspective of international law.

The political treatment of the crises as a "hybrid aggression" is not only national. The European Commission, in its Proposal on Council Decision for provisional emergency measures, stressed that the EU considers it a "hybrid attack on the EU as a whole".[22] Consideration of the crisis as a hybrid attack against the EU might result in legal and practical consequences in the future.

3.2. Semantic paradoxes: "non-detention" and "non-entry"

On July 13, 2021, the Parliament also passed significant amendments to the Act on the Legal Status of Foreigners in Lithuania.[23] By amendments, rights of migrants and asylum seekers were significantly restricted, and detention was permitted under another word – a mandatory "accommodation". Due to the limited extent of this chapter, no detailed analysis of specific

19 European Convention for the Protection of Human Rights and Fundamental Freedoms, as amended by Protocols Nos. 11 and 14 (adopted 4 November 1950, entered into force 3 September 1953) ETS 5, Art. 15 (1).

20 European Convention of Human Rights, Art 15 (2).

21 Resolution on Countering Hybrid Aggression, 13 July 2021, No XIV-505, point 5.

22 COM(2021) 752 final, see Context for the Proposal in the Explanatory Memorandum to the Proposal.

23 Act Amending Articles 5, 71, 76, 77, 79, 113, 131, 136, 138, 139, 140 of Act No IX-2206 on the Legal Status of Foreigners and supplementing the Act with Chapter IX-1, TAR, 22 July 2021, No. 16266.

provisions of the Act on the Legal Status of Foreigners is provided. Instead, the reader is offered this summary:

> To put it simply, the formulations of the Act in practice have meant that all asylum seekers, without any individual assessment of their situation (solely due to coming to Lithuania without a passport or a visa), by administrative decision (without a court decision) and without legal aid of a lawyer (neither at the time the administrative decision is taken, nor at the time of its appeal to court), were accommodated in various centres without the right to leave the territory.[24]

The authors, Laurynas Biekša and Ilona Ivašauskaitė, further explain that they consider the term "accommodation" misleading in the Act on the Legal Status of Foreigners and note that people who were provided such "accommodation" in the summer of 2021 were de facto *detained.* The interpretation of this compulsory "accommodation" as *de facto* detention was also confirmed by the Lithuanian Supreme Administrative Court in its case law.[25] It must also be noted that the Supreme Administrative Court in one recent asylum seeker's case had doubts about the compatibility of the updated Lithuanian legislation with EU law[26] and in April of 2022 addressed the European Court of Justice (the ECJ) with the request to adopt a preliminary ruling. The case at the national level and the case pending at the ECJ do not include issues on the rights of the child. However, children in some instances are also arbitrarily detained under the pretext of "accommodation", as can be understood from reports of the Ombudspersons (the ombudsperson on the rights of the child and the parliamentary ombudsperson).[27]

Another semantic paradox in the enactment of July 13 was that arrival to Lithuania without the necessary documents was considered legally nonexistent. A "presence" of asylum seekers in transit zones or places of temporary accommodation is not "entry" to the territory of Lithuania until the decision is made to allow them to enter the territory of Lithuania.[28] The head of the state border guard service, Ruslamas Liubajevas, explained the situation as follows:

> Physical presence of migrants in Lithuanian territory does not mean that they were allowed to enter. It is the officer approaching the group

24 Laurynas Biekša and Ilona Ivašauskaitė, 'Lietuvos Reakcija į Prieglobsčio Prašytojų Antplūdį Tarptautinės ir Europos Sąjungos Teisės Kontekste', in Lyra Jakulevičienė and Vytautas Sinkevičius (eds), *Lietuvos Teisė 2021: Esminiai pokyčiai* (Mykolas Romeris University, Vilnius, 2021), 156–167. Translated by Laima Vaige, at 159.

25 Supreme Administrative Court of Lithuania, Decision of 6 October 2021 in Case no. AS-653–492/2021; decision of 27 October 2021 in Case no. AS-747–442/2021.

26 Supreme Administrative Court of Lithuania, Case No. A-1091–822/2022, pending.

27 Se further in Section 5 of the chapter.

28 Act on the Legal Status of Foreigners, Article 5 (2).

> of illegal migrants who must take the decision to allow them in or not. If the person is approached in the border zone, the same procedure applies, the situation is evaluated if the person needs help or so on. Such approaching could happen at the border, or in the state border protection territory, in the border zone, and beyond it.[29]

The interpretation is that a person might physically be deep in the territory of Lithuania but legally be considered *not* in Lithuania before the decision is taken to grant that person entry. The Act on the Legal Status of Foreigners was also amended in December 2021,[30] but the key ideas that are criticised in this chapter have not changed. Article 5 (2) of the Act on Legal Status of Foreigners provides that the "presence" of foreigners in transit zones, border crossing points or temporary accommodation facilities "shall not be considered as entry into the territory of the Republic of Lithuania".[31]

3.3. Asylum request in inaccessible places

The Act on Legal Status of Foreigners was subsequently amended in August 2021 and December 2021. The amendments of August 2021 specified in which places the asylum seekers can submit their requests for asylum and allowed a refusal of entry in situations where the requirements were not complied with.[32] No possibility of asylum seeking in a Lithuanian embassy was provided at the time, but it was opened later, in September 2021.[33] This possibility does not seem to be working in practice, because people are not allowed to enter an embassy without proper documents.

As reported by Laurynas Biekša and Ilona Ivašauskaitė, only two people submitted their requests for asylum through a Lithuanian embassy in Minsk.[34] Furthermore, despite the fact that border control points were supposed to be the primary places for asylum seekers to enter legally, only one person was reported to use this route. The reason, according to Laurynas Biekša and Ilona Ivašauskaitė, is that people simply could not enter the border control zone without the proper documents (passport and visa).

29 Ignas Jačauskas, 'VSAT Vadas: Migrantai į Lietuvą Neįleidžiami Nepaisant To, Kur Šalyje Yra Sulaikyti' ('The Head of VSAT: Migrants Are Not Allowed into Lithuania, Regardless of Where They Are Approached in the State'), *Delfi*, Vilnius, 14 October 2021, www.delfi.lt/news/daily/lithuania/vsat-vadas-migrantai-i-lietuva-neileidziami-nepaisant-to-kur-salyje-yra-sulaikyti.d?id=88425839, accessed 12 November 2022.

30 Act Amending Articles 2, 3, 5, 26, 32, 40, 50, 67, 71, 76, 77, 79, 113, 125, 126, 130–1, 136, 138, 139 and 140 of Act No IX-2206 on the Legal Status of Foreigners, Repealing Article 69 and Chapter IX-1 and Supplementing the Act with Chapter X-2, 23 December 2021, no. XIV-816. Furthermore, the Act was also amended in March of 2022, with the view of facilitating intake of refugees from Ukraine, attacked by Russia on 24 February 2022.

31 Act on the Legal Status of Foreigners, Article 5(2) as amended on 23 December 2021.

32 Act Amending Article 67 of Act No IX-2206 on the Legal Status of Foreigners, TAR, 11 August 2021, No. 17359.

33 Ministry of the Interion of the Republic of Lithuania, Order On Submission of Applications for Asylum by Foreigners No. V-393, 21 September 2022.

34 Biekša and Ivašauskaitė (n 24), 161.

By March 2022, a fence of almost 500 kilometres was constructed, including 300 kilometres of barbed wire fence (concertina).[35] The number of people crossing the Lithuanian border decreased in quantity, but to this date, people continue to arrive and continue to be refused entry.[36] It can be expected that more people will arrive during warmer periods, but the "wall project" also continues until September 2022. The "wall project" has broad political support in Lithuania. The EU has contributed to funding the increased presence of guards at the border and repatriation costs to "voluntary returns" of foreigners to countries of origin but refused to pay for the wall project, especially for the barbed wire.[37]

In the judgment of 30 June 2022, the European Court of Justice held that EU law is infringed, if "illegally staying third-country nationals are effectively deprived of the opportunity of access, in the territory of that Member State, to the procedure in which applications for international protection are examined." (para 75). This means that once the migrants manage to enter Lithuania, it no longer should matter that the officers did not allow them to enter. The possibility to apply for an asylum should be given. However, by the time this judgment was adopted, the wall was in place, and illegal crossings of the border were made very hard. The only possibility for an illegal crossing is via dangerous areas, in which it was too difficult to construct the wall. Some people still attempt it, because the access to asylum procedure should legally be available in the territory of Lithuania.

4. Key violations of human rights

Pushbacks and the turn-around policy in Lithuania could be evaluated as problematic from the perspective of prohibition of *collective expulsions* and *refoulment.* This is the conclusion of Laurynas Biekša and Ilona Ivašauskaitė, who noted that

> Officers of the Lithuanian Republic do not adopt any decision and do not perform any evaluation, when they turn foreigners around and when they return them back to Belarus.[38]

35 'Kiek Pasistūmėta Statant Barjerą: Pasienyje Nutiesta 300 Kilometrų Koncertinos ir 150 Kilometrų Tvoros' ('How Much Progress with the Barrier: 300 km of Concertina and 150 km of Fence Constructed at the Border'), *LRT,* Vilnius, 24 March 2022, www.lrt.lt/naujienos/lietuvoje/2/1653640/kiek-pasistumeta-statant-barjera-pasienyje-nutiesta-300-kilometru-koncertinos-ir-150-kilometru-tvoros, accessed 24 March 2022.

36 On the same day, 24 March 2022, when the minister of the interior and the person in charge for extreme situations, Agne Bilotaitė, announced the updates on the "wall project", 20 people were refused entry to Lithuania from the side of Belarus.

37 Daniel Boffey, 'Ursula von der Leyen Says EU Will Not Fund 'Barbed Wire and Walls', *The Guardian,* London, 22 October 2021, www.theguardian.com/world/2021/oct/22/ursula-von-der-leyen-says-eu-will-not-fund-barbed-wire-and-walls, accessed 12 January 2021.

38 See Biekša and Ivašauskaitė (n 24), 164.

A border guard anonymously talked to the media, claiming that one migrant is given less than two minutes in practice,[39] which does not make it possible to perform an individual assessment of their circumstances. In many cases, the people have no opportunity to request asylum. It could also be claimed that Belarus was not a particularly safe state to asylum seekers, because violence has been widely reported from the side of border guards in Belarus, and shots have been heard many times from the territory of Belarus.

In a couple of cases, the European Court of Human Rights (the ECtHR) adopted interim measures, ordering Lithuania to ensure the right to apply for asylum of applicants who came from Afghanistan.[40] It appears that after being stranded on the border for a while, the applicants managed to enter Lithuania physically but were not willing to stay on. The interim measures with respect to these applicants were not extended by the Court and lapsed in September 2021.[41]

Asylum seekers have also reported psychological pressure to leave voluntarily. They are offered a lump sum of 1000 Euros[42] and convinced that there is no other way but to leave the state. For instance, a lesbian asylum-seeker from Cameroon says:

> I was told to return to my country voluntarily because I came to Lithuania while illegally crossing the border. The return was, according to them, the fastest and simplest way. They explained that this decision could be taken at any time, and it would solve the situation very fast: flight tickets would be bought, and a lump sum would be paid. It just feels that they are not even listening to what we are saying to them.[43]

With respect to the asylum seekers and migrants who are mandatorily accommodated in Lithuania, it could be considered unlawful detention,

39 Benas Gerdžiūnas and Artūras Morozovas, '2 Minutės Nustatyti – "Nelegalas" ar Pabėgėlis: kaip Realybėje Atrodo Reikalavimai Išvykti Savo Noru' ('2 Minutes to Determine Whether a Person Is "Illegal" or a Refugee: How Requirements to Leave Voluntarily Look Like in Reality'), *LRT*, Vilnius, 10 September 2021, www.lrt.lt/naujienos/lietuvoje/2/1491915/2-minutes-nustatyti-nelegalas-ar-pabegelis-kaip-realybeje-atrodo-reikalavimai-isvykti-savo-noru, accessed 17 March 2022.

40 ECtHR, case no. 44205/21 and case no. 61159/21.

41 European Court of Human Rights, 'Update on Interim Decisions Concerning Member States' Borders with Belarus' (21 February 2022), ECHR 051.

42 The lump sum has gradually increased by a factor of 3. The Minister of the Interior claims that one asylum seeker costs the state about 11,000 Euros per year; hence such a lump sum is a cheaper option. 'Savanoriškas Migrantų Grįžimas į Kilmės Šalis Bus Skatinamas Triskart Didesne Pinigų Suma' (n 13).

43 Artūras Morozovas, 'Tarp Prieglobsčio Prašytojų Istorijų – Lesbiečių Pora, Raginimai Išvykti Savo noru ir Kamerūnietis, Kuris Ieškodamas Pareigūnų Nuėjo iki Kauno' ('Among Asylum Seekers, a Lesbian Couple, Given Encouragements to Leave Voluntarily, and a Cameroonian Who Went to Kaunas in Search of Officers'), *LRT*, Vilnius, 16 September 2021, www.lrt.lt/naujienos/lietuvoje/2/1494874/tarp-prieglobscio-prasytoju-istoriju-lesbieciu-pora-raginimai-isvykti-savo-noru-ir-kamerunietis-kuris-ieskodamas-pareigunu-nuejo-iki-kauno, accessed 12 February 2022.

as previously stressed. It is also problematic from the perspective of the prohibition of inhuman and degrading treatment. In October 2021, the parliamentary ombudsperson concluded that accommodation conditions of the asylum seekers in Lithuania, in some instances, met the criteria for inhuman and degrading treatment.[44] In January 2022, the parliamentary ombudsperson raised concerns regarding the conditions at Kybartai foreigners' registration centre, again claiming the conditions met the criteria for inhuman and degrading treatment.[45]

The parliamentary ombudsperson is a non-specialised office that investigates activities of state agents. Meanwhile, there are also two specialised ombudspersons in Lithuania: the Office of the Ombudsperson on the Rights of the Child and the Office on the Equal Opportunities Ombudsperson.

5. Children in crisis

5.1. The child's perspective and the OP3 CRC in Lithuania

The rights of the child are often defended by those who represent children or care about children's rights rather than directly by children themselves. From the perspective of agency, it is important that children be heard and seen in all juridical and legislative processes where decisions concern them. Children who have come via the Eastern route are very different but share similar experiences of restricted rights. For instance, Hivi is a 13-year-old teenager who came to Lithuania in the summer of 2021 (prior to the adoption of the pushback policy):

> She's a Kurdish teenager who has been living in one of the detention centers with her parents for more than nine months.
>
> At the moment, the days of Hivi's family are marked by waiting for their final answer regarding their asylum status.
>
> Hivi, who left Kurdistan when she was in 7th grade, has no educational prospects apart from a daily Lithuanian lesson in Pabradė.[46]
>
> Yet the use of English in Hivi's daily routine is already constant – she translates and interprets for everyone around her, from the morning till [sic] the end of the day.[47]

44 Report of the Parliamentary Ombudsperson, No. NKR-2021/1- of 7 October 2021.

45 Report of the Parliamentary Ombudsperson, No. NKP-2021/1–4 of 24 January 2022.

46 Pabradė is a remote town in Lithuania, where one of the foreigners' registration centres is situated. The interview was taken remotely, because journalists are not allowed in the premises, and those who live there cannot leave. Hivi would get a question via Instagram and would record an answer and send it to the journalist.

47 Martyna Šulskutė, 'Language Shouldn't Be a Curse, It Should Be a Blessing', *NARA*, Vilnius, 13 April 2022, https://nara.lt/en/articles-en/language-shouldn-t-be-a-curse-it-should-be-a-blessing, accessed 14 April 2022.

In order to integrate the child right's perspective more directly, the Optional Protocol to the CRC on a Communications Procedure was introduced in 2011. Lithuania signed the Optional Protocol in 2015 and ratified it in the autumn of 2022, with entry into force on 1 January 2023.[48] Lithuania ratified the CRC in 1995[49] and adopted the Act on the Fundamentals of Protection of the Rights of the Child in 1996,[50] and the Office of the Ombudsperson for Child's Rights was established in 2000.[51] One of the key tasks of the institution is to monitor the implementation of children's rights in accordance with the CRC. It is an independent institution, which receives funding from the state. In contrast to court judgments, the decisions of this institution are only recommendatory, but they are respected due to the authority of the Office of the Ombudsperson for Child's Rights.

The discussion on the rights of children is causing intense political conflicts. Hot topics include the meaning of family values, freedoms and responsibilities and national identity. The most significant breakthrough in this political debate was the amendment of the Act on the Fundamentals of Protection of the Rights of the Child, which for the first time prohibited all forms of violence against children, including corporal punishment in all areas of life. Considering how recent this legal change was – 2017 – partially explains why the rights of migrant children are not always protected effectively.

Moreover, the ratification of the Optional Protocol, which entered into force on 1 January 2023 in Lithuania, can be considered a landmark event that a strong potential for further reforms.

5.2. The migrant child at the intersections of vulnerabilities

It has already been stated that pushbacks and detention of migrants constitute serious human rights violations. Pushbacks of children and migration-related detention of children must immediately be abolished. This has been demanded by the ombudsperson for the rights of the child, parliamentary ombudsperson, and various non-governmental organisations in Lithuania.[52]

Intersectionality is a tool for conceptualising an individual as affected by multiple, overlapping and intersecting disadvantages and discriminations.

48 UNGA, 'Optional Protocol to the Convention on the Rights of the Child on a Communications Procedure' (adopted 19 December 2011, entered into force 14 April 2014, in accordance with article 19(1)) 66th session (2011), A/RES/66/138, https://e-seimas.lrs.lt/portal/legalAct/lt/TAD/febe0872da9211ecb1b39d276e924a5d?jfwid=hfzmf8tpo, accessed 3 March 2023.

49 The Convention on the Rights of the Child was published, in Lithuanian, in the Official Gazette (Valstybės žinios) on 21 July 1995 No. 60–1501.

50 Act on the Fundamentals of Protection of the Rights of the Child, Official Gazette, 12 April 1996, No. 33–807.

51 Act on the Ombudsperson for Children, 25 May 2000, No VIII-1708.

52 Joint Statement of Human Rights Monitoring Institute and the Global Detention Project, submitted to the UN Committee against Torture (18 October 2021), https://tbinternet.ohchr.org/Treaties/CAT/Shared%20Documents/LTU/INT_CAT_NGO_LTU_47040_E.pdf, accessed 18 March 2022.

The metaphor of people at traffic intersections is often used to understand that injury may come from various directions and at the same time. All children are vulnerable, but migrant children are in a uniquely vulnerable situation, where even their lives and health could be threatened. State authorities might consider that they do not bear any responsibilities and refer instead to parental responsibilities.[53] At the same time, the parents and guardians who are in detention or pushback situations are not in a position to protect the life and health of a child, or they are altogether missing when the child travels alone.

Migrant children are at intersections of disadvantages, discriminations and vulnerabilities. Their age and migration create a unique set of vulnerabilities, which must be "seen" in law. Children are often unable to prove their identity and have a high chance of being treated as "illegal" (illegal migrants). In case of migrant children coming via Belarus, the risk of sustaining injury at the intersections is higher when they are pushed back to Belarus. As mentioned at the outset, human rights instruments do not function in that state, and multiple violations are reported, *inter alia*, against migrants and against children.

The ombudsperson for equal opportunities has consistently argued for an intersectional approach to discrimination in Lithuania.[54] It is currently possible to complain to the ombudsperson for equal opportunities regarding multiple discrimination grounds (such as age and gender, age and social status), rather than just one (such as age). However, the work of this ombudsperson is limited, with the focus on the discrimination of adults. The ombudsperson for equal opportunities is currently monitoring the legal position of migrants and asylum seekers in relation to intersecting vulnerabilities[55] – in particular, problems faced by LGBTQIA+ (lesbian, gay, bisexual, trans, queer intersex and asexual) migrants. Meanwhile, the work of the ombudsperson for child's rights is focused on children, but so far, it does not work with intersectional vulnerabilities. Children in migration also face multifaceted challenges, and

53 The situation described in the Statement of the Office of the Ombudsperson for Child's Rights on the Alleged Violations of Rights and Interests of the Children, who Were Refused Entry to the Territory of Lithuania on 2021–11–06 and 2021–12–01, 13 January 2022, No. (6.7.-2021–51/53)PR-3.

54 In 2011, the ombudsperson for equal opportunities adopted its first decision on multiple discrimination. The situation concerned a preference of people with military training in civil-service employment. Such preference was considered discriminatory based on gender, disability and age, 108–127. Annual Report of the Ombudsperson for Equal Opportunities for 2011, https://lygybe.lt/data/public/uploads/2015/12/lgkt-ataskaita-2011.pdf, accessed 3 March 2022, 108–127.

55 Vilma Venckutonytė, 'Po Apsilankymų Migrantų Sulaikymo Vietose: Kiekvienas iš Mūsų Galėtų Būti Tokioje Pačioje Situacijoje' ('After Visiting Migrant Detention Places: Each of Us Could Be in the Same Situation'), (*Office of the Equal Opportunities Ombudsperson*, 21 February 2022), www.lygybe.lt/lt/po-apsilankymu-migrantu-sulaikymo-vietose-kiekvienas-is-musu-galetu-buti-tokioje-pacioje-situacijoje, accessed 4 March 2022.

when dealing with unaccompanied migrants or migrant children with disabilities, it would be useful to consider intersectionality in the future.[56]

5.3. Key issues for the ombudsperson for child's rights

The objective of the ombudsperson for child's rights is to represent the rights of the children in Lithuania. At the moment of the crisis and up to the time this chapter was finalised (April 2022), the ombudsperson was Edita Žiobienė, who has held this post for three terms. It is significant that the ombudsperson chose to represent the rights of children who are considered "illegal migrants" in Lithuania. In some respects, the "illegal migrant" child is not considered a child when such a child experiences pushbacks at the borders or is detained or refused education. This could be called the third semantic paradox: besides "non-detention" and "non-entry" is the child who is not treated as a child.

The Office of the Ombudsperson for Child's Rights adopted three statements relevant to the analysed crisis. All of the statements include a thorough analysis from the perspective of the best interests of the child. The ombudsperson offered certain suggestions for improving the situation: legislative changes, practical improvements and conceptual policy changes. In order to make sure that the case-practice did not deviate from children's rights standards, the ombudsperson organised a joint event with the Supreme Court of Lithuania and held meetings at a ministerial and parliamentary level about the rights of unaccompanied migrant children. She also criticised legislative attempts to legalise infringements of migrant children's rights in relation to "accommodation" without the freedom to move.[57]

The first ombudsperson's statement concerned the situation of unaccompanied minors,[58] the second one focused on the situation of children in accommodation centres,[59] and the third was an investigation of the pushbacks of a specific family with children.[60] Officially, the first two investigations were initiated by the Office of the Ombudsperson for Child's Rights; however, the incentive to do so was strong pressure from politicians and the concerns of human rights organisations. Both investigations are thorough and include detailed information from various actors. They also provide

56 Also see Section 5.6 further in the text.

57 For instance, in the annual report for the year 2021, presented on April 1, 2022, the ombudsperson criticised a new version of the Act on the Legal Status of Foreigners, suggesting her own legislative amendments instead.

58 Statement of the Office of the Ombudsperson for Child's Rights on Investigation, on Own Motion, of the Situation of Unaccompanied Minor Foreigners, 16 November 2021, No. (6.7–2021–42)PR-142.

59 Ibid.

60 Statement of the Office of the Ombudsperson for Child's Rights on the Alleged Violations of Rights and Interests of the Children, Who Were Refused Entry to the Territory of Lithuania on 2021–11–06 and 2021–12–01, 13 January 2022, No. (6.7.-2021–51/53)PR-3.

overviews of legal obligations, including overviews of international obligations of the state with respect to migrant children.

5.4. Treatment of unaccompanied minors

The first statement was adopted in November of 2021 and concerned unaccompanied minors. In its analysis, the Office of the Ombudsperson for Child's Rights noted great inconsistencies in the treatment of unaccompanied minors in courts and by state authorities. It concludes that child right's protection officers must be informed in all cases, regardless of whether unaccompanied migrant children asked for asylum. The child rights protection officers must also be present at interviews.[61] The ombudsperson criticised the fact that the border guard office did not always inform child protection offices about unaccompanied migrants. Sometimes they were informed only after the age was medically confirmed. Child rights protection officers were not always invited to interviews with minors.

The medical determination of the age of unaccompanied children has been used in 85% of cases in Lithuania, despite the fact that it should be a last resort rather than a standard procedure.[62] The ombudsperson also criticised "a bad practice of age determination without appointing a representative and without his or her consent, without a possibility to appeal".[63]

The ombudsperson made a number of conclusions on the prospective code of conduct and made many suggestions on the changes needed in law and in practice. In particular, the legal changes that were needed regarding an *immediate* appointment of a guardian who could represent the migrant child. The ombudsperson also noted in this statement that living conditions of unaccompanied minors were not always adequate and facilities were not always suitable to accommodate children. The comparability of "accommodation" conditions to detention was discussed in a separate investigation, which concerned all children, not only unaccompanied children (see further in Section 5.5).

In 2022, the Supreme Court of Lithuania adopted a decision that could be considered a precedent on the treatment of unaccompanied migrant children. This case concerned an appeal in cassation – meaning there was no dispute of facts, but an issue of law had to be clarified. The appealing institution was a territorial child protection agency. The relevant issue was whether, in order to assign a guardian for a migrant child in Lithuania, the regional child protection office must initiate a procedure for "taking the child" from

61 Statement of the Office of the Ombudsperson for Child's Rights on Investigation, on Own Motion, of the Situation of Unaccompanied Minor Foreigners, 24.

62 Ibid., 34.

63 Ibid., 38.

the parents who remained in the state of origin – which was the position of the child protection agency. The Supreme Court replied in the negative.

> 32. In consideration of the relevant case-practice of the court in cassation, an issue of compatibility between these fundamental family law principles arises: 1) parental rights and responsibilities belong, firstly, to the parents. 2) intervention into private life of parents and children can only be justified by law, and provided that there is a legitimate goal and it is necessary in a democratic society. 3) while deciding on the restrictions of parental rights and duties, in all cases the right to fair trial must be ensured. 4) interests of the child are the most significant in deciding all issues related to the child.
>
> 33. The plaintiff considered that the parental rights belong to the parents of the child (Art. 3.165 of the Civil Code), and other persons can only acquire it, when the parents are inadequately exercising these rights in respect of their children (Art. 3.160 (2) of the Civil Code), thus, in order to protect the child it is necessary to take (restrict) the relevant part of parental rights and transfer it to the State. However, this approach of the child protection agency is in principle focused not on the child's rights or their protection, but in the wish to restrict the parental rights because of the neglect of the child who finds themselves in an undesirable situation. The court in cassation assesses that the State must take operative actions to protect such children because of their vulnerability (the child is in a foreign State alone, where they do not have any social connections, has not managed to feel comfortable or safe in the State so far).[64]

The Supreme Court stressed that it is not the restriction of parental responsibilities that need be in focus but instead a direct concern for the protection of the migrant child. The Court further explained, with references to the case-law from the European Court of Human Rights, that the protection of children is the primary concern in such situations. It could be expected that in the future, migrant children who are unaccompanied in Lithuanian territory will be immediately appointed a temporary guardian.

5.5. Detention and pushbacks of children

The second report of the ombudsperson for the rights of the child was published at the beginning of December 2021 and concerned children held in "accommodation" centres. The ombudsperson made a number of

64 Supreme Court of Lithuania, decision of January 12, 2022, civil case No. 3K-3–117–943/2022.

suggestions regarding conditions of accommodation and the vulnerability assessment of children. The investigation revealed that migrant children:

> were accommodated in closed environments with control mechanisms, the places of accommodation are fenced, the perimeter is guarded by officers, and in some of the accommodation centres, the windows of living premises were barred.[65]

The Office of the Ombudsperson for Child's Rights criticised the fact that children born to migrants without identity documents are not registered in the civil registry and recommended that some legal solution be found.[66] A number of positive suggestions were made regarding the treatment of children in accommodation centres, with the use of holistic and thoughtful approaches to child's rights.

The third investigation of the Office of the Ombudsperson for Child's Rights concerned the situation of a specific Iraqi family with four children, who were pushed back repeatedly from the border of Lithuania in November and December 2021. The third statement was on December 31, 2021. The opinion of the border guards in the analysed situation was that the parents were responsible for the wellbeing of the children and their right to life and health. The ombudsperson was critical of this approach and warned that:

> a practice is formed that children accompanied by parents are not considered as vulnerable persons, which does not comply with the interests of migrant children.[67]

The ombudsperson suggested a review and amendment of the current legislation on vulnerability assessment and also stressed that the state has certain international obligations with respect to child's rights. Following the decision of the ombudsperson, there have not been any significant amendments of the Act on the Legal Status of Foreigners regarding the concept of a vulnerable person or other provisions in the act regarding vulnerability. However, not much time has passed since the investigation of the ombudsperson, and amendments might be adopted in the future.

It is worth noting that prior this crisis, Lithuania and other neighbouring states argued that Belarus is a state where human rights are violated. It is hence difficult to understand why that state is treated as sufficiently

65 Statement of the Office of the Ombudsperson for Child's Rights on Investigation, on Own Motion, of the Situation of Foreign Migrant Children in Accommodation Centres, 11.

66 Ibid., 50.

67 Statement of the Office of the Ombudsperson for Child's Rights on the Alleged Violations of Rights and Interests of the Children, Who Were Refused Entry to the Territory of Lithuania, 15.

safe for migrant families with children to be pushed back at the border. As mentioned, shots are fired at the border territory from the Belarussian side, and migrants have reported that border guards in Belarus used physical violence to push them towards Lithuania; destroyed their documents; taken their water, food and communication devices; and drugged children with psychotropic medicines.[68]

5.6. Child's rights to education and health

The ombudsperson repeatedly emphasised that the right to education must be ensured to all children without discrimination, regardless of their legal status (migrant or refugee) and various identity aspects. In her final annual report, she suggested including a legal provision in Lithuanian law that a child's right to education must be ensured no later than three months after the arrival of the migrant children.[69] The ombudsperson also criticised the Act on the Legal Status of Foreigners with respect to the right to health. She suggested that migrant children should have the right not only to the necessary medical aid but also to security in cases of physical sickness and mental health. The problem is isolation of the children in the so-called "accommodation centres". Such isolated accommodation may equate to detention, which affects the physical and mental health of the migrant child.

As previously mentioned, there have not been deaths at the border of Belarus and Lithuania. However, one migrant child died in the territory of Lithuania in 2021 (the Rukla refugee centre) due to various health problems and a disability caused by previous injuries in the state of origin.[70] The child was brought by the father to the Belarus–Lithuania border on August 6, 2021. When dealing with migrant children, it is important to address intersectionality, and even more so when dealing with migrant children with disabilities. An intersectional approach would help identify the groups of children who are in particularly vulnerable situations and make

---

68 Two children were drugged in Belarus and ended up in emergency care in Lithuania, immediately after crossing the border (the border could be crossed because the event took place prior to the pushback policy). A police investigation was opened in Lithuania. Dominykas Griežė, 'Dėl Baltarusijos Režimo Apnuodytų Pabėgėlių Vaikų Lietuviai Pradėjo Ikiteisminį Tyrimą: Įtaria Sunkiai Sutrikdžius Sveikatą' ('Lithuanians Started Pre-trial Investigation Regarding Refugee Children Drugged by the Belarussian Regime: Suspicions of Serious Harm to Health'), *Vakarų ekspresas*, Klaipėda, 19 August 2021, https://ve.lt/aktualijos/lietuva/del-baltarusijos-rezimo-apnuodytu-pabegeliu-vaiku-lietuviai-pradejo-ikiteismini, accessed 12 March 2022.

69 Annual Report of the Ombudsperson for the Rights of Children, 31 March 2022. No. 4–3, p. 55.

70 Karolina Stažytė, 'Pabėgėlių Centre Miręs Vaikas Palaidotas Musulmonų Kapinėse the Child Who Died in Refugee Centre, Buried in the Muslim Cemetery'), *15 min*, Vilnius, 28 September 2022, www.15min.lt/naujiena/aktualu/lietuva/pabegeliu-centre-mires-vaikas-palaidotas-vilniaus-musulmonu-kapinese-56-1572246, accessed 5 March 2022.

sure that they are never treated *en masse* with all migrants. It is suggested that the ombudsperson for the child's rights could address intersectional vulnerabilities of particularly vulnerable migrant children in the future. The good practice by the ombudsperson for equal opportunities could be used. Both ombudspersons could cooperate more closely for the purpose of monitoring intersecting vulnerabilities.

6. Concluding remarks

Migrants and asylum seekers coming from Belarus have been treated as "instrumentalised" weapons in a hybrid attack against the (vulnerable) Eastern route states and the EU. It must be stressed that only human beings, not states or the EU, have a "vulnerability" in need of protection. Migrant children coming via Belarus are in a particularly vulnerable situation due to their age and the hardships of parents or guardians responsible for their health. They are literally stranded at intersections with multiple sources of potential injury, especially when they are pushed back to Belarus, where violent human rights violations are reported, *inter alia*, against migrants and children. Migrant children have also been accommodated in conditions comparable with detention, and some of them have had their freedom of movement limited.

Prompt legal changes were introduced in Lithuania in 2021, restricting international obligations with respect to migrants and asylum seekers. The legal situation and human rights violations have been constructively criticised by ombudspersons in Lithuania, with regard to children's rights in particular, by the ombudsperson for the child's rights, who published several detailed reports in 2021.

One concern of the ombudsperson for child's rights was the precarious situation of unaccompanied migrant children; another issue was the treatment of children in registration and accommodation centres, and finally, the pushbacks of a family with children were analysed. The ombudsperson for the child's rights also organised various events, including a seminar with the Supreme Court on the legal situation of unaccompanied migrant children, and discussed the practice of non-registry of babies born in Lithuania to migrant parents with civil registry officials. In 2022, the Supreme Court of Lithuania adopted an important case on the legal status of unaccompanied migrant children, stressing that a guardian and legal representative must be appointed in Lithuania without the procedure for legal restriction of the original parents' rights. Rather than sanctioning the parents and restricting their rights, the crucial concern was the need for the protection of the child's rights in migration and the migrant child's vulnerability. Both national litigation, as well as applications to the ECtHR, have proved effective and could significantly improve the situation of migrant children. In the future, the CRC mechanisms could also be used, considering that Lithuania held its promise to ratify the OP3. Potentially, the ratification of the OP3 opens a new era for children's rights in Lithuania, and could introduce significant changes, if that potential is realised.

The ombudsperson for equal opportunities has consistently applied an intersectional approach for at least a decade. This institution is currently monitoring the humanitarian crisis discussed in this chapter. The objective is the identification of multiple forms of discrimination, but the focus is on vulnerable adults rather than children. It is suggested that the ombudsperson for the child's rights could also use the good practice of the ombudsperson for equal opportunities and integrate the intersectional approach in their work in the future. This would follow the spirit and vision of the CRC – and strengthen the protection of rights of migrant children at intersections of vulnerabilities.

Bibliography

Legal documents

Act Amending Articles 2, 3, 5, 26, 32, 40, 50, 67, 71, 76, 77, 79, 113, 125, 126, 130-1, 136, 138, 139 and 140 of Act No IX-2206 on the Legal Status of Foreigners, Repealing Article 69 and Chapter IX-1 and Supplementing the Act with Chapter X-2, 23 December 2021, No. XIV-816.

Act Amending Article 67 of Act No IX-2206 on the Legal Status of Foreigners, TAR, 11 August 2021, No. 17359.

Act Amending Articles 5, 71, 76, 77, 79, 113, 131, 136, 138, 139, 140 of Act No IX-2206 on the Legal Status of Foreigners and supplementing the Act with Chapter IX-1, TAR, 22 July 2021, No. 16266.

Act on Legal Status of Foreigners, 29 April 2004, No. IX-2206.

Act on the Fundamentals of Protection of the Rights of the Child, 12 April 1996, No. 33–807.

Act on the Ombudsperson for Child's Rights, 25 May 2000, No VIII-1708.

European Convention for the Protection of Human Rights and Fundamental Freedoms, as amended by Protocols Nos. 11 and 14 (adopted 4 November 1950, entered into force 3 September 1953).

Ministry of the Interion of the Republic of Lithuania, Order On Submission of Applications for Asylum by Foreigners No. V-393, 21 September 2022.

Optional Protocol to the Convention on the Rights of the Child on a Communications Procedure' (adopted 19 December 2011, entered into force 14 April 2014).

Resolution of the Government on Announcing State-Level Emergency and Appointing State-level Head of Emergency Operations, No. 517 of 2 July 2021, TAR, No. 15235.

Resolution of the Parliament of Lithuania on Countering Hybrid Aggression, 13 July 2021 No XIV-505.

Case-law

European Court of Human Rights, *M.A. v Lithuania*, judgment of 11 December 2018, app. no. 59793/17.

European Court of Human Rights, *M.K. v Poland*, judgment of 23 July 2020, app.nos 40503/17, 42902/17 and 43643/17.

European Court of Human Rights, *A.S. and Others v. Lithuania*, ECHR app. no. 44205/21, app.no. 61159/21, pending.

Court of Justice of the European Union (Grand Chamber), decision on 30 June 2022 in case C-72/22 PPU.

Supreme Administrative Court of Lithuania, Decision of 6 October 2021, Case no. AS-653-492/2021.

Supreme Administrative Court of Lithuania, Decision of 27 October 2021, Case no. AS-747-442/2021.

Supreme Court of Lithuania, Decision of 12 January 2022, Civil Case No. 3K-3-117-943/2022.

Literature

Bennets, M, 'Lukashenko Willing to Flood EU with Drugs and Migrants to Stop New Sanctions', *The Times,* London, 28 May 2021. www.thetimes.co.uk/article/lukashenko-willing-to-flood-eu-with-drugs-and-migrants-to-stop-new-sanctions-vtrwndw82, accessed 4 November 2021.

Biekša, L and Ivašauskaitė, I, 'Lietuvos Reakcija į Prieglobsčio Prašytojų Antplūdį Tarptautinės ir Europos Sąjungos Teisės Kontekste' ('Reaction of Lithuania to Influx of Asylum Seekers, in the Context of International and European Union Law'), in Jakulevičienė, L and Sinkevičius, V (eds), *Lietuvos Teisė 2021: Esminiai pokyčiai.* Mykolas Romeris University. Vilnius, 2021, 156–167.

Bilal, A, 'Hybrid Warfare – New Threats, Complexity, and "Trust" as the Antidote', *NATO,* 20 November 2021. www.nato.int/docu/review/articles/2021/11/30/hybrid-warfare-new-threats-complexity-and-trust-as-the-antidote/index.html, accessed 2 March 2022.

Boffey, D, 'Ursula von der Leyen Says EU Will not Fund 'Barbed Wire and Walls', *The Guardian,* London, 22 October 2021. www.theguardian.com/world/2021/oct/22/ursula-von-der-leyen-says-eu-will-not-fund-barbed-wire-and-walls, accessed 12 January 2021.

Crenshaw, K, 'Demarginalizing the Intersection of Race and Sex: A Black Feminist Critique of Antidiscrimination Doctrine, Feminist Theory and Antiracist Politics', *University of Chicago Legal Forum,* 1(8), 139–167, 1989.

Gerdžiūnas, B and Morozovas, A, '2 Minutės Nustatyti – "Nelegalas" ar Pabėgėlis: kaip Realybėje Atrodo Reikalavimai Išvykti Savo Noru' ('2 Minutes to Determine Whether a Person Is "Illegal" or a Refugee: How Requirements to Leave Voluntarily Look Like in Reality'), *LRT,* Vilnius, 10 September 2021. www.lrt.lt/naujienos/lietuvoje/2/1491915/2-minutes-nustatyti-nelegalas-ar-pabegelis-kaip-realybeje-atrodo-reikalavimai-isvykti-savo-noru, accessed 17 March 2022.

Griežė, D, 'Dėl Baltarusijos Režimo Apnuodytų Pabėgėlių Vaikų Lietuviai Pradėjo Ikiteisminį Tyrimą: Įtaria Sunkiai Sutrikdžius Sveikatą' ('Lithuanians Started Pre-trial Investigation Regarding Refugee Children Drugged by the Belarussian Regime: Suspicions of Serious Harm to Health'), *Vakarų ekspresas,* Klaipėda, 19 August 2021. https://ve.lt/aktualijos/lietuva/del-baltarusijos-rezimo-apnuodytu-pabegeliu-vaiku-lietuviai-pradejo-ikiteismini, accessed 12 March 2022.

Jačauskas, I, 'VSAT Vadas: Migrantai į Lietuvą Neįleidžiami Nepaisant to, kur Šalyje Yra Sulaikyti' ('The Head of VSAT: Migrants Are not Allowed into Lithuania, Regardless of Where They Are Approached in the State'), *Delfi,* Vilnius, 14 October 2021. www.delfi.lt/news/daily/lithuania/vsat-vadas-migrantai-i-lietuva-neileidziami-nepaisant-to-kur-salyje-yra-sulaikyti.d?id=88425839, accessed 12 November 2022.

'Kiek Pasistūmėta Statant Barjerą: Pasienyje Nutiesta 300 Kilometrų Koncertinos ir 150 Kilometrų Tvoros' ('How Much Progress with the Barrier: 300 km of Concertina and 150 km of Fence Constructed at the Border'), *LRT,* Vilnius, 24 March 2022. www.lrt.lt/naujienos/lietuvoje/2/1653640/kiek-pasistumeta-statant-barjera-pasienyje-nutiesta-300-kilometru-koncertinos-ir-150-kilometru-tvoros, accessed 24 March 2022.

Morozovas, A, 'Tarp Prieglobsčio Prašytojų Istorijų – Lesbiečių Pora, Raginimai Išvykti Savo noru ir Kamerūnietis, Kuris Ieškodamas Pareigūnų Nuėjo iki Kauno' ('Among Asylum Seekers, a Lesbian Couple, Given Encouragements to Leave Voluntarily, and a Cameroonian Who Went to Kaunas in Search of Officers'), *LRT,* Vilnius, 16 September 2021. www.lrt.lt/naujienos/lietuvoje/2/1494874/tarp-prieglobscio-prasytoju-istoriju-lesbieciu-pora-raginimai-isvykti-savo-noru-ir-kamerunietis-kuris-ieskodamas-pareigunu-nuejo-iki-kauno, accessed 12 February 2022.

Stažytė, K, 'Pabėgėlių Centre Miręs Vaikas Palaidotas Musulmonų Kapinėse' ('The Child Who Died in Refugee Centre, Buried in the Muslim Cemetery'), *15 min,* Vilnius, 28 September 2022. www.15min.lt/naujiena/aktualu/lietuva/pabegeliu-centre-mires-vaikas-palaidotas-vilniaus-musulmonu-kapinese-56-1572246, accessed 5 March 2022.

Šulskutė, M, 'Language Shouldn't be a Curse, It Should be a Blessing', *NARA,* Vilnius, 13 April 2022. https://nara.lt/en/articles-en/language-shouldn-t-be-a-curse-it-should-be-a-blessing, accessed 14 April 2022.

Venckutonytė, V, 'Po Apsilankymų Migrantų Sulaikymo Vietose: Kiekvienas iš Mūsų Galėtų Būti Tokioje Pačioje Situacijoje' ('After Visiting Migrant Detention Places: Each of Us Could Be in the Same Situation'), *Office of the Equal Opportunities Ombudsperson,* 21 February 2022. www.lygybe.lt/lt/po-apsilankymu-migrantu-sulaikymo-vietose-kiekvienas-is-musu-galetu-buti-tokioje-pacioje-situacijoje, accessed 4 March 2022.

Other

Annual Report of the Ombudsperson for Equal Opportunities for 2011. https://lygybe.lt/data/public/uploads/2015/12/lgkt-ataskaita-2011.pdf, accessed 3 March 2022.

Annual Report of the Ombudsperson for the Rights of Children, 31 March 2022. No. 4-3.

Department of Statistics, Official Statistics Portal, 'Monitoring of Illegal Migration from 1 January 2021'. https://osp.stat.gov.lt/gyventoju-migracija, accessed (updated daily) 4 March 2021.

European Commission, 'Proposal On Council Decision for Provisional Emergency Measures for the Benefit of Latvia, Lithuania and Poland' 1 December 2021, COM(2021) 752 final.

European Court of Human Rights, 'Update on Interim Decisions Concerning Member States' Borders with Belarus' (21 February 2022) ECHR 051.

Human Rights Monitoring Institute and the Global Detention Project, *Joint Statement of Human Rights Monitoring Institute and the Global Detention Project,* submitted to the UN Committee against Torture (18 October 2021). https://tbinternet.ohchr.org/Treaties/CAT/Shared%20Documents/LTU/INT_CAT_NGO_LTU_47040_E.pdf, accessed 18 March 2022.

'Į Iraką sSugrįžę Migrantai Papasakojo, Ką š Tikrųjų Patyrė Baltarusijoje' ('Migrants Who Returned to Iraq Told of What They Had Really Experienced in Belarus'),

Delfi, Vilnius, 19 November 2021. www.delfi.lt/news/daily/world/i-iraka-sugrize-migrantai-papasakojo-ka-is-tikruju-patyre-baltarusijoje.d?id=88724767, accessed 12 January 2022.

'Lithuanians Form "Freedom Way" Human Chain in Solidarity with Belarus Opposition', *Radio Free Europe,* Prague, 23 August 2020. www.rferl.org/a/30798715.html, accessed 24 March 2022.

'Mixed Migration', *Migrationsdatenportal,* 21 February 2022. www.migrationdataportal.org/de/node/3152, accessed 14 March 2022.

Report of the Parliamentary Ombudsperson of the Republic of Lithuania No. NKR-2021/1- of 7 October 2021.

Report of the Republic of Lithuania, 5th and 6th joint periodic report on the implementation of the Convention on the Rights of the Child, CRC/C/LTU/5-6, 9 April 2020.

'Savanoriškas Migrantų Grįžimas į Kilmės Šalis Bus Skatinamas Triskart Didesne Pinigų Suma' ('Voluntary Return of Migrants to States of Origin Shall Be Fostered by Three Times Higher a Sum'), *Migris Electronic Migration Services,* 8 December 2021. www.migracija.lt/-/savanori%C5%A1kas-migrant%C5%B3-gr%C4%AF%C5%BEimas-%C4%AF-kilm%C4%97s-%C5%A1alis-bus-skatinamas-triskart-didesne-pinig%C5%B3-suma, accessed 20 March 2022.

Statement of the Office of the Ombudsperson for Child's Rights on Investigation, on Own Motion, of the Situation of Foreign Migrant Children in Accommodation Centres, 31 December 2021, No. (6.7-2021-45)PR-167.

Statement of the Office of the Ombudsperson for Child's Rights on Investigation, on Own Motion, of the Situation of Unaccompanied Minor Foreigners, 16 November 2021, No. (6.7-2021-42)PR-142.

Statement of the Office of the Ombudsperson for Child's Rights on the Alleged Violations of Rights and Interests of the Children, who Were Refused Entry to the Territory of Lithuania on 2021-11-06 and 2021-12-01, 13 January 2022, No. (6.7.-2021-51/53)PR-3.

UN High Commissioner for Human Rights, 'Situation of Human Rights in Belarus in the Run-up to the 2020 Presidential Election and in its Aftermath' (4 March 2022) A/HRC/49/71.

UNGA, 'Optional Protocol to the Convention on the Rights of the Child on a Communications Procedure' (adopted 19 December 2011, entered into force 14 April 2014, in accordance with article 19(1)) 66th session (2011), A/RES/66/138 for the Lithuanian ratification, see https://e-seimas.lrs.lt/portal/legalAct/lt/TAD/febe0872da9211ecb1b39d276e924a5d?jfwid=hfzmf8tpo, accessed 3 March 2023.

8 Forced migration, gendered violence and the child rights perspective

Modalities of violence against marginalised groups in Turkey

*Rukaya Al Zayani**

1. Introduction

Violence is, for most human beings, an inevitable component of everyday life. We humans inflict, endure, witness and discuss it. But social groups in various situations are differently immersed in violence in their lives, and its modality (how it is experienced and expressed) takes various forms. Investigation reveals a parallel universe of diverse clusters among refugee women and LGBTIQ+ individuals who incur violence, and its impact varies. This chapter addresses the modalities of violence in the lives of asylum-seekers, refugees and immigrants.

My cognitive framing of violence as a phenomenon is influenced by the notion of modality in terms of how violence travels spatially and how we sense, perceive, undergo and embody it. Here, my interpretation is based on people's lived experiences of violence. The notion of modality has its historical roots in philosophy, aesthetics, media studies and comparative literature, to name a few fields.[1] Four modalities – material, sensory, spatiotemporal and semiotic – are derived from media studies, and each has modes. Sensory modality, for example, concerns physical and mental experience through our five senses (sight, hearing, touch, taste and smell), and spatiotemporal modality relates to our sensory perceptions of the material world (virtual, perceptual and cognitive space and time, for example).[2] The modality of violence correlates with sensory modality, temporality and spatiality.

Forced migration and displacement do not generate violence, but they exacerbate it. Being compelled to leave one's home and to separate from others by migrating in search of a refuge intensifies violence. Violence does not 'just happen' and is no random anomaly. Gender-based and all other forms of

* Rukaya Al Zayani is a doctoral student in gender studies at Örebro University researching the modalities of violence against the queer community in Turkey. Rukaya holds an MA in international relations from Istanbul Bilgi University.

1 Lars Elleström, *Media Borders, Multimodality and Intermediality* (Palgrave Macmillan, NY, 2010).

2 Ibid.

DOI: 10.4324/9781003187493-8

violence associated with forced migration and displacement result from conditions, policies and migration agencies' actions.[3] Comprehending and analysing the underlying issues in situations and institutions where violence emerges are essential steps towards its prevention by breaking the vicious circle.

This chapter seeks to highlight the various modalities of violence targeting marginalised groups and individuals, including refugees, children and LGBTIQ+ individuals, in Turkey. 'LGBTIQ+' stands for lesbian, gay, bisexual, trans, intersex, queer and questioning, and the plus sign refers to gender and sexual identities other than the non-heteronormative gender and sexual characteristics specified by the acronym.

The following section illustrates some of my findings about how certain financial assistance policies trigger violence against refugee women, children and LGBTIQ+ individuals in Turkey. During their journey, migrants tend to be subjected to violence by border control regimes and in detention centres, camps, hospitals and bureau offices owing to deficient social welfare policies. They also suffer from policies that enable and reinforce violence against girls and women in particular.[4] The vicious circle of forced migration and displacement causes violence to permeate the private sphere as well.

Refugees are removed from their everyday lives. Their accustomed social norms and familiar circumstances rapidly give way to doubts and challenges posed by the new location: novel demands, different institutions and relationships and often unfamiliar languages and cultures. Refugees find themselves dependent on institutions and individuals in authority who are frequently aware of their vulnerable situation and choose to exploit and abuse them. This dependence creates a power-relationship dynamic between refugees and those who exert control over them.

This chapter also contains an overview of gender issues, focusing particularly on refugee women, girls and LGBTIQ+ individuals obliged to migrate and of intersectionality as a framework for analysing the various modalities of violence. This is followed by an overview, with an intersectional approach, of migrant women, gender aspects of forced migration and gender-based violence. Subsequent sections cover the empirical material I collected during my fieldwork projects in Istanbul in 2018–2020.[5]

1.1. Gender and forced migration

Gender and women are topics that migration analysis has invariably lacked. The male has always been assumed to be the dominant migrant figure.

3 S Buckley-Zistel and U Krause (eds), *Gender, Violence, Refugees* (Berghahn Books, UK, 2017).

4 S Jansen and S Löfving, *Focaal* (Berghahn: Oxford, 2007), 3–14.

5 A small part of the selected material was collected during a research project entitled *Counting Our Losses: Social Entrepreneurship, Refugees and Urban Transformation in Turkey*. The remainder was derived from my MA dissertation, *Intersectionality of Violence: Discrimination and Gender-Based Violence against Syrian Refugees in Turkey*. See https://transcityistanbul.org.

Women's invisibility as migrants used to be a salient feature of migration research and studies, but attitudes changed with the realisation that women have always been migrants. Today, their numbers are rising.[6] The feminisation of migration has rapidly captured researchers' attention, and Castles and Miller cite it as one of the five main trends in contemporary migration.[7]

Women compose 50% of most migratory flows, and in some they outnumber the men. In Europe, for example, women make up nearly 52% of migrants, and the same tendency has characterised North America since the 1970s.[8] Reasons and motives for migration vary, making it difficult – indeed, almost impossible – to generalise about female migration motives and patterns.

Among contemporary women's motives are the wish to migrate, with or without a partner and/or family. Many women migrate for study and work purposes and some to escape from precarious conditions in their countries: poverty, violence, conflict and war. Women's migration experience varies greatly, and any generalisation about the 'feminisation' of migratory trends is elusive. Women's position and agency are major factors influencing their own migratory experience, while other factors include ethnicity, socio-economic category, age and sexual orientation.[9] Thus, the intersectional dynamics of migration play an influential part in women's migration experience. It is crucial to note, too, that this experience is structured by policy regimes and legislation in their countries of origin, transit and arrival. Importantly, this illustrates how processes of local, regional, national and international legislation and regulations shape women's experience.

Kofman (2004) argues that much of the literature on migration ignores the experience of skilled migrants. Migrant experience varies greatly, and it is essential to remember that even the experience of two refugee women diverge greatly according to their journeys and countries of origin, transit and arrival. Nonetheless, connections may be made among the experiences of different migrant women; national policy regimes, for example, have an overall impact on refugee women and families.

To understand the injustices and inequalities that arise in forced migration, a focus on gender is vital. It also illustrates the heteronormative focus of the male as the migrant figure. Donato (2006) traced trends in forced migration that focused solely on the male figure, but also went further by

6 J Freedman, Z Kıvılcım and N Özgür Baklacıoğlu (eds), *A Gendered Approach to the Syrian Refugee Crisis*, Routledge Studies in Development, Mobilities and Migration (London and New York: Routledge, Taylor & Francis Group, 2017).

7 MJ Miller and S Castles, *The Age of Migration: International Population Movements in the Modern World* (Macmillan Press, UK, 1993), 8–9.

8 E Kofman, 'Gendered Global Migrations', *International Feminist Journal of Politics*, 6(4) (2004), 643–665.

9 J Freedman, 'Women's Experience of Forced Migration: Gender-Based Forms of Insecurity and the Uses of "Vulnerability"', in *A Gendered Approach to the Syrian Refugee Crisis*.

examining forced migration in a gendered analysis.[10] Since the 1970s, feminists have been using the term 'gender' to distinguish the socially constructed, binary matrix of femininity and masculinity.

Clearly, migration policies, processes and responses are gendered and tend to make women invisible and portray them as fragile or vulnerable. Currently, we are all observing the overwhelming proportion of women and children among refugees fleeing within and out of Ukraine because of the Russian invasion. With military conscription, Ukraine banned cis men aged 16–60 from leaving the country. The majority of people crossing the borders are therefore women, children and elderly men.[11] This asserts the notion that women, children and the elderly, being fragile, need to be protected. In contrast, trans people are not allowed passage to other countries because their gender identification is not matched by the information on their passports.[12] There are claims that trans women are refused entry and are pushed back from the borders for this reason.[13]

Feminist scholars have challenged the processes in social sciences and policy-making that render refugee women's experience invisible, although these women's agency is of major importance in migration. Similarly, in scholarly research on forced migration there is overrepresentation of men's stories, and women's experiences are interpreted accordingly. Sattel, in his review of Reiter (1975), pointed out the existence of abundant information about women but also the fact that its source was often men's replies to questions about their womenfolk. This information was 'too often presented as a group's reality, rather than only part of a cultural whole', and too often, women and their roles were 'glossed over, under-analysed or absent from all but the edges of the description'.[14]

Contemporary feminists of the period advocated placing women at the centre of analysis to make refugee women's experience visible and combat sexist bias (Stacey and Thorne, 1985). Feminists' advocacy brought about radical progress in Development Studies, which led to parallel gendered analyses of displacement and refugee studies in the 1980s. These

10 KM Donato, D Gabaccia, J Holdaway, M Manalansan and PR Pessar, 'A Glass Half Full? Gender in Migration Studies', *International Migration Review*, 40 (2006), 3–26.

11 The New York Times, 'A Crisis for Mothers: The War in Ukraine Has Led to Familiar, but Heightened, Problems for Women', *The New York Times*, 14 April 2022, www.nytimes.com/2022/04/14/briefing/ukraine-refugeesmotherschildren.html, accessed 18 April 2022.

12 Euronews, '"Lawful Transphobia" Stopping Ukraine's Trans Community from Fleeing', *Euronews*, 22 March 2022, www.euronews.com/2022/03/22/lawful-transphobia-stopping-ukraine-s-trans-community-fromfleeing, accessed 20 April 2022.

13 The Guardian, '"I Will Not Be Held Prisoner": The Trans Women Turned Back at Ukraine's Borders', *The Guardian*, 22 March 2022, www.theguardian.com/global-development/2022/mar/22/i-will-not-be-heldprisoner-the-trans-women-turned-back-at-ukraines-borders, accessed 20 April 2022.

14 JW Sattel, review of RR Reiter, 'Toward an Anthropology of Women', *Contemporary Sociology*, 5(3) (1976), 284.

developments ultimately led to the emergence of the women in forced migration (WIFM) and gender and forced migration (GAFM) paradigms.[15]

In contrast to the emergence of gender-oriented paradigms in scholarship, feminists have criticised the 1951 Geneva Convention, and specifically its definition of 'refugee', which includes 'portraying as universal that which is, in fact, a male paradigm . . . women refugees face rejection of their claims because their experiences of persecution go unrecognized'.[16] Feminist critics of the Convention argue that it is androcentric and heteronormative. Other critiques seek to redefine refugees inclusively in terms of gender and sexual orientation. Although feminist advocacy has directed attention to LGBTIQ+ refugees and asylum-seekers, this is a relatively new area of policy implementation.

Nevertheless, these LGBTIQ+ refugee issues have recently been receiving more attention from scholars and policy-makers,[17] who have begun to highlight challenges and obstacles facing LGBTIQ+ refugees and asylum-seekers in their own countries, during their journeys and upon arrival. Those challenges include homophobia, transphobia, criminalisation of same-sex relationships and persecution of LGBTIQ+ individuals. This persecution has included forced marriage, 'corrective rapes', coercive sterilisation and 'corrective surgery' on intersex individuals.

Recognition of such refugee LGBTIQ+ challenges has led to policy guidelines to accommodate their needs and protection. The UNHCR published its *Guidance Note on Refugee Claims Relating to Sexual Orientation and Gender Identity* in 2008,[18] followed by the *UNHCR Need to Know Guidance on Working with LGBTI Persons* in 2011. Both publications were revised in 2012,[19] but Article 10(1)(d) of the EU's *Qualification Directives*, as revised in 2011, recognises sexual orientation and gender identity as included under 'membership of a particular social group'.[20] Understanding oppression and inequalities based solely on gender facilitates comprehension of how violence is targeted, expressed and experienced.

15 E Fiddian-Qasmiyeh, G Loescher, K Long and N Sigona, 'Gender and Forced Migration', in E Fiddian-Qasmiyeh, G Loescher, K Long and N Sigona (eds), *The Oxford Handbook of Refugee and Forced Migration Studies* (Oxford: Oxford University Press, 2014).

16 J Greatbatch, 'The Gender Difference: Feminist Critiques of Refugee Discourse', *International Journal of Refugee Law*, 1 (1989), 518–527.

17 I Skjelsbæk, 'Sexual Violence and War: Mapping Out a Complex Relationship', *European Journal of International Relations*, 7(2) (2001), 211–237.

18 UNHCR (no date), http://help.unhcr.org/turkey/information-for-syrians/temporary-protection-in-turkey/.

19 UNHCR, 'Working with Lesbian, Gay, Bisexual, Transgender, Intersex and Queer Persons in Forced Displacement' (2011), www.refworld.org/pdfid/4e6073972.pdf.

20 Directive 2011/95/EU of the European Parliament and of the Council of 13 December 2011 on standards for the qualification of third-country nationals or stateless persons as beneficiaries of international protection, for a uniform status for refugees or for persons eligible for subsidiary protection, and for the content of the protection granted.

1.2 Expressions of violence

Conceptually, it is meaningful to think of violence as a phenomenon. As described by Hearn et al. (2020), a regime of violence is an approach developed to 'interrogate if and how the institutionalization and production of violence co-vary to constitute violence regimes and distinct systems'.[21] The theoretical approach to how violence and a violence regime can enable a framework to regulate and govern every domain is, empirically, both challenging and promising. However, it helps to broaden our current conceptualisation of violence rather than limiting its scope, thus minimising and/or neglecting other forms of violence that may be coherent and have a harmful impact.

In addressing violence, significant aspects to consider are the methodological level of a violence regime in allowing broader co-variance with other forms of violence and how far those forms correspond with one another rather than shifting the focus towards other domains, such as civil society. The four manifestations of violence illustrated in Hearn et al. (2020) – 'deadly', 'damaging', 'diffuse' and 'dispersed' – articulate a regime of violence that transcends time and space, without restricting any potential form of violence.

My previous research findings have shown that forms of violence frequently reported by Syrian trans women in Turkey are (1) street violence, (2) kidnapping, (3) transphobia and hate crimes, (4) physical violence and (5) intimate partner violence (IPV). The forms of violence most reported by cis Syrian women, on the other hand, are (1) domestic violence, (2) verbal harassment, (3) psychological violence and (4) structural violence.[22] As mentioned at the beginning of this chapter, certain policies (such as cash assistance) trigger other forms of structural[23] and indirect violence and lead to the manifestation and acceleration of direct and physical violence. Examples are (1) marital rape, (2) coercion and (3) coerced polygamous marriage. It may be observed which forms of violence operate at micro, meso and macro levels, stemming from interpersonal, societal and intergovernmental factors.

Research on the implications of gendered violence in forced migration is structured through tunnel-visioning of the journey, which is thus

21 J Hearn, S Strid, AL Humbert, D Balkmar and M Delaunay, From Gender Regimes to Violence Regimes: Re-thinking the Position of Violence, *Social Politics: International Studies in Gender, State & Society*, 29 (2020), 1–24.

22 'Structural violence', a term coined by John Galtung, a Norwegian sociologist, refers to a form of violence in which social institutions and social structures prevent people from their safeguarding rights and care, and from meeting their own needs. J Galtung, 'Violence, Peace, and Peace Research', *Journal of Peace Research*, 6 (1969), 167–191.

23 S Ocurumez, S Akyuz and H Bradby, 'The Conceptualization Problem in Research and Responses to Sexual and Gender-Based Violence in Forced Migration', *Journal of Gender Studies*, 30 (2021), 66–78.

Table 8.1 The various forms of violence against cisgender Syrian women and girls and Syrian trans women

Cisgender women and girls	*Trans women*
Forms of violence	
Domestic violence	Street violence
Verbal harassment	Kidnapping
Psychological violence	Transphobia
Structural violence	Hate crimes
Coercion	Physical violence
Forced pregnancies/forced marriages	Intimate partner violence (IPV)
Child marriages	Structural violence

overemphasised. Conclusions from general discussions and findings in scholarly literature on sexual and gendered violence give undue emphasis to conflicts and wars and generally exclude postwar and post-conflict sexual and gendered violence and such violence after resettlement and displacement. Conceptualisation of violence is thus fragmented and does not encompass the complexity of gendered violence.[24]

Sexual, gender-based violence (SGBV) is conceptualised with an emphasis on cis women and on protection and only recently came to include LGBTIQ+ folks.[25] Most of the studies focus on the causes and consequences of sexual and physical violence, while fewer have addressed structural and symbolic violence.[26] The focus on and the classification of SGBV in the literature reflects a framework introduced by Skjelsbæk (2001), which assigns SGBV to the contexts of war and conflict, rather than forced migration, and most of the relevant general academic literature concerns war and conflict situations and excludes forced migration.

2. Intersecting forms of violence

During my fieldwork in Istanbul and after finalising the collection of material, I concluded that various modalities of violence both reproduce and reinforce violence. In particular, financial assistance regulations encourage reproduction among Turkey's Syrian community solely for the purpose of eligibility for beneficiary status. Given the sensitivity of this topic, the ethical concerns and the risks of repeated traumatisation, I refrained from asking direct questions about marital rape and/or reproductive coercion.[27] The

24 Sattel, review of Reiter (n 14), 284.

25 Freedman (n 9), 125–141.

26 H Myrttinen, L Khattab and M Charbel, '"Trust No One, Beware of Everyone": Vulnerabilities of LGBTI Refugees in Lebanon', in *A Gendered Approach to the Syrian Refugee Crisis* (2017).

27 Importantly, various women I spoke to referred to coerced pregnancies through their tone and body language. They conveyed a strong impression of ambivalence when they narrated their experience of the cash assistance programme.

term 'intersecting' in the subheading refers not to intersectionality but to the intertwined forms of violence. In this section, I present my findings thematically, in terms of the emerging forms of violence.

2.1. Coercive reproduction and marriage, unregistered marriage and child marriage

Having children as a proxy means of coping with forced migration has been a common practice among Turkey's Syrian community. A Syrian woman told me her opinion about bringing more children into the world.

> We've heard of this a lot, and we've seen it a lot too. There are people that have children around the ages of seven and eight, and they're still conceiving more children. . . . They have five children in total. I'm against this. It's not logical . . . okay, you are receiving extra money now but aren't you going to spend that money on the new-born? The child brings a lot of expenses. Now, I have two kids and, because of the current situation, I don't want to have another child.
>
> (24-year-old Syrian woman, Yedikule)[28]

At a local Turkish NGO where I conducted interviews, the project coordinator stressed the domestic issues that arise because of such practices:

> Her husband told her: 'I'll divorce you and kick you out of the house and I'll get another one [wife] to conceive a baby with. It's your choice!'
>
> (Project Coordinator, Cultural Centre, Yedikule)

Unregistered marriages are common among the Syrian community in Turkey, and such marriages are also often early and/or forced ones. All the Syrian women I have interviewed referred to their daughters' marriages by saying (in Arabic) 'I married her off', showing how the family view young women and girls as a financial burden, instead of 'She got married', which would have shown willingness and independent agency for the bride's part. Although in Turkey's Syrian community, the reasons are far more complex and may involve various factors, the common practice of forced and early marriage has served to ease financial burdens and also to protect the daughter and safeguard her future. According to the literature, such marriages are arranged to protect young women and girls from sexual assault and to protect the 'family honour'. Early and forced marriages are more common in camps.[29]

28 Yedikule ('Seven Towers'), part of the Fatih district of Istanbul, is named after its seven-towered fortress.

29 Freedman et al. (n 6).

A 45-year-old Syrian mother I interviewed in the Association for Solidarity with Asylum Seekers and Immigrants (ASAM)[30] informed me that her 20-year-old daughter had been 'married off' to another Syrian man, who had subjected her to abuse.

> My daughter Fatma got a divorce, and her husband is threatening us with a mafia. He is threatening us with other things too, so I came here for a consultation. My daughter doesn't have a marriage certificate, they can't help us.
>
> (45-year-old Syrian mother, ASAM)

According to the mother, she tried to seek legal help through ASAM. Owing to the nature of the marriage, which was not registered in court and was conducted through a religious ceremony, no legal help is available. When I asked about the nature of the marriage, the Syrian mother informed me that this practice is quite common in the Syrian community in Turkey. Upon arrival in the country, her Syrian neighbours informed her that this was the norm for getting married in the community, but there may be other reasons this practice has been widespread. The mother went on to narrate how it happened:

> They fooled us, darling. He told us if we get an official marriage in court, the Syrian regime will take away my son and his life will depend on the Syrian regime. They fooled us, they fooled her father, fooled her brother. We're isolated, we didn't know what her rights are. The regime will take our son away from us and his papers will end up with the regime . . . I don't know . . . whenever I asked, the neighbours said no one's getting an official marriage, they said we're all getting married without a marriage certificate.
>
> (45-year-old Syrian mother, ASAM)

When I asked about early/forced marriages and child marriages, the programme director and the NGO's psychologist informed me that those cases are monitored within the organisation. When I asked whether they consider child and early marriages forms of forced marriage, they informed me that they are all forced, because consent is lacking. According to the organisation, there are two reasons this practice has increased sharply among the Syrian community in Turkey.

> The families are afraid that something bad will happen to their daughters, so they force them to get married and most of the husbands are relatives, first cousins. The family have this mindset if their daughter

30 ASAM is a non-profit humanitarian NGO in Turkey that provides help and support to refugees, asylum-seekers and internally displaced individuals.

stays within their family, she's going to be safe and protected, I think that's the main motive. The second motive is a financial motive . . . because marrying someone off would mean there will be less burden in the household and that will somehow enhance their financial situation.
(psychologist, Mavi Kalem)[31]

Child marriage and child pregnancies tend to be invisible. Refugee Rights Turkey's child officer informed me that the organisation finds out about a child's pregnancy only when the girl gives birth in hospital:

> We mostly know about child marriages when the child gives birth in hospital. Before that it was not easy to see child marriage because it's not registered. When a child gives birth in hospital, the hospital authorities, like the hospital's social services, need to call the prosecution office and there should be some implementation of that, depending on the child's age and consent as well.
> (child officer, Refugees Rights Turkey)

Throughout the conversation, the child officer informed me about the laws and regulations in Turkey regarding child protection and violence against women. However, according to the officer, implementation was inadequate:

> In law everything is great, especially for foreigners and international protection. There are good articles about asylum, but we can't see it all being implemented. If you look at the news, you'll see the difference. Maybe you followed the recent cases of the two women who were abused and killed by their husbands or partners . . . we can clearly see that law enforcement officers don't do their work well. If a woman gets murdered by her partner, we see that in the process there were many things that should have been done but were never done by the police, authorities, prosecutors and so on.
> (child officer, Refugee Rights Turkey)

Most child marriages were between cousins and/or other family members, according to the Mavi Kalem psychologist. The age gap between the spouses ranges from a few years to up to ten. When I asked whether they considered it a form of incest, they had no hesitation in saying no. The programme director identified another dimension of this problem:

> I witnessed a childcare provider (that's more like a legal caregiver) marrying the child. . . . They're not related but, according to the law, the

31 Mavi Kalem ('Blue Pen') is a local Turkish NGO located in the Balat area of Fatih, Istanbul. Established by a group of volunteers in Düzce, Turkey and later relocated in Balat as a hub of internal migration, Mavi Kalem provides psychosocial support for women and children.

> person was a caregiver and because of that it's also considered incest. We saw two or three cases.
>
> (programme director, Mavi Kalem)

According to the material collected, incest intersects with marriage within the family, and early or forced marriage intersects with financial instability. Most of the Syrian women I interviewed had married early, at the age of 16 or 17. The majority came from a rural background, with elementary to middle-school educational attainment, except for one woman who was illiterate. Although reasons for early marriage in Syria have cultural dimensions, it did not take place on an extremely large scale. According to UNICEF, before the Syrian war broke out, 17.7% of girls married below the age of 18 and 3.4% below 15.[32]

Gender oppression, inequality and constructed gender relations impose societal expectations of how women should act, live their lives and behave, not only in society but in a family unit.[33] Gendered patriarchal cultural norms and expectations reinforce violence against women. This often results from societal attitudes that consider men superior to women. The result is the rigid dominance of men in the world and the power endowed to them to make decisions about women's livelihoods and how family units should function and behave in the real world.[34] That increases the inequality gap between sexes and genders. Women are expected to follow the expectations of a worldview put forward by the patriarchal system, to which they are also expected to be amenable. As for Syrian women and girls, according to the material collected, although they are expected to follow the constructed patriarchal societal norms, in forced migration, these norms shift towards survival mechanisms and sacrifices to sustain a liveable life.

2.2 Lived experiences of violence in the private sphere and gendered immobility in state shelters in Istanbul

A project coordinator at a local Turkish NGO in Yedikule stressed that domestic violence is an issue that is extremely sensitive topic of discussion. The organisation lacks the training courses and support to provide psychological help to refugee women who have been subjected to gender-based

32 Central Bureau of Statistics/UNICEF, *'TO PROTECT HER HONOUR': Child Marriage in Emergencies – The Fatal Confusion between Protecting Girls and Sexual Violence* (Care Child Marriage in Emergencies, May), https://resourcecentre.savethechildren.net/document/protect-her-honour-child-marriage-emergencies-fatal-confusion-between-protecting-girls-and/, accessed 10 February 2022.

33 D Western, 'A Conceptual and Contextual Background for Gender-Based Violence and Depression in Women', in *Gender-based Violence and Depression in Women*, by Deborah Western (Caufield East, Victoria: Springer New York, 2013), 1–101.

34 Ibid., 27.

violence.[35] The project coordinator emphasised that women do not feel safe living with their husbands:

> Maybe around three women out of ten are being subjected to gender-based violence at their homes by their husbands.
>
> (project coordinator, Cultural Centre, Yedikule)

According to another Turkish NGO that supports refugees by providing legal aid, a majority of the Syrian women beneficiaries sought assistance from the organisation to divorce their abusive husbands:

> Syrian women have sought our help mostly to divorce their husbands because of domestic violence and emotional, psychological and physical abuse. For these reasons, they also contact our organisation to change their cities of registration because they have someone who is harassing them in the city where they're registered. As you know, they can't just change the city where they registered in.
>
> (child officer, Refugee Rights Turkey)

Syrian refugees are not allowed to move from their city of registration in Turkey to another province. Major cities in Turkey are closed for registration, and many Syrian refugees are not allowed to travel to other cities without a permit.[36] The child protection officer informed me that many Syrian minors flee their homes because of domestic violence. There is also a gendered dimension to Syrian minors fleeing from domestic violence: according to the child protection officer, 80% of the minor beneficiaries are male. The low percentage of girls is due to cultural control, which restricts their mobility. Girls' movements are therefore much more limited than boys'. Refugee Rights Turkey's child officer stressed that some Syrian girls have sought refuge in a state shelter because of domestic abuse and child marriage and that, given the gendered nature of Turkish state shelters, the girls' mobility was restricted:

> They're mostly locked in the shelter because they are girls. They can't use their mobile phones and they only have one day off. It is more like

35 It is worth mentioning that at the time of the fieldwork project, I observed that there is a language barrier in the centre. The staff spoke Turkish and English, and the refugee women spoke only Arabic. The founder of the centre spoke Arabic, and I was told that refugee women were not comfortable talking about problems they face at home because the founder was a man. The language barrier also imposes limitations on how refugee women report issues.

36 European Council on Refugees and Exiles, 2019. See UNHCR, https://help.unhcr.org/turkey/information-for-syrians/reception-and-registration-with-the-turkish-authorities/, and Human Rights Watch, www.hrw.org/news/2018/07/16/turkey-stops-registering-syrian-asylum-seekers.

> prison than a shelter. This information came from the girls from the shelter.
>
> (child officer, Refugee Rights Turkey)

Gendered inequality and control in state shelters raise many concerns about the livelihoods of women and girls on the one hand and abuse due to lack of transparency and monitoring by local organisations on the other:

> We weren't allowed to go into the shelters, but we were more able to visit the shelters where male unaccompanied minors stay. Those are state policies. And the girls were staying with other Turkish girls, but there are more special shelters for male refugees and male foreigners in Istanbul than for girls. As you can imagine, female children are more vulnerable to abuse, so they are more careful with NGOs. For political reasons, an NGO that was established by the wife of the president was allowed to enter shelters more easily than us.
>
> (child officer, Refugee Rights Turkey)

Violence, both gender based and otherwise, has been a common practice in detention centres, shelters and camps. An exploitative discourse prevails, so that these gendered issues are not perceived as a serious problem by nation-states, although violations of human rights are involved. Common European Asylum System (CEAS) directives indicate the obligation of taking gendered issues into consideration, but in practice these directives have only slightly improved refugee women's livelihoods and protection in European asylum systems. Victims and survivors of gender-based violence face both legal and practical obstacles within European asylum systems when they try to exercise their rights by, for example, accessing services and protection.[37]

A 30-year-old single Syrian mother I had interviewed at ASAM in a previous fieldwork project revealed to me that her ex-husband was physically abusing her and her children. It went on until the landlord evicted her from her home because of neighbours' complaints, alleging that she was causing a lot of problems as grounds for the eviction. At the time of the interview (in 2018), her ex-husband kept threatening to take away her children. The woman sobbed throughout the interview as she talked about her suffering and the state of limbo she has been in.

> I live in fear. I live in terror because of the threats from his relatives. They're all threatening me.
>
> (30-year-old Syrian single mother, ASAM)

Although the single mother was divorced, she was waiting for the judge to issue the final decree. This was the last document required for the UNCHR

37 Freedman (n 9).

third-country resettlement programme, and the waiting period made her feel extremely insecure:

> I really feel that my fate is unknown, I don't know what will happen by then, what my situation will be like, and how I'll manage to stay in Turkey. I have four children and they aren't responsible for all of this. I spoke to my lawyer, and I started crying a lot. . . . I went and told him I have four children and I'm on my own. I ended up in the street and the government will take five months to sign my divorce certificate. . . . What am I going to do during these five months? On top of all of this, the actual process of processing my papers, the system . . . the government . . . something has to be done about this, fast.
>
> (30-year-old Syrian single mother, ASAM)

A Syrian woman confided her problems to a project coordinator who was concerned about her absence and her lack of activity and motivation at the centre.

> 'Why don't you come every week?' I ask. Then they say: 'My husband doesn't like me coming here every time, even though he is working. He doesn't want me to spend my time outside the house.'
>
> (project coordinator, Cultural Centre, Yedikule)

Forced migration and flight from a war have created a space for allowing such practices as early marriage to breed more violence and abuse. The psychologist from Kadınlarla Dayanışma Vakfı (KADAV,[38] the Women's Solidarity Foundation) concluded that forced migration exacerbates violence:

> Violence is the gun of the system, rape is the gun of the system, against women and LGBTI+. The people that are in power are using violence as a gun. Sexual violence especially is increasing in wartime, against not only women but men as well. In prisons, during the migration journey, while you're transitioning from one country to another, it exists in the military, practised by military forces and religious groups. They're all using this gun against marginalised people.
>
> (psychologist, KADAV)

Forms of violence inflicted on Syrian women and girls range from domestic violence, forced marriage, child marriage and reproductive coercion to structural violence and threats of violence. These shape their livelihoods and lived experiences in Turkey. Inadequate protection and life in a closed community further intensify violence against women and girls.

38 KADAV, a Turkish NGO, provides legal aid, gender-based violence support, psychosocial support and shelter to women in Turkey.

2.3 Violence is not binary: Syrian LGBTIQ+ and sex worker refugees

The various forms of violence that target Syrian LGBTIQ+ individuals are multifaceted. The shifting, intersecting dynamics of violence form a combination that includes violence inflicted spatially and across cyberspace.

According to the KADAV psychologist, Syrian LGBTIQ+ people have been subjected to online violence. Specifically, they have received unsolicited online threats and text messages from family members and people in extremist groups such as ISIS. According to KADAV's psychologist, ISIS-affiliated members uncover the LGBTIQ+ individuals' identity in various ways. First, living in a closed community may increase their chances of finding out who their victims are. Second, family members in Syria confront LGBTIQ+ people about their sexual orientation, causing them to flee to Turkey to escape violence, possible prosecution and other repercussions. Because of stigmatisation, the family in Syria arranges a deal with ISIS-affiliated individuals located in Turkey to threaten and harass the LGBTIQ+ individuals.

> When they come out, generally, families begin to threaten the person. Many of these people, facing violence and abuse from family members, escape this by smuggling themselves into Turkey. Of course, some similar events have taken place when the LGBTI+ person runs away. Some families make arrangements with organisations to find the person, and in most cases, murder them. Sometimes this is done directly by an extremist religious group, without any deal being arranged. When these Syrians arrive in Istanbul or any other Turkish city, the group finds their mobile phone numbers and harass[es] them with threatening text messages. Or if they find their social media accounts and specific content that shows the person is 'gay' or 'acts gay', they use the content to threaten the person with blackmail. So many people constantly change their mobile phones and social media accounts. As you know, it's a very closed community, so it's not easy to 'run away'. Many have been harassed in real life too, stalked and followed.
>
> (psychologist, KADAV)

Living in a closed community can both provide a safe space and enable violence. In most cases, closed communities are a safe space for cis heterosexual men, protecting them from other men. Forced migration fosters and intensifies violence, and living in a closed community can exacerbate violence against marginalised groups.

The behaviour, intentions and acts of individuals are also crucial for understanding and analysing violence as a phenomenon. According to a 23-year-old bisexual Syrian girl in Mersin, one of her gay-identifying Syrian friends was threatened and stalked by an ISIS member in Gaziantep.[39]

39 Gaziantep is a province located in southwestern Turkey, bordering Syria.

Living in a closed and crowded community there, the person's sexual orientation and identity were exposed. A neighbour found out about his sexual orientation and proceeded to threaten, stalk and terrorise him.

> Some of his neighbours found out that he was gay. One of them is an ISIS member. My friend lived in Gaziantep. . . . The ISIS man used to scare my friend. Sometimes he waited until my friend came out of the house, and then he broke in. He didn't steal anything; it was just a way of scaring my friend away by showing him that he knows about him. The ISIS man would send him text messages saying he knows when my friend is inside the house and when he's out, and telling him things like 'I'm watching you and I know everything.' My friend was terrified, and used to sleep with the lights on. He changed house two or three times, but the man still followed and terrorised him . . . that man was real.
>
> (23-year-old bisexual Syrian woman, Mersin)

Online violence is an acute problem that targets Syrian LGBTIQ+ individuals in Turkey. I interviewed staff at Hêvî LGBT[40] (the Kurdish word *hêvî* means 'hope'), an LGBTIQ+ NGO in Istanbul concerned with online and digital violence. The coordinator informed me that this kind of violence against Syrian LGBTIQ+ individuals in Turkey has been increasing sharply. The social worker affirmed the allegations that Syrian LGBTIQ+ are threatened by Islamic groups and/or people affiliated with them, mostly ISIS. Syrian LGBTIQ+ people are threatened by unsolicited text messages, online harassment and abuse that culminate in physical stalking, and many have had to change their phone numbers and accommodation.

> We have a beneficiary in Urfa, Turkey. She contacted us from Urfa because she was being threatened by her family and a religious group there. We appointed a lawyer, who tried many ways to help her out, but we can't do more than that. Because LGBT killings and murders in Turkey aren't considered hate crimes, it's like telling the woman [beneficiary]: 'Go and die, and then we'll see what we can do about it.'
>
> (social worker, Hêvî LGBT)

The staff at Hêvî LGBT related that Syrian trans women face physical and sexual violence by clients and intimate partners and are subjected to street violence as well. Syrian trans sex workers find clients[41] in the Tarlabaşı[42]

40 Hêvî LGBT is a local NGO that provides support and legal aid to LGBTI+ people in Turkey.

41 The social worker from Hêvî LGBT informed me, at the time of the fieldwork project, that Syrian trans sex workers charge as low as 20–30 Turkish Liras (EUR 1.15–1.73) and up to a maximum of 50 Turkish Liras (EUR 2.88).

42 Tarlabaşı, part of the district of Beyoglu in Istanbul, is dominated by dilapidated buildings, gentrification, poverty, homelessness, sex work and illegal drugs.

area in Istanbul, which is known for its gentrification, sex work and poverty. Syrian sex workers are marginalised in society and even more so in their sex work because of their social status and identity. According to Hêvî LGBT, 80% of the sex workers in Tarlabaşı are Syrian.

When I approached the former manager of Aman Shelter for an interview, he told me about the various intersectional forms of violence that Syrian trans women face on a daily basis in Istanbul. Given the fact that Syrians tend to live in a closed community, an aggravating amount of homophobia and transphobia is highly likely to occur. According to the manager of the LGBTI+ shelter, Syrian trans women and sex workers prefer to live in the Taksim area, mainly because Taksim is not populated by Syrian refugees, and they prefer to live away from areas populated by Syrians for safety reasons. Moving away from the community could serve as a protection mechanism to protect one's identity and liberty; however, it could cause more isolation. According to Aman's former manager, Syrian trans women prefer to stay away from the Syrian community as much as possible, and the Syrian trans community tries to avoid potential interactions with fellow Syrians. Violence against Syrian trans women takes various intertwined forms, the most frequently reported being IPV; if they are sex workers, violent acts perpetrated by clients; street violence; and transphobia. IPV was mentioned five times in the interview with the ex-shelter manager, while incidents of IPV were also reported to have taken place both inside and outside the shelter.

> A trans woman was beaten by her ex-boyfriend. She was wounded, her eyes were injured and swollen, she was beaten up!
>
> (ex-manager, Aman LGBTI)

The manager informed me that there had been a kidnap situation where a trans woman was kidnapped by one of her clients and kept captive for three consecutive days, until she escaped to the shelter. Police protection for trans women is conspicuously absent. According to the material I collected and the stories told to me, trans women are ignored and invalidated by authorities and belittled and dehumanised by the police. When the former shelter manager went to report the kidnapping to the police, the police officers said: 'How do you know she was kidnapped? Give us proof!' And when a group of trans women were assaulted by a group of people in Taksim Square, the police dismissed the victims by shouting: 'Get out of here! You're prostitutes'.

Evidently, protection and support for victimised trans sex workers are lacking. Their absence aggravates the violence against trans sex workers. The intersectional identities of Syrian trans sex workers are important in an examination of the abuse and injustices that take place. Their primary identity is as Syrian trans sex workers in an intolerant society, while being a refugee is secondary.

Violence takes place in both public and private spaces. According to the material I have gathered and analysed, transphobia intersects with hate crime. A surge in this kind of crime can occur at any given moment in the streets of Tarlabaşı. The absence of police protection enables more violent acts and crimes against trans women. Hate crimes can occur at any time, and the scale of the personal danger and risk for sex workers creates an omnipresent atmosphere of menace. Many of the perpetrators were not clients or intimate partners; some of the violent acts were committed by strangers in the street.

> The other assaults were carried out by strangers, and once by a taxi driver. They ganged up on two transwomen and beat them.
>
> (Aman LGBTI shelter manager)

The material I have analysed illustrates the harm and violence perpetrated against Syrian trans sex workers. In public, street violence is the manifestation; in private, intimate partner violence predominates. Violence against trans women embodies various modalities. The patriarchal system views gender as binary – two binary genders at the ends of the spectrum, blurring every other gender identity that exists outside the heterosexual and heteronormative matrix. Not only does the system oppress people who do not adhere to heteronormative norms of gender; it also provides scope for further injustice to take place.

According to my observations, violence, abuse and injustices towards Syrian LGBTI+ emerge from the social presence of homophobia and transphobia among the local population, people in authority and the Syrian local community. Homophobia and transphobia transcend all social and ethnic divisions and are sharply evident in the lives of LGBTIQ+ individuals. Trans women are exposed to violence from the police, on the streets, from clients, in the community and by intimate partners. The lack of protection for LGBTIQ+ people in Turkey intersects with regulations on temporary protection in the country.

3. Conclusion

This chapter has addressed the lived experiences of Syrian refugees, as narrated by project officers, NGO staff and social workers in Turkey within the scope of a fieldwork project in Istanbul. In response to the stated aim of this chapter, I have explicitly addressed the various modalities of violence that targets refugees in their everyday lives in Istanbul. Everyday violence takes place in their homes, in the streets and in shelters and is structurally facilitated by authorities, regulations and subtle embodied norms.

Violence transcends our social and political realms at macro, meso and micro levels. The levels and dichotomies of different modalities of violence vary by gender, and the forms of violence most reported by cis Syrian women are discrimination, domestic violence, verbal harassment, psychological abuse, structural violence, reproductive coercion and forced marriage. The forms of violence most reported by LGBTIQ+ individuals are street violence, kidnapping, hate crime, sexual assault and/or rape, physical violence, intimate partner violence and structural violence.

In terms of social policies and crisis response, what is needed is a focus on the lived experiences of marginalised groups. The purpose is, by contextualising their embodied experiences of navigating forced migration and experiencing violence, to formulate an approach to enhance these groups' livelihoods. Only when we understand how violence operates at macro, meso and micro levels, and its repercussions at the level of individual lived experience, can this be achieved.

List of references

Literature

Buckley-Zistel, S and Krause, U (eds), *Gender, Violence, Refugees*. Berghahn Books. 2017.

Çelik, Ç and White, H, 'Forced Migration and Protection: Turkey's Domestic Responses to the Syrian Refugees', *European Review*, 1, UK, 2021.

Directive 2011/95/EU of the European Parliament and of the Council of 13 December 2011 on standards for the qualification of third-country nationals or stateless persons as beneficiaries of international protection, for a uniform status for refugees or for persons eligible for subsidiary protection, and for the content of the protection granted, 18.

Donato, KM et al, 'A Glass Half Full? Gender in Migration Studies', *International Migration Review*, 40, 3, 2006.

Elleström, L and Bruhn, J, *Media Borders, Multimodality and Intermediality*. Palgrave Macmillan. UK, 2010.

Facundo Cuevas, P, Kaan Inan, O, Twose, A and Çelik C, 'Vulnerability and Protection of Refugees in Turkey: Findings from the Rollout of the Largest Humanitarian Cash Assistance Program in the World', World Bank. 2019. https://reliefweb.int/report/turkey/vulnerability-and-protection-refugees-turkey-findings-rollout-largest-humanitarian.

Fiddian-Qasmiyeh, E et al, 'Gender and Forced Migration', in Fiddian-Qasmiyeh, E et al. (eds), *The Oxford Handbook of Refugee and Forced Migration Studies*. Oxford University Press. UK, 2014.

Freedman, J, 'Women's Experience of Forced Migration: Gender-Based Forms of Insecurity and the Uses of "Vulnerability" ', in Freedman, J et al. (eds) *A Gendered Approach to the Syrian Refugee Crisis*. Routledge, Taylor & Francis Group, UK, 2017.

Freedman, J, Kivilcim, Z and Özgür Baklacioğlu, N (eds), *A Gendered Approach to the Syrian Refugee Crisis*. Routledge, Taylor & Francis Group. UK, 2017.

Galtung, J, 'Violence, Peace, and Peace Research', *Journal of Peace Research*, 6, 167, 1969.

Greatbatch, J, 'The Gender Difference: Feminist Critiques of Refugee Discourse', *International Journal of Refugee Law*, 1, 518, 1989.

Jansen, S and Löfving, S, 'Introduction', *Focaal*, 3, 2007.

Kilby, J, 'Introduction to Special Issue: Theorizing Violence', *European Journal of Social Theory*, 16, 261, 2013.

Kofman, E, 'Gendered Global Migrations', *International Feminist Journal of Politics*, 6, 643, 2004.

McCall, L, 'The Complexity of Intersectionality', *Signs: Journal of Women in Culture and Society*, 30, 1771, 2005.

Miller, MJ and Castles, S, *The Age of Migration: International Population Movements in the Modern World*. Macmillan Press. UK, 1993.

Myrttinen, H, Khattab, L and Maydaa, C, '"Trust No One, Beware of Everyone": Vulnerabilities of LGBTI Refugees in Lebanon', in Freedman, J, Kivilcim, Z and Özgür Baklacioğlu, N (eds), *A Gendered Approach to the Syrian Refugee Crisis*. Routledge Taylor & Francis Group. UK, 2017.

Ozocerites, S, Akyuz, S and Bradby, H, 'The Conceptualization Problem in Research and Responses to Sexual and Gender-Based Violence in Forced Migration', *Journal of Gender Studies*, 30, 66, 2021.

Sattel, JW, review of Reiter RR, 'Toward an Anthropology of Women', *Contemporary Sociology*, 5, 284, 1976.

Skjelsbæk, I, 'Sexual Violence and War: Mapping Out a Complex Relationship', *European Journal of International Relations*, 7(2), 211, 2001.

Sosa, L, *Intersectionality in the Human Rights Legal Framework on Violence against Women: At the Centre or the Margins?* Cambridge: Cambridge University Press. 2017.

The Guardian, '"I Will Not Be Held Prisoner": The Trans Women Turned Back at Ukraine's Borders', 22 March 2022. www.theguardian.com/global-development/2022/mar/22/i-will-not-be-held-prisoner-the-trans-women-turned-back-at-ukraines-borders, accessed 20 April 2022.

The New York Times, 'A Crisis for Mothers: The War in Ukraine Has Led to Familiar, but Heightened, Problems for Women', *New Your Times*, 14 April 2022. www.nytimes.com/2022/04/14/briefing/ukraine-refugees-mothers-children.html, accessed 18 April 2022.

Turkish Red Crescent Society, 'Emergency Social Net Safety Offering a Lifeline to Vulnerable Refugees in Turkey', 2018. www.ifrc.org/emergency-social-safety-net-essn, accessed 8 February 2022.

Vogt, WA, 'Lives in Transit: Violence and Intimacy on the Migrant Journey', *California Series in Public Anthropology*, 267, 2018.

Walby, S, 'Violence and Society: Introduction to an Emerging Field of Sociology', *Current Sociology*, 61, 95, 2013.

Other sources

CARE, 'To Protect Her Honour: Child Marriage in Emergencies – The Fatal Confusion between Protecting Girls and Sexual Violence', International and Central Bureau of Statistics/UNICEF, May 2015. https://resourcecentre.savethechildren.net/document/protect-her-honour-child-marriage-emergencies-fatal-confusion-between-protecting-girls-and/ accessed 10 February 2022.

Euronews, '"Lawful Transphobia" Stopping Ukraine's Trans Community from Fleeing', 22 March 2022. www.euronews.com/2022/03/22/lawful-transphobia-stopping-ukraine-s-trans-community-from-fleeing, accessed 20 April 2022.

European Council on Refugees and Exiles, 'Turkey: Mass Detention Following Istanbul Push for Return of Refugees to "Satellite Cities"', August 2019. https://ecre.org/turkey-mass-detention-following-istanbul-push-for-return-of-refugees-to-satellite-cities/

European Institute for Gender Equality (EIGE), *Intersecting inequalities: Gender Equality Index,* 2019. https://eige.europa.eu/publications/intersecting-inequalities-gender-equality-index, accessed 12 February 2022.
UNHCR, 'Registration with the Turkish Authorities'. https://help.unhcr.org/turkey/information-for-syrians/reception-and-registration-with-the-turkish-authorities/, http://help.unhcr.org/turkey/information-for-syrians/temporary-protection-in-turkey/.
UNHCR, 'Working with Lesbian, Gay, Bisexual, Transgender, Intersex and Queer Persons in Forced Displacement', www.refworld.org/pdfid/4e6073972.pdf.

9 Child rights respect

Global pandemics call for conscious change

*Cornelia C. Walther**

1. Introduction – the issue

This chapter briefly lays out the contours of a novel approach to social change for the realization of all rights for all children. Although applicable in all circumstances, this perspective is particularly relevant in case of crisis, such as most recently the COVID pandemic and shortly after it the war in Ukraine.

COVID-19 is a reminder that humans around the world are fundamentally all the same: the result of four dimensions – soul, heart, mind and body, which find their expression in aspirations, emotions, thoughts and sensations, thus influencing their experiences and expressions. Through these four dimensions, which constantly interact and impact each other, each person reflects the four dimensions of the society in which they evolve. The latter not only influences who they are and become but it is influenced by them in return. Nothing happens in a vacuum. Individuals are part of communities that form countries, which together with the natural environment constitute planet Earth; they are an integral part of the universe. Micro, meso, macro, meta – everything is connected. Adopting this perspective makes the abstract statement that 'we can change the world' a concrete and pragmatic undertaking that begins at the core of the centre, with the aspiration of individuals to realize the rights of everyone everywhere.[1]

The individual and collective dimensions of human existence stand in a constant interplay, which can be understood and systematically addressed in view of gradual optimization. Optimization is an ongoing process, which can be pursued systematically. It is necessary to achieve and sustain the universal respect and realization of all rights for all children. Accepting and

* Cornelia C. Walther, PhD. Following two decades with the United Nations, Dr Cornelia C. Walther founded the POZE movement in Haiti, from where it has spread around the world. Based between Europe and the United States, she has published multiple books and presently concentrates on scaling POZE whilst offering executive coaching to non-profit leaders.

1 C Walther, *Development, Humanitarian Aid and Social Welfare* (Palgrave Macmillan, 2020a).

DOI: 10.4324/9781003187493-9

addressing such a logic of interconnectedness serves everyone involved; it is crucial for children to survive and thrive and essential for humanity to fulfil its potential of prosperity.

Each individual child regardless of their race or location, socio-economic background or special needs, represents a part of the micro dimension that stands at the centre of everything else and must receive special care and protection. This has been recognized in the legal space. The Convention on the Rights of the Child (CRC) has found a reflection in various regional and national legal instruments in almost all countries. From families to schools, children are constitutive components of society, and, at least in theory, they are to be respected as such. The recognition of their status as rights-holders in general in terms of human rights, and as especially protected human beings thanks to international treaties such as the CRC and its related protocols, must be considered as part of a framework that can be enforced, not just paid lip service to.

The politically thorny and practically challenging part of the equation that links entitlement and enforcement or obligation and fulfilment, theory and practice, arises with further acuity in a (situation of) natural disaster or armed conflict where the formal duty-bearer (state/macro) is unable to address the entitlements of their citizens (individual/micro). This will be touched upon here yet not explored in depth, since the focus is on the shift from obligation to desire. Here we concentrate on the voluntary action taken by individuals to respect not only the *rights* of others but to invest their own *resources* in line with the values that underpin these *rights*; this behaviour is anchored on the one hand in awareness of the risk that derives from inaction and on the other hand in an acute understanding of the *responsibilities* deriving from one's own human nature.

Durable social change starts at the centre (individuals) and is nurtured from the periphery (external factors) through a web of interactions between manifold dimensions. Analysing the interactions that are conducive to the respect of children's legal entitlements (enshrined rights) and the actual manifestation of these rights or, inversely, the gap between theory and practice (unsatisfied needs), the present chapter offers a holistic framework to assess and addresses the organic interplay of individuals, institutions, countries and society overall. What follows is based on the POZE paradigm,[2]

2 POZE has various meanings. In particular it reflects the paradigm's 1) outcomes: perspective (a holistic view on life), optimization (through influence on the dimensions that shape existence), zeniths (the gradual progression towards ones best self), exposure (experience of reality as it is) and its 2) parameters: purpose (the innate quest for meaning which expresses the human soul), om (the universally recognized word of emotional harmony), zoom (a focus on the essential), expression (the translation of our inner reality in the world); The noun 'poze' translates as 'inner peace' in Haitian Creole. 'Poze' reflects the prototype of the approach in Haiti 2017, which planted the seeds for an expanding network of likeminded thinkers and doers around the world (P-O-Z-E: People On Zenith Exploration).

which addresses change from the inside out – with the aspiration of individuals for meaning, whilst nurturing it from the outside in, with the expressions and experiences deriving from this quest. Fulfilling the latter echoes deference to the legal obligations deriving from the legal framework dedicated to protecting and promoting the rights of those who cannot protect themselves, such as children.

Beyond formal duty-bearers, a natural responsibility arises from our human nature to care for others (Haidt, 2016).[3] The benefits that derive from respecting this responsibility – which has partially found a reflection in the collective dimension of certain rights (Section 2.3) – are mutual, in the sense that they are there for the one who fulfils the duty as well as the one for whom that duty is fulfilled.[4] Respecting everyone's rights lies in everyone's ultimate interest. In a society marked by inequality, everyone is worse off, including those at the top of the food chain.[5]

Human rights have been fought for by generations, yet they remain at risk of being drained of all content. Unfortunately, the influence of formal rules that are not respected is worse than the missed potential of rules that were never put in place.[6] Theory and practice rely on each other. One is mired without the other; just like soul and body, expertise and expression, theory and practice are pairs that complement each other. The Universal Declaration of Human Rights (UDHR) and the CRC have been signed and ratified by almost all member states of the United Nations, and yet the rights of billions of individuals are disregarded or openly violated every day. The existence of these rights is an asset but does not equal a game that is won.

The ongoing pandemic represents a conundrum because it has put the spotlight on a systemic social paradox that has been lingering for centuries due to human inertia in the face of suffering. The acute crisis that was triggered by COVID is compounded by a chronic crisis that is the result of individual and collective inaction.[7] Inequality is rising and thriving; human rights in general and children's rights in particular are neglected and abused. Moving through this schism together is an opportunity to grow,

3 J Haidt, 'The Moral Roots of Liberals and Conservatives', TED (2006), https://rb.gy/fep1gt, accessed August 2020.

4 C Walther, 'Le droit au service de l'enfant', University d'Aix-Marseille, 2014.

5 RG Wilkinson and K Pickett, *The Spirit Level: Why More Equal Societies Almost Always Do Better* (Allen Lane, New York, 2009).

6 When people experience that official rules are disregarded by others without consequences, they are inclined to follow their example, especially if respect of the rule comes with a cost or involves discomfort. Gradually a disregarded norm can thus erode the collective normative setting. The attitude towards bribery in many countries, where corruption is forbidden according to the national law yet widely practised by government officials, businesses and individuals illustrates that. C Bicchieri, *Norms in the Wild. How to Diagnose, Measure, and Change Social Norms* (Oxford: Oxford University Press, 2016).

7 C Walther, *Connection in the Times of COVID. Corona's Call for Conscious Choices* (Palgrave Macmillan, New York, 2020c).

individually and collectively. Whether the outcomes of the present quagmire are beneficial depends on our ability to finally build a society where rights are translated into practice. Our aspiration and ability to give every child a fair chance to use their full potential is the point of departure for the argumentation laid out in this chapter.

Following the present introduction, the next section offers a brief overview of the POZE paradigm (Section 2) that underpins the subsequent argumentation. Building on the understanding of a twice four-dimensional reality that influences the individual and collective sphere, we look at certain legal implications of this perspective, the possibilities deriving from it to optimize the social interplays conditioning them and possible ways forward to move not only through but beyond the COVID conundrum (Section 3). The conclusion sums up the main arguments (Section 4).

2. A new perspective

COVID has put the spotlight on the interconnectedness of everything and everyone. A minor fact, such as the bite of a bat in China, may almost paralyse the largest economies on far-off continents. The sooner we adopt a holistic understanding of the world that we evolve in, the better it is for us as individuals and for society overall. Only laws that are conceived, perceived and enforced with that understanding can actually represent a central pillar in the endeavour to ensure that children's rights really are universal.

This section outlines a paradigm that considers human existence as a composition of twice four dimensions which are influenced by four principles that influence their interaction. Awareness and acceptance of these dynamics is helpful not only to understand but to gradually optimize the outcomes. This matters in the ambition of overcoming the chronic (dis-) regard of human rights in general and of children's rights in particular.

2.1. Collective notions

Four universal principles are at play in the world:

Connection – Everything is linked. Nothing exists in a vacuum.
Change – Everything evolves, constantly. Nothing is permanent.
Continuum – Everything is part of something else. Nothing is strictly separated.
Complementarity – Everything needs something else to be complete. Nothing is perfect in isolation.

Each one of these principles is described in turn in the following, as the rest of this chapter is anchored in these inter-connected and mutually reinforcing mechanisms. Certain deriving aspects which may serve to unravel parts of the collateral damage caused by COVID-19 are also included in the discussion.

Connection – Everything is connected. COVID-19 illustrates the extent to which nature and humankind are linked. Humans are part of an ongoing chain that facilitates the transition of a virus from one realm to another. This ongoing crisis also shows how connected individuals around the world are. Globalization is no empty word but a reality that shapes social behaviour – from communication to consumption – and is shaped by it. Whatever happens in one dimension has direct and indirect consequences in the others, immediately or eventually. This external connection mirrors the internal connectedness that influences who an individual is and becomes. The aspirations, emotions, thoughts and experiences of every person, which impact how they express themselves in their environment, are influenced by the four dimensions of their being – soul, heart, mind and body.

Change – Evolution is inherent to nature. Nothing remains as it was. Human beings, animals, plants, societies and the universe keep on changing. It is futile to seek permanence by holding on to material assets as a guarantee for certain stages of life. Health, wealth and relationships inexorably shift through time. This principle of transformation is the only constant of human existence.

Continuum – Individuals trying to describe and understand the natural world often pinpoint to symmetry and the existence of 'pairs'. However, according to the evolutionist Stephen Jay Gould, the division by two as a natural principle of objective order does not hold. The universe is too complex for such simplification. Reality comes in many colours that transition via gradients in between. In his words,

> Nature does not dictate dualities, trinities, quarterings, or any 'objective' basis for human taxonomies; most of our chosen schemes, and our designated numbers of categories, record human choices from a cornucopia of possibilities offered by natural variation from place to place and permitted by the flexibility of our mental capacities.[8]

Complementarity – Antipodes complement each other[9] whilst representing different stages of one and the same scale. What may appear disconnected and opposed is part of a continuum within which one extreme represents at least a piece of its apparent opposite – and makes it whole. Acknowledging and accepting complementarity opens the door to internal and external acceptance, alignment and the use of existing resources in ways that achieve the utmost added value for everyone and everything.

Perceiving life and living, individuals and society as part of an organically evolving kaleidoscope places seemingly disconnected disciplines and sectors in one and the same realm of interdependent action and reaction. Within a continuum of change that links everything and everyone in an

8 SJ Gould, *Wonderful Life* (New York: W. W. Norton & Co, 1989).

9 In ways reminiscent of Hegel's dynamic notions of contradiction and overcoming which he used to criticize Aristotle's view of a world composed of discrete identities.

ongoing dynamic of rights and responsibilities, resources and risks are different faces of the same polyhedron. Adopting such a holistic perspective makes respecting rights, especially those that represent the future of this planet – the children – a natural choice.

In summary: Whatever we are and whatever we do is part of a spectrum of connected extremes that stand in complementarity. Everything is connected, mind and matter, within and without, inside and outside, rights and responsibilities. Internal synchronization ensues when a person's aspirations, emotions, thoughts and physical sensations unfold their complementary features. In the interaction with other people, the ability to recognize and respect differences and similarities between the self and others allows individuals to optimize the interpersonal dynamics that they are part of. Respecting the rights of others is one way to optimize this interaction.

2.2. Individual dimensions

How individuals live in this world is shaped by the four dimensions that shape their being. Engaged in an ongoing spiral dynamic, from the centre to the periphery and from the periphery inwards, these dimensions continuously interact and influence each other. Starting from birth, this internal two-way interaction influences who a person is and becomes and how they interact with the environment. Every step a child takes in this world is thus coloured not only by the child's inner dimensions but in addition by the inner dimensions of the caretakers. It is a constantly shifting kaleidoscope that must be taken into consideration when we contemplate sustainable solutions to address the wellbeing of children. In a crisis, individual agendas and group dynamics, all influenced by this prism of an internal and external multidimensionality, clash. It is impossible to control these manifold layers. However, gradually widening one's scope offers insights to understand the dynamics at play and see entry-points to influence them consciously. Such awareness conditions the ability to carve out space for children by paying particular attention to the needs and rights that are at most risk of being jeopardized. A word on each of the dimensions follows as the basic structure to organize subsequent reflections related to the collective challenge of promoting and respecting children's rights:

Starting at the core of our being, the *soul* represents the essence of who we are. It embodies our aspirations, encompassed in the desire to find meaning in everyday existence. Whatever a person feels, thinks and does is rooted in this craving for a purpose.[10] The quest of WHY is anchored here.

The second dimension is the *heart*. Schematically and metaphorically speaking, it harbours our emotions, determining how we feel in a given situation. WHO an individual is and how they behave are significantly influenced by emotions.

10 VE Frankl, *Man's Search for Meaning* (Simon and Schuster, London, 1985).

Although we commonly assume that human decisions are rational, science has proven that often the opposite is true.[11] Emotions are fundamental in the intellectual process of forming opinions and decisions; thus they shape much of human behaviour. Conversely, the kind of thoughts that a person entertains impacts their mood and emotional attitude towards themselves, others and life in general.

The third dimension of the human being is the *mind*. Thoughts are the result of an intricate mixture of genetic disposition, education, beliefs, memories, upbringing and environment. They influence emotions and aspirations, physical experiences and expressions and are influenced by them in return.[12] The mind, which is determined by hardware aspects such as neurological pathways, hormones, blood supply and nutrition and by software elements such as past and present expressions and experiences, stands in constant connection with the rest of one's being. The long-held, hermetic separation of mind and matter is discarded.[13] How a person thinks in the present is not only influenced by who they are currently; it is influenced by their past being, and it influences whom they evolve into. Every thought, every action leaves physical traces in an individual's mental hardware.[14] WHERE one stands in life at present is thus the cause and consequence of one's ever-changing perception of reality, perception of the self and re-action to the environment in line with this perceived 'reality'.

The fourth dimension is the *body*, which is the outer membrane that connects and separates internal and external realms. As an interface between the inside and the outside, it is the layer on which one experiences the world and expresses oneself in it. WHAT a person physically manifests is influenced by their mental setup, and vice versa.[15] Exteroceptive and interoceptive stimuli experienced through the body impact the way one thinks and feels. Countless invisible factors such as the state of one's microbiome, blood-sugar level, hormone balance and immune system affect our perception of a situation and thus the action we choose to take in it.

Nothing happens in a vacuum. The body reflects an individual's internal circumstances. Conversely, our experience of the environment impacts our internal circumstances, shaping our perspective of the world and hereby our reaction to it. Whatever happens at the centre radiates out, like the ripple effects of a stone cast into the water. Whichever state our internal realm is in – our emotions and thoughts, which are influenced by our aspirations – impacts our experience of and interaction with the outside world (Figure 9.1).

11 J Lehrer, *How We Decide* (Boston: Mariner Books, 2010).

12 D Kahneman, *Thinking, Fast and Slow* (London: Penguin Books, 2011).

13 A Schnabel, 'Antonio Damasio: "Descartes' Irrtum" ', in K Senge and R Schützeichel (eds), *Hauptwerke der Emotionssoziologie* (Springer VS, Wiesbaden, Wiesbaden, 2013).

14 N Doidge, *The Brain That Changes Itself: Stories of Personal Triumph from the Frontiers of Brain Science* (New York: Viking Press, 2007).

15 Ibid.

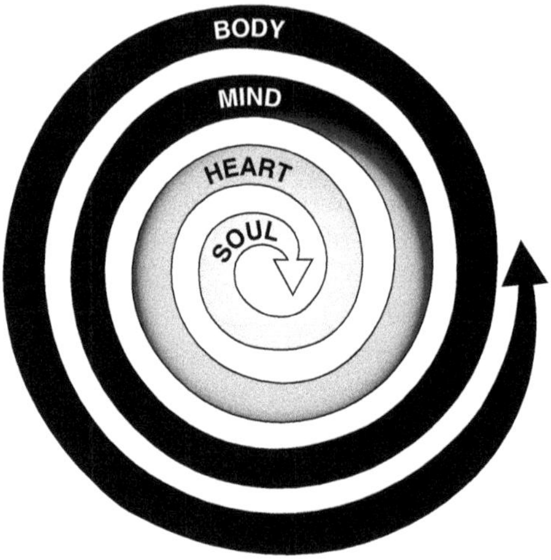

Figure 9.1 Spiral soul to body

Everything is connected, from the inside out and from the outside in. From the inside out – the soul finds its expression in human aspirations. These influence the heart, which is the source of emotions. How we feel impacts our mind. How and what we think impacts our overall wellbeing and our behaviour. From the outside in – the body is the interface between our inner and outer realities. Experiences influence our mind and heart, our thoughts and our feelings. Whether child or adult, physical experiences influence the inner realm, while the latter shapes an individual's expressions, attitude and behaviour in the outside world.

2.3. Social interplay

Like every acute crisis, whether humanmade or not, COVID-19 has reshaped how we perceive others and how we interact with them; it has changed the way we work, shop, eat and socialize. These behavioural changes affect the environment in which the virus was able to get a foothold. Depending on the choices that we make now, individually and collectively, and our underpinning intentions, these temporary modifications of our behaviour are gradually turning into new habits, which in a positive-case scenario will eventually lead to an environment that is hospitable to children and their rights and hostile to future pandemics. To understand and modify these relationships, it is necessary to explore the relationship between individual and social dimensions.

As seen, the four dimensions that determine an individual's experiences and expressions mirror the social interrelations that shape life in society. The *micro* level refers, on the one hand, to the four-dimensional internal composition of every individual's being, while on the other, it denotes the role of the individual in society. Every person is at the same time part of various *meso*-entities, different types of communities and institutions, such as a family, church, workplace, organization, school, political party or sports club. These meso-entities function as an intermediary between the person and the subsequent *macro* level. States (macro) comprise cultural, political and economic systems, including the governing structures and institutions that oversee, influence and manage society and provide the incentive that help or hinder the decisions, actions and beliefs of individuals and institutions.[16] Respectively and combined, these three dimensions form part of the *meta*-dimension.[17] The latter also includes supra-national organizations and entities such as the United Nations, due to their global mandate and impact. Furthermore, the commitments and entitlements that derive from international human rights like those enshrined in the Convention on the Rights of the Child are situated at this level, though their influence is and must be woven through all four dimensions. Finally, the meta level embraces nature and everything else in the universe. Consciously or unconsciously, willingly or unwillingly, every individual is simultaneously part of several meso and macro dimensions and of the overall meta-dimension. This perceptive will herein be referred to as the *m4-matrix* (Section 3.2).

Whatever happens in one dimension has repercussions within and upon the others. The effectiveness and evolution of one component within this interconnected matrix influence the effectiveness and evolution of the others. Human rights frameworks such as the UDHR and the CRC were meant to ensure that the result lives up to a minimum standard for all. Whether and how this setup is used with the ambition of mutual optimization is a matter of choice. One can either choose to seek modifications in a restrictive manner, focusing on one dimension while leaving the others aside, or put the panoply of pieces into a holistic vision which capitalizes on synergy and systematically influences causal interplays. One can either leave the outcome of the underpinning constellations to chance or choose to consciously influence them in view of results that lead humanity closer towards higher standards of quality of life that are shared by all.

COVID-19 is a test to see whether human beings are now mature enough to use their individual and collective power for the common good rather than personal profit or nationalistic ambitions. The rights enshrined in the CRC provide a minimum standard to orient an individual's inner compass, thus offering a solid point of departure for the tasks to be tackled for children.

16 H Plotkin, 'Human Nature, Cultural Diversity and Evolutionary Theory', *Philosophical Transactions of the Royal Society of London. Series B, Biological Sciences*, 366(1563) (2011), 454–463.

17 International trade, ODA, FDI, remittances and so on belong to a supra-national (interlinked) system: the international economy. However, as is often the case with meta systems, it emanates from actions and activities at the other levels. For example, an individual migrant (micro) uses the system to send remittances back home; an exporting company (meso) sells its wares across borders to another company; a government (macro) sends a grant, such as ODA, to finance development programmes in another country. Each type of behaviour happens in a different collective dimension, depending on the actor behind it. Thus, when referring to this behaviour, we locate it at the country (macro) level, whereas the action of individuals who participate in a community (meso) occurs at the micro level.

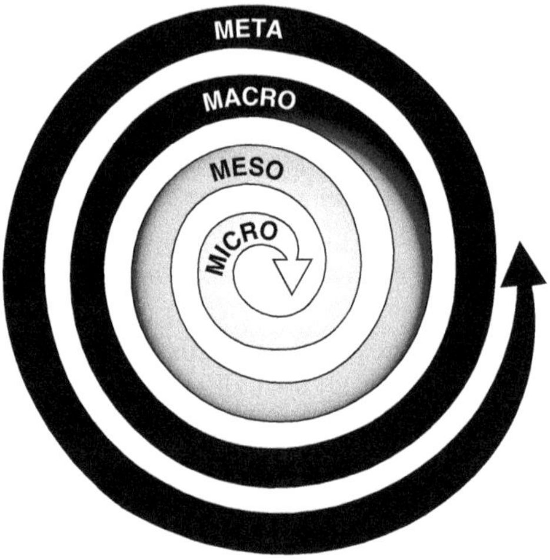

Figure 9.2 Spiral micro to meta

Everything is connected, from the inside out and from the outside in. Individuals represent the micro dimension of a multi-dimensional system. They form, shape and experience the meso level, which results from the communities they are part of (voluntarily or biologically, directly or indirectly). The contours of economic, political and cultural systems form the macro level. Micro, meso and macro dimensions operate within a meta system. Within a seamless continuum, one dimension is influenced by the others and influences them in return.

Making life worth living for every child is dependent on everyone's involvement. Since individuals (micro) and sub-national institutions (meso) shape the macro-dimension and are major components of the meta-dimension, society hinges on the course of these two spheres of life (Figure 9.2).[18] How the world emerges from COVID-19, as from any other crisis, centres on the attitude and behaviour of individuals, including civil courage and collective resolve.

Translating rights into reality entails more than an obligation to respect the law. It requires an individual and collective commitment to the intentions that underpin the regulations in place (i.e., the written law). When it comes to the gigantic task of manifesting the ideals of human rights treaties in general and those dedicated to the weakest link of the human community in particular – children – the focus on this aspiration is even more acute.

18 While the meso-dimension is sub-national, certain institutions at the meso level have counterparts at the supra-national level (i.e. churches, multinational companies). This double nature illustrates the inseparable nature of dimensions which are connected through an ongoing dynamic of mutual interaction. A similar double-sized nature marks the meta-dimension which, on the one hand, entails supra-national institutions such as the United Nations and, on the other, the sum of all entities and spheres that are not human related, such as Nature.

The macro dimension can be tailored to become a conducive environment for the protection of children's rights. Yet only if the intention behind this endeavour is genuinely geared towards impact will the outcomes ensue. This entails, on the one hand, an institutional disposition to promote the meaningful participation of children in line with their entitlement per the Optional Protocol to the CRC – to state and defend their concerns and needs – and, on the other, the state's proactive identification and support of localized entities at the community level; the latter may serve not only as a passive watchdog that monitors child right violations; it may also reach out to children in need and serve as a catalyst for community-based support mechanisms that systematically cater to those needs.

The aspiration of every individual within the social kaleidoscope is thus at stake. To make the rights deriving from the CRC a universal reality for children, these rights must be taken beyond the commitments of states (macro) and past the cloud of supranational institutions (meta). Individuals and institutions must respectively and together take on the complementary role of identifying and supporting the most vulnerable children in their areas of access. The responsibility to serve those whose legal entitlements are disregarded cannot be delegated to the state alone; seeing the immensity of the task, and the natural binomen of human privilege and responsibility, everyone has a part to play.

The aspiration of individuals (micro), be they caretakers or not, is central in the endeavour to create communities (meso) that offer an environment in which children can thrive. Legal instruments such as the 'Optional Protocol to the Convention on the Rights of the Child on a Communications Procedure',[19] which enables children to submit a claim to the Committee on the Rights of the Child when their rights have been violated, are useful because they recognize that children are active rights-holders who must be treated as such. However, these tools merely offer mechanisms that come into play when the dynamic has gone awry. The aspirations that underpin a holistic social transformation and gradually result in an environment in which all children have a chance to unfold their potential start far earlier.

International law in general and the CRC in particular entail the potential of a supportive framework to nurture dynamics that are conducive to enacted interpersonal responsibility. Although it may appear difficult to shift from a perspective that is self-centred to an all-inclusive attitude, the return on such personal energy investment is manifold. In particular, a proactive respect of the reciprocity principle underneath the prevailing rights schema pays off for individuals who are willing to get involved.

19 Adopted and opened for signature, ratification and accession through General Assembly resolution A/RES/66/138 of 19 December 2011; entered into force on 14 April 2014. Office of Human Rights, www.ohchr.org/en/professionalinterest/pages/opiccrc.aspx, accessed May 2021.

2.4. Reciprocity – the return on realized rights

The principle of reciprocity has been recognized and reflected in cultures for centuries. Commonly referred to as 'the Golden Rule', it states that we should do to others what we desire for ourselves and refrain from doing to them what we would not want to be done to us.[20] It has found entry into religions and belief systems around the world, manifesting in simple terms such as solidarity with those in need. Solidarity reveals the combination of compassion (heart) with an understanding of the context (mind) and the aspiration of purpose (soul).[21] When individuals combine the understanding of their own possibilities (mind) with the caring for (heart) and connection with others and manifest the result as tangible action for others (body), they move towards completion (soul). Modern science increasingly proves that this wisdom of the past is a natural reflection of humanity's 'moral blueprint'.[22]

Developmental psychology has shown that humans are born with an innate 'draft' of the world. 'The initial organization of the brain does not depend on experience to a large extent. Nature provides a first draft, which experience then revises. Built-in doesn't mean unmalleable; it means organized in advance of experience'.[23] This leads to the content of a person's

20 Z Rakhshani, 'The Golden Rule and Its Consequences: A Practical and Effective Solution for World Peace', *Journal of History Culture and Art Research*, 6 (2017), 465. https://doi.org/10.7596/taksad.v6i1.754.

21 The term 'solidarity' refers to the awareness of shared interests, objectives, standards and sympathies creating a psychological sense of unity of groups or classes. It means looking at the ties that bind people together as one in a society. It is included in all major religions and closely related to the golden rule. It has found its way into the Charter of Fundamental Rights of the European Union and is mentioned in the Universal Declaration on Bioethics and Human Rights. Different types of social solidarity correlate with different types of societies. In a society exhibiting mechanical solidarity, its cohesion and integration come from the homogeneity of individuals – people feel connected through similar work, educational and religious training and lifestyle. Mechanical solidarity normally operates in 'traditional' and small-scale societies. In simpler societies (e.g., tribal), solidarity is usually based on kinship ties of familial networks. Organic solidarity comes from the interdependence that arises from the specialization of work and the complementarities between people – a development which occurs in 'modern' and 'industrial' societies. P Thijssen, 'From Mechanical to Organic Solidarity, and Back: With Honneth beyond Durkheim', *European Journal of Social Theory*, 15 (2012), 454–470. For Peter Kropotkin, solidarity is essential since mutual aid does not result from the expectation of a reward but rather from instinctive feelings of solidarity. P Kropotkin, *Mutual Aid: A Factor of Evolution* (New York: Freedom Press, 1998).

22 Anchored in the soul are our values – the cornerstone of our belief systems, which in turn underpin our short-term desires and longer-term aspirations. Cross-cultural studies have shown that five human values come from a common pool innate in human nature: harm/care, fairness/reciprocity, in-group/loyalty, authority/respect, and purity/sanctity. (Haidt (n 3)).

23 GF Marcus, 'What Developmental Biology Can Tell Us about Innateness', in P Carruthers, S Laurence and S Stich (eds), *The Innate Mind: Structure and Content* (Oxford: Oxford University Press, 2005).

innate moral draft. Across continents and cultures, there is commonality on 'five foundations of morality':[24] The first one is harm/care. Humans are mammals whose neural and hormonal programming renders them prone to bond with others, to care for them. We have evolved to feel compassion for others, especially those who appear to be weak and vulnerable, which in turn gives us strong feelings about those who cause harm. The second foundation is fairness/reciprocity. It is illustrated by 'the Golden Rule', which forms a central part of many religions.[25] The third foundation is in-group/loyalty. Humans are unique in their ability to cooperate and form groups among those that share no filial links.[26] We are social beings by birth. The fourth foundation is authority/respect. It is not only based on power and violence but also voluntary deference and love. The fifth foundation is purity/sanctity, the idea of virtue which comes from controlling what you do with your body. It relates to the purposeful orientation of one's being and becoming towards something that is larger than one's own life. As we grow up, we gradually and subconsciously, based on these moral foundations, distil the values that matter most to us as a person. Depending on culture and context, experiences and environment, the weighting attributed to these values is different among individuals and among societies. Whichever weight is given by a critical mass of people in society influences the prevailing social norms, which then influence the individuals who involve in this environment.[27] As we will see, accepting and acting in line with this perspective lies in our own best interests.[28]

24 Anchored in the soul are our values – the cornerstone of our belief systems, which in turn underpin our short-term desires and longer-term aspirations. Cross-cultural studies have shown that five human values come from a common pool innate in human nature: harm/care, fairness/reciprocity, in-group/loyalty, authority/respect, and purity/sanctity. (Haidt (n 3))

25 For centuries, there have been attempts by philosophers to contradict, limit, expand or modify it. Good summaries and discussions are found in: Jeffrey Wattles, *The Golden Rule* (New York: Oxford University Press, 1996). David E Cortesi, *Secular Wholeness* (2001), Trafford on Demand Publishing. Wattles' summary is pertinent and probably the way forward: 'For responding to all these objections, there are three possible strategies: abandon the rule, reformulate it, or retain it as commonly worded, while taking advantage of objections to clarify its proper interpretation. I take the third way' (Wattles 2013), www.psychologytoday.com/us/blog/evolution-the-self/201303/the-golden-rule-part-1-dont-take-it-literally.

26 M Nowak and R Highfield, *Supercooperators: Altruism, Evolution, and Why We Need Each Other to Succeed* (New York: Simon & Schuster, 2011).

27 Bicchieri (n 6).

28 Humans are hardwired to cooperate, and whatever you do for others benefits both – the one who acts and the one who receives. Moreover, benefits of pro-social action occur on four levels. The very act of giving back to the community boosts a person's happiness, health and sense of physical well-being. TG Plante, 'Helping Others Offers Surprising Benefits', *Psychology Today* (2012), www.psychologytoday.com/us/blog/do-theright-thing/201207/helping-others-offers-surprising-benefits-0). Beyond the benefits for the one who acts and the one who receives, others who witness altruistic acts experience renewed hope, appeasement and the desire to take similar action. S Ramey, 'There Are Also Benefits for Those Witnessing Acts of Kindness' (2016), https://exploringyourmind.

We dive into the meaning of life and living when we acknowledge that we are not alone and act accordingly. When we acknowledge the complementarity of our own resources and the resources of others, the respective rights and responsibilities appear naturally, and once these rights and responsibilities are acted upon, the 360° benefits that derive from such action become felt among all parties involved.

In the long term, individual wellbeing depends on actions that are performed by the person for the wellbeing of others in the short term. Rights enshrine this understanding. Even though the longstanding paradigm of *homo homini lupus est* (Latin for 'man is wolf to man') has served for centuries as an unspoken justification for egocentric behaviour, it is invalid. An attitude of *homo homini lux est* (Latin for 'man is light to man') is part of human evolution. Cooperation, and deriving from it the intuition to express solidarity towards those in need, is an integral part of the human DNA; it is the principal reason humanity has survived and evolved thus far.[29]

Solidarity is a win-win-win-win, because 'compassion is a question of human survival'.[30] Solidarity is an action, a behaviour that translates the attitude of compassion. If a mindset of compassion prevails, solidarity flows naturally. Perceived from a standpoint of compassion, the obligation to translate the CRC into practice becomes a desire.

Empathy enables humans to feel with those who suffer from the gap that separates the world that could be if rights were translated from theory to practice and the prevalent reality. Compassion is an emotional manifestation of the desire to reduce that gap, whereas solidarity is the action that channels this desire into external results. This internal primal part of the human setup has left an imprint on the fundamental human rights that (should) guide society. Acting accordingly fosters subjective and collective wellbeing and happiness.

Solidarity translates empathy (feeling with) into action. It matters for giver and receiver whether the action is rights based or out of a mere desire to relieve the suffering of another person. Too much empathy can be debilitating, paralysing the person who 'suffers with' rather than motivating her to act for the person who suffers.[31] Studies have found that a focus on empathy may be experienced as uncomfortable and troublesome, while

---

com/benefits-witnessing-acts-kindness/). From such an expanding attitude of kindness and care among individuals, society overall benefits, as the occurrence and acceptability of inequality and deprivation shrink. Wilkinson and Pickett (n 5).

29 Cooperation may appear to go against our ingrained instinct of seeing first and foremost to our own needs. However, supporting others in an effort of sharing is part of our DNA. It is the reason humankind has reached the present stage of evolution. Nowak and Highfield (n 26).

30 HH Dalai Lama, the Fourteenth, *Policy of Kindness: An Anthology of Writings by and about the Dalai Lama* (Shambhala, Delhi, 1990), 112.

31 T Well, 'Compassion Is Better Than Empathy', *Psychology Today* (2017), www.psychologytoday.com/us/blog/the-clarity/201703/compassion-is-better-empathy.

compassion creates mental positivity.[32] What we do for others furthers our own interests as well as theirs, because when our inner beliefs and external behaviour are aligned, inner peace and collective harmony ensue. Individuals who not only respect the rights of others but act with the genuine intention to promote their wellbeing benefit in four direct and four indirect ways that influence the twice four-dimensional prism looked at earlier.[33]

2.4.1. *Direct benefits – micro level*

Win-1 – Acting in line with one's personal values, and the inherent human aspiration of being a 'good person', contributes to a positive self-image, which is an essential part of an individual's self-confidence and inner coherence (soul).

Win-2 – Helping others results in the emission of endorphins (body), which influence the hormonal interplay that is related to the subjective feeling of happiness (heart).

Win-3 – Experiencing how the receiver of the benevolent act benefits enhances the positive experience of the one who acted because they understand further the connection between their own action and the influence it has on others (mind).

Win-4 – Contributing to an overall atmosphere of lawfulness and solidarity within the meso and macro environment that they are part of benefits individuals because the prevailing interpersonal relationship arena is strengthened. Within institutions, the accumulation of such behaviour eventually affects the organizational culture that the individuals evolve in, which is beneficial to them and others (body).

2.4.2. *Indirect benefits – micro, meso, macro, meta levels*

Win-5 – The repetition of a certain behaviour strengthens the underpinning synaptic connections (micro). This makes that behaviour easier over time. Thus, what was initially a conscious effort turns into a natural action that still yields the aforementioned benefits (micro).

Win-6 – Behaving in a kind, helpful manner influences how a person is perceived by others. When that type of behaviour is repeated over time, it leads others to trust and appreciate them more (meso).

32 In a behavioural experiment, people who were tasked to concentrate on compassion ended up feeling kinder and more eager to help others than those in the empathy group T Singer and OM Klimecki, 'Empathy and Compassion', *Current Biology*, 24 (2014), 875–878.

33 For a detailed outline of the win-win-win-win effect and its scientific underpinnings, please see Walther (n 1, 7) and the references about humans being hardwired for cooperation (previously). Some interesting background reading includes the following: on the link between emotion, thought and action (Lehrer (n 11)), on our (ir)rational thought processes. Bicchieri (n 6) regarding the connection between behaviour and brain structure. Doidge (n 14) regarding the neuroscientific implications of such processes; on the impact that short and long-term behaviour changes have on society, Biccheri (n 6).

Win-7 – Bystanders who observe an act of kindness not only see their own mood enhanced, they are also inspired to echo the pro-social behaviour themselves. This has the aforementioned benefits for the bystander (micro) and benefits other people in their environment, including the person who took the initial action (micro). Witnessing others perform according to the values that one admires confirms the observer's own ability to engage in a similar behaviour whilst increasing the desire to do so.[34] A domino chain is set off that affects the social setting in which it takes place positively (meso).

Win-8 – The snowball effect of a pay-it-forward dynamic can affect entire states if a sufficient number of people gets involved (macro). Conversely, what a state does through its leaders, for instance, in regard to treaty obligations in general and CRC obligations in particular, influences the social dynamics at play. A 'tipping point' in the social arena is reached when a critical mass of people shifts their behaviour; a new social norm emerges (macro).[35] The latter could entail the proactive pursuit of courageous kindness or solidarity as a natural drive that weaves through society. Ultimately, a fresh pro-social dynamic can have ripple effects across the planet (meta). 'Boomerang benefits' ensue, or the person who planted the seeds of kindness harvests the fruits of the initial action in multiple ways, directly and indirectly (micro).

It lies in everyone's interests to acknowledge and actively address not just the rights of others but the underpinning intentions of the legal framework. Yet the path from awareness of this fact, to appreciating how relevant it is for each individual, to accepting the deriving behavioural consequences as a necessity, to choosing one's action accordingly is not always straightforward. Emotional inertia and psychological maladjustment may lead individuals to stick with their acquired modus operandi even once they have come to know better.[36] This has costs for others but also for themselves due to cognitive dissonance.[37] It is necessary for the wellbeing of individuals to act in coherence with their beliefs and values. When a person's aspirations and actions are misaligned, it takes a toll; their health and life expectancy are jeopardized, and their reputation suffers due to the perception of inauthenticity that is triggered in others.

Theory must be translated into practice to make rights a universal reality. This will happen only when individuals shift from the perception of

34 Nettleship, Richard Lewis, 'Chapter 4 – The Four Stages of Intelligence', in *Lectures on the Republic of Plato*, (London: Macmillan & Co, 1955).

35 M Gladwell, *The Tipping Point: How Little Things Can Make a Big Difference* (Little, Brown, 2000).

36 P Kuppens, NB Allen and LB Sheeber, 'Emotional Inertia and Psychological Maladjustment', *Psychological Science*, 21(7) (2010), 984–991, https://doi.org/10.1177/0956797610372634

37 L Festinger, 'Cognitive Dissonance', *Scientific American*, 207(4) (1962), 93–107.

obligation (intellectual/must) to a natural *desire* of involvement (emotional/want). Beyond the citizen-sphere, this is relevant also in the context of state obligations. Because even though states are impersonal entities (macro), backstage human, decision-makers are at play (micro) whose aspirations, emotions, thoughts and behaviour determine the 'action' of a government. The aspirations of these individuals must be aligned with the purpose of the CRC to yield the desired pro-social outcomes.

Building on this multidimensional perspective, the deriving implications for human rights will be looked at.

3. Implications

COVID-19 has pulled the veil away from a systemic social paradox that has lingered under the radar for a long time. For centuries children have grown up in this setting, many of them losing out because their rights were disregarded. The pandemic illustrates the impact of snubbed human rights. Neither the profit-driven globalization of the past few decades nor the powerplay of nationalistic agendas were motivated by a desire to ensure the best possible outcomes for children. Three negative trends stick out in particular – although, unfortunately, they are not the only persisting rights violations: violations of the rights to life, health and social protection; gender-based violence and threats to sexual and reproductive rights; and repression of dissent (Amnesty International 2021). All of them put the CRC to shame, showing a blatant disregard of children's needs and rights. Although the repression of dissent may seem less relevant when talking about children, it is jeopardizing the future of children by putting their caretakers in danger and while tarnishing the social environment in which they grow up. The recent evolution has

> taught us, yet again, lessons that we ignore at the peril of generations to come: the interdependence of the human family; the universality of what we, the peoples' require of governance in times of crisis, and just how indivisible is our own future from the future we are creating for our children and the planet that is hosting this generation and those who follow. It taught us again the essence, in other words, of human rights. The question that remains to be answered is: will we be bold enough to see what must be done and courageous enough to get on and do it, at scale and at pace?
>
> (Agnès Callamard, AI Secretary General, April 2021)[38]

38 The Amnesty International Report 2020/21 documents the human rights situation in 149 countries in 2020, as well as providing a global and regional analysis. It presents Amnesty International's concerns and calls for action from governments and others. (Amnesty International (2021). Index number: POL 10/3202/2021).

Nothing happens in a vacuum. Not only are individuals and institutions, communities and countries intrinsically connected; the past influences the present, thereby laying the foundation of the future. The rights abuses that are witness today have been nurtured and enabled by abuses that were condoned in the past. The implications of the status quo are felt by many today and will impact billions more tomorrow. Children are and will be the first to suffer the consequences. The present section offers an overview of certain causes and consequences that become visible from the holistic perspective that was presented in the previous section.

3.1. Legal considerations

'Everyone has the right to life, liberty and security of person' (UDHR, Article 3). Although theoretically inalienable,[39] the right to health and life that ascribes for everyone an entitlement to the best possible care (which has been a hypocritical word-on-paper statute for too long in too many countries) has been redefined during COVID-19. Further and beyond, freedom and safety, access to social services and a minimum standard of living – long taken for granted by those of us who live in high- or middle-income countries – have revealed their fragility.

> States Parties recognize that every child has the inherent right to life. States Parties shall ensure to the maximum extent possible the survival and development of the child.
>
> (CRC Art.6)

The establishment of these general principles within the CRC implies 'that they were intended to enjoy an additional status over and above the other substantive rights'.[40]

The Convention on the Rights of the Child offers an inclusive catalogue of rights that seeks to protect the material and immaterial needs of a child, covering their physiological, intellectual, emotional and social requirements. These rights are based on the non-discrimination principle, and all actions must be in line with the best interests of children. Every child has the right to obtain adequate support for their development in terms of their physical, moral, mental, social and spiritual aspects (Lundy and Byrne, 2017; CRC, 1989).[41] If one were to visualize these entitlements through the schema introduced earlier regarding the individual dimensions of our being (Figure 9.1), the following schematic overview would appear, showing the interplay between all rights. (Figure 9.3).

39 Office of the United Nations High Commissioner for Human Rights (OHCHR) and World Health Organization (WHO). (2000). The Right to Health. Fact Sheet No. 31.

40 Laura Lundy and B Bronagh, *The Four General Principles of the United Nations Convention on the Rights of the Child: The Potential Value of the Approach in Other Areas of Human Rights Law* (Taylor & Francis, London, 2017).

41 Ibid.

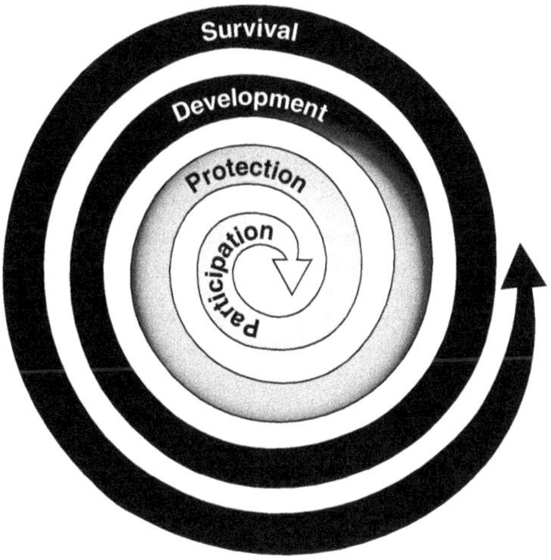

Figure 9.3 Spiral CRC pillars

Everything is connected, from the inside out and from the outside in. Participation, or the aspiration to be an integral part of society, is a central need of children. It is anchored in the quest for meaning (Soul). Protection from harm is essential to shield the soft emotional core of children, which is still evolving (Heart). Development relates to the ongoing leaning process of the intellectual and perceptual status of the person (Mind). Survival entails all of the above and the material conditions to unfold one's inherent potential (Body).

States' obligations deriving from the CRC may be divided into three categories: to respect, to protect and to fulfil; the latter component includes an obligation to facilitate and an obligation to provide (CESCR, General Comment (GC) 12 and reiterated in various subsequent GCs of the CRC Committee). Even though the CRC Committee has recognized that a state may not be able to address all the rights of all children immediately, it has clearly stated that the principle of 'progressive realization' applies. This reflects a positive obligation for each state to fulfil and to protect what is due to each child. Governments must take proactive steps and establish targets and benchmarks to measure the progressive achievement of all goals. This has been particularly emphasized regarding the 'right of the child to the highest attainable standard of health' (CRC Art.24).

> All States are required to take immediate action to implement these obligations as a matter of priority and without discrimination of any kind. Where the available resources are demonstrably inadequate, States are still required to undertake targeted measures to move as expeditiously and effectively as possible towards the full realization of the child's right to health.
>
> (CRC GC 15)

The situation that has emerged with COVID-19 shows that the realization of a right is never acquired once and forever. Since 2019, the pandemic has driven between 120 and 150 million children into poverty whilst widening the gender gap in employment (World Health Organization (WHO) 2021). In 2020 an estimated 1.6 billion children worldwide had been affected by disrupted access to education (John Hopkins, World Bank, UNICEF, 2021).[42] Routine immunization services were cut in half or stopped altogether; services for basic healthcare and reproductive health were disrupted.[43] The systems in place were not ready to cope with the pandemic or its medium-term fall-outs. Human rights abuses that were condoned for a long time have been rising to the surface in the aftermath of the outbreak, leading to a further deterioration of the situation of those who were worst off from the start. The pandemic has sadly exemplified once more that 'the management of social issues is subject to historical contingency and strategic re-articulation. And thus, the risk of regress'.[44]

Access to all rights for all people has never been a reality. Although the CRC has been signed and ratified by all countries but the United States, the reality that billions of children around the world, on all continents, have been facing for a long time is a far cry from the enshrined legal commitments. There is no equitable access to health care and other social services. The pre-existing inequities have been exacerbated during the pandemic with consequences on education, food, and healthcare for (non-)Covid diseases. Children are affected by what happens to their families. The fallout of inadequate social protection schemes to help those who lost their employment and their income during the pandemic has taking its toll on caregivers and thus their ability to protect their children. Even countries in which COVID is presently under control will be hit by the consequences if they reject the notion of borderless solidarity. Because eventually, the virus and its effects will boomerang. Globalization has never been as acutely felt as today. Shifts are required at the micro (individual), meso (institutions) and macro (state) levels, and their lack will be felt everywhere.

'The COVID-19 pandemic has thrived amid the inequalities in our societies and the gaps in our health systems' (Director-General Tedros Adhanom Ghebreyesus 2021).[45] 'It is vital for all governments to invest in strengthening their health services and to remove the barriers that prevent so many

42 Johns Hopkins University, World Bank, UNICEF (2021), 'Tracker to Measure COVID Impact on Education', Joint Press Release, www.unicef.org/press-releases/new-global-tracker-measure-pandemics-impact-education-worldwide, accessed April 2021.

43 UNICEF Data, 'Covid and Children' (2021), https://data.unicef.org/covid-19-and-children/ accessed April 2021.

44 A Minujin and A Grondona, 'Poverty, Needs and Rights: Definitions in Dispute', No. 22 of Voces en el Fénix/Voices in the Phoenix (2013).

45 Xinhua, Huaxia (ed), 'WHO Calls for Addressing Inequality in Health during the Pandemic', April 2021.

people from using them, so more people have the chance to live healthy lives.' International solidarity to translate rights into reality is needed in a timely fashion. At the time of writing, COVAX, a WHO-led global vaccine initiative geared to ensure cross-border solidarity, still faces not only an insufficient sharing of vaccine doses because countries are hoarding their stocks but also a significant financing gap.

Is the right to life and health of a child born in Afghanistan worth less than the right of a child in the United Kingdom? Is it possible to relate a person's right to health to a place and to the socio-economic status of their family? The answers are obvious on a theoretical level, and yet the right to life and living is *de facto* being valued very differently. This was the case before COVID, and the pandemic has illustrated the consequences. And yet humanity is stuck in this together. COVID puts a spotlight on the universal need for rights that are not just written but respected. At the same time, it is a reminder of the human foundation that preceded those rights and the laws that emanate from it. This foundation offers a stable ground to move forward, provided the mindsets at all levels of the micro-meso-macro-meta dynamic are geared towards outcomes that matter and last.

*3.2. **Optimizing the** m4-matrix*

Individuals are part of a living kaleidoscope that constantly changes. Therefore, realizing children's rights is not a one-off achievement, which can be forgotten about once it has been achieved. To understand the dynamics of social transformation, we must acknowledge the components of the status quo, including the role of interconnected players and their internal (mis-)alignment. For individuals and states alike, it is an ongoing journey that requires efforts at all levels of the micro-meso-macro-meta *(m4)-matrix*. Internal synchronization of each dimension is a decisive factor for a smooth interaction between the dimensions.

3.2.1. Micro shapes meso, and vice versa

Individuals cannot control the meso, macro and meta dimensions that they are part of, but they can influence their own attitude and action and thereby what happens around them or in the dimensions that they are part of. Human beings may have no control over the game that is being played, but how one player choses to move influences others who are involved in same dynamic, which ultimately impacts the overall outcomes. It is a constantly falling and rising domino chain, which has no beginning nor end. Values and aspirations offer stability in this context.

The status quo is framed by the values of those who constitute society. Two evolutionary advantages play in favour of humans who want to change and bring change: creativity and the natural quest for happiness. The ability to imagine something that does not exist (yet) and the desire for happiness are unique human features that come with practical benefits for the species.[46] Using the capacity to think (mind) and feel (emotion), humans can envision a different tomorrow and translate this vision into tangible results by choosing the related behaviour consciously (body). Building onto the pursuit of happiness is the motivational driver (aspiration) that triggers humans to take action. 'Evolution uses happiness to guide us toward what's in our genes' best interest, giving us the best chance of reproduction'.[47] It is the pleasant counterpart of purpose orientation that is framed by values and of respecting rights that is steered by the intellect. On top of these comes the inherent human affinity for cooperation.

Humans evolved into their current state thanks to the intrinsic ability to collaborate,[48] which is conditioned by the capacity for self-control.[49] Caring and sharing are part of our DNA (Section 2). It is a self-interested instinct that conditions our survival. A social setup in which isolation and inequity are condoned and supported goes against that inherent setup and is thus detrimental in the short run because it affects individual wellbeing and in the long term because it endangers the survival of the species (meta).

A seamless interplay between actors requires that individuals (micro), institutions (meso) and states (macro) operate according to the same high values and a shared mindset. Simply put, the best possible outcomes, including the realization of all rights for all children, depend on the collective resolve and ability to optimize the *m4-matrix* and thus society.

The sum is believed to be greater than its parts. However, in some circumstances, competing agendas lead to the mutual impediment of parts within a system which has repercussions on the environment in which it operates, on other systems and ultimately on the dysfunctional system itself. The result is a growing number of disregarded rights and responsibilities, deprived children, unhappy people, dysfunctional organizations and imbalanced systems. Optimizing the twice-four-dimensional reality that influences each individual and which every person influences every moment of every day is a constantly evolving task.

States (macro) comprise cultural, political and economic systems, including the governing structures and institutions that oversee, influence and manage society, and provide the incentive that help or hinder the decisions,

46 W Von Hippel, *The Social Leap: The New Evolutionary Science of Who We Are, Where We Come From, and What Makes Us Happy* (New York, NY: Harper Collins, 2018).

47 Ibid.

48 Nowak and Highfield (n 26).

49 Supra (n 46). Self-control has major social advantages. If I can control the way I respond to you, then I can give you the kind of impression that I want to give you. I can refrain from expressing my thoughts/emotions unless the time is right.
It is an evolutionary advantage that humans have. The level of self-control increases with the understanding of and influence on the dimensions that shape the instinctive drivers of our behaviour.

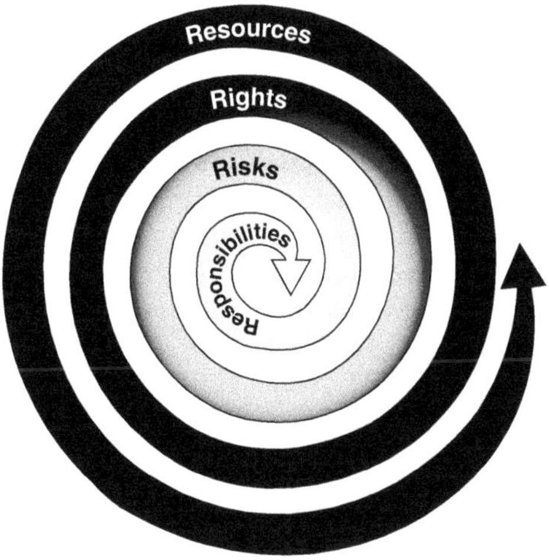

Figure 9.4 Spiral R4

Everything is connected, from the inside out and from the outside in. Individual responsibilities are inherent in every individual's human nature, or the moral blueprint that colours our aspirations (micro). Risks are caused by ignoring the fulfilment of these obligations, for the individuals directly and the communities that they evolve in (meso). Rights have been envisioned (and are supposed to be enforced) to ensure the possible social setup for every member in every country (macro). Resources are abundantly available (meta); they can and must be distributed equally to optimize the m4-matrix and thus life on Planet Earth. The interplay between these dimensions matters crucially when it comes to the (dis)respect of children's rights.

actions and beliefs of individuals and institutions.[50] Herein institutions (meso) are duty bearers, too. Their nature and the form of their obligations evolves organically in line with the social dynamics of the times, culture and environment in which they are situated.

Awareness of the *m4*-perspective that all individuals operate in makes it easier to accept the statement that every child's *Rights* are worth the same and that disregarding them has *Risks* for everyone. It makes it also obvious that the *Resources* of everyone are needed to address and fulfil these rights in a sustainable manner. Access to these resources is conditioned by individual and collective *Responsibilities* that are respected and translate rights into reality. (Figure 9.4) This may involve uncomfortable choices and consequences. In an interconnected society, everyone is accountable, individually and collectively, for the choices that are (not) made.

Expanding our mental scope to take in not just the pieces but their interplay is the first step towards conscious influence on the multiple tectonic plates that shape society. Such influence entails thinking about behaviour

50 Plotkin (n 16), 454–463.

by thinking about the thinking, feelings and aspirations that precede it. It is a mental habit that is useful to adopt because it puts the individual in a driver position in the overall scheme of life.

It is in one's personal interest to enact Kant's 'categorical imperative:' 'Act only according to that maxim by which you can at the same time that it should become a universal law'. Or, in the words of Gandhi, 'We need to be the change we want to see'. Even where internal and external valuations as well as intrinsic and extrinsic values clash, remaining aligned to one's internal compass will be more conducive to a person's inner peace than the pursuit of a social codex that stands in contrast to their internal belief system (Gino et al. 2015).[51]

4. Conclusion

Everything always changes. Amid the natural uncertainty of life, respecting and promoting the existing rights framework and, beyond that, making sure that it is tangible and implemented, represents an aspect of certainty that one can invest in. It is this injection of practical legal features that is required to optimize the *m4-matrix.* Individuals represent the centre of this optimization. COVID-19 has confirmed that everything can change, always and unexpectedly – and the direction that a change takes affects all the dimensions of the *m4-matrix.*

Using the aforementioned ability of creativity let us suppose for a moment that a critical mass of individuals,

- agrees that they from now on wish to live in a society where solidarity and the pro-active respect of all rights for all people, including children, prevails, and based on this aspiration, they
- re-shape their day-to-day behaviour to set an example.

Now imagine this critical mass of people

- operates within a system – whether it is their community (meso), their country (macro) or the world (meta) – that is conducive to their aspiration. This setup facilitates their decision to get proactively involved in realizing the rights of children in their vicinity.

Furthermore, imagine that the ensuing pro-social dynamics

- result in the decentralized development of social, economic and legal assets that are designed with the stated intention to not only ensure full respect of the CRC but to support, scale and sustain inclusive social change. The assets could be fine-tuned with an understanding of the

51 F Gino, M Kouchaki and AD Galinsky, 'The Moral Virtue of Authenticity: How Inauthenticity Produces Feelings of Immorality and Impurity', *Psychological Science,* 26 (2015), 983–996.

internal individual interplay, their interactions within the *m4-matrix* and their influence on the outcomes of COVID. (Figure 9.5)

Human rights treaties represent the overall legal framework in which most national and local regulations operate; this underpinning is a major asset in the quest for a more inclusive post-COVID future, because treaties like the CRC illustrate the values and aspirations that have inspired individuals for centuries, long before these treaties were drafted and manifested. The time has come to put them into practice unconditionally. The basic entitlements that derive from them for every human being, in particular

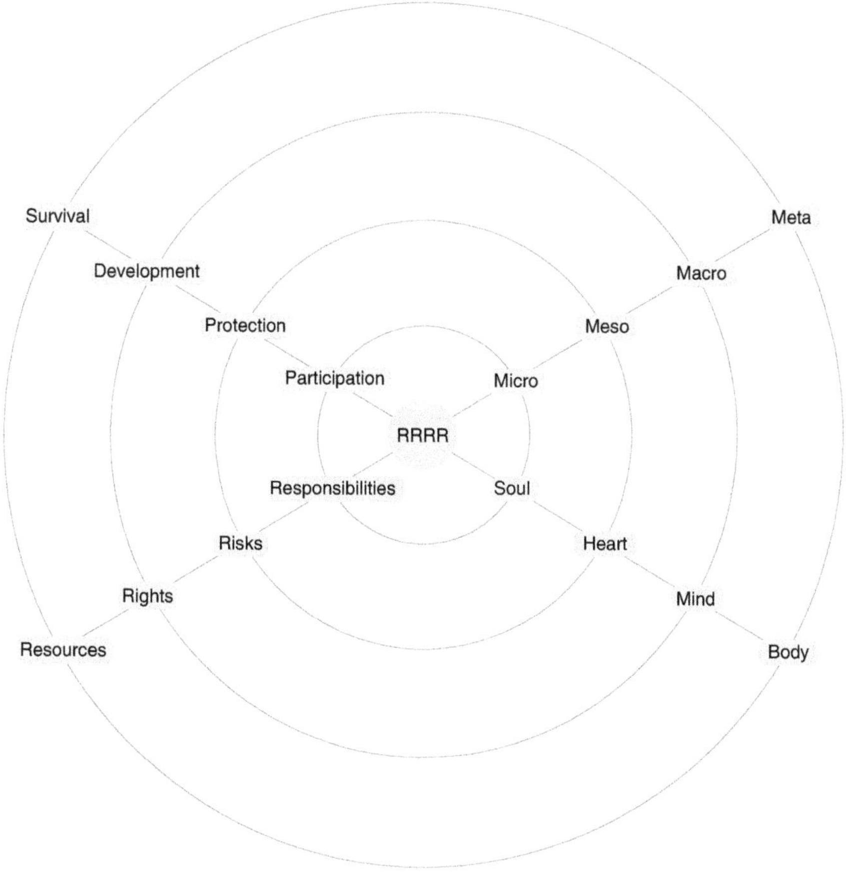

Figure 9.5 MindMap m4 and R4

Everything is connected. The four dimensions of our being (soul, heart, mind, body) relate to the components that characterize the human being and society as a community of human beings (responsibilities, risks, rights, resources). Both arenas are reflected in the CRC (participation, protection, development, survival). Ultimately awareness and action that respect the interdependency of the multi-layered reality that shapes life conditions the optimization of the m4-matrix (micro, meso, macro, meta).

the ones who are most in need of special protection such as children, must move from paper to practice.

Whatever happens around us has a counterpart inside of us. The COVID conundrum that haunts humanity today began with factors that had been inherent in the prevailing social system for decades, manifesting as human rights neglects in general and children's rights abuses in particular; these were condoned by individuals and institutions alike.

The micro level represents the catalytic core where change starts and stalls. The aspiration of individuals to translate the rights of others into reality, in their immediate vicinity and beyond, is the trigger that shifts the social scale. Embracing a holistic perspective concerning risks and responsibilities as well as rights and resources is a step that can be undertaken by everyone everywhere. The consequences of waiting can be felt at all levels, and gradually the fallout is becoming worse, because the resulting environment becomes ever more pervasive. Humans are accountable, individually and collectively, for the choices they do (not) make. The time for action is now.

List of references

Literature

Amnesty International, Index number: POL 10/3202/2021.

Bicchieri, C, *Norms in the Wild. How to Diagnose, Measure, and Change Social Norms.* Oxford: Oxford University Press. 2016.

Cortesi, DE, 'Secular Wholeness. Trafford on Demand', *Psychology Today,* 2001. www.psychologytoday.com/us/blog/evolution-the-self/201303/the-golden-rule-part-1-dont-take-it-literally

Dalai Lama, HH, *The Fourteenth Policy of Kindness: An Anthology of Writings by and about the Dalai Lama.* Shambhala. Delhi, 1990.

Doidge, N, *The Brain That Changes Itself: Stories of Personal Triumph from the Frontiers of Brain Science.* New York, NY: Viking Press. 2007.

Festinger, L, 'Cognitive Dissonance', *Scientific American,* 207 (4), 1962.

Frankl, VE, *Man's Search for Meaning.* Simon and Schuster. New York, 1985.

General Assembly Resolution A/RES/66/138 of 19 December 2011; entered into force on 14 April 2014. Office of Human Rights. www.ohchr.org/en/professionalinterest/pages/opiccrc.aspx, accessed May 2021.

Gino, F, Kouchaki, M and Galinsky, AD, 'The Moral Virtue of Authenticity: How Inauthenticity Produces Feelings of Immorality and Impurity', *Psychological Science,* 26, 2015.

Gladwell, M, *The Tipping Point: How Little Things Can Make a Big Difference.* Little, Brown. New York, 2000.

Gould, SJ, *Wonderful Life.* New York: W. W. Norton & Co. 1989.

Haidt, J, *The Moral Roots of Liberals and Conservatives.* TED. 2006. https://rb.gy/fep1gt, accessed August 2020.

Kahneman, D, *Thinking, Fast and Slow.* London: Penguin Books. 2011.

Kropotkin, P, *Mutual Aid: A Factor of Evolution.* New York: Freedom Press. 1998.

Kuppens, P, Allen, NB and Sheeber, LB, 'Emotional Inertia and Psychological Maladjustment', *Psychological Science,* 21(7), 2010.

Lehrer, J, *How We Decide.* Boston: Mariner Books. 2010.

Lundy, L and Bronagh, B, *The Four General Principles of the United Nations Convention on the Rights of the Child: The Potential Value of the Approach in Other Areas of Human Rights Law.* London, 2017.

Marcus, GF, 'What Developmental Biology Can Tell Us about Innateness', in Carruthers, P, Laurence, S and Stich, S (eds), *The Innate Mind: Structure and Content.* Oxford University Press. London, 2005.

Minujin, A and Grondona, A, 'Poverty, Needs and Rights: Definitions in Dispute', No. 22 of Voces en el Fénix/Voices in the Phoenix, 2013.

Nettleship, RL, 'Chapter 4 – The Four Stages of Intelligence', in *Lectures on the Republic of Plato.* London: Macmillan & Co. 1955.

Nowak, M and Highfield, R, *Supercooperators: Altruism, Evolution, and Why We Need Each Other to Succeed.* New York: Simon & Schuster. 2011.

Office of the United Nations High Commissioner for Human Rights (OHCHR) and World Health Organization (WHO), *The Right to Health.* Fact Sheet No. 31. 2000.

Plante, TG, 'Helping Others Offers Surprising Benefits', *Psychology Today,* 2012. www.psychologytoday.com/us/blog/do-theright-thing/201207/helping-others-offers-surprising-benefits-0

Plotkin, H, 'Human Nature, Cultural Diversity and Evolutionary Theory', *Philosophical Transactions of the Royal Society of London. Series B, Biological Sciences,* 366, 2011.

Rakhshani, Z, 'The Golden Rule and Its Consequences: A Practical and Effective Solution for World Peace', *Journal of History Culture and Art Research,* 6, 2017.

Schnabel, A, 'Antonio Damasio: Descartes' Irrtum', in Senge, K and Schützeichel, R (eds), *Hauptwerke der Emotionssoziologie.* Springer VS. Wiesbaden. Wisbaden, 2013.

Singer, T and Klimecki, OM, 'Empathy and Compassion', *Current Biology,* 24, 2014.

Thijssen, P, 'From Mechanical to Organic Solidarity, and Back: With Honneth beyond Durkheim', *European Journal of Social Theory,* 15, 2012.

Von Hippel, W, *The Social Leap: The New Evolutionary Science of Who We Are, Where We Come from, and What Makes Us Happy.* New York, NY: HarperCollins. 2018.

Walther, C, *Connection in the Times of COVID. Corona's Call for Conscious Choices.* Palgrave Macmillan. New York, 2020a.

Walther, C, *Development, Humanitarian Aid and Social Welfare.* Palgrave Macmillan. New York, 2020b.

Walther, C, 'Le droit au service de l'enfant', University d'Aix-Marseille, 2014.

Wattles, J, *The Golden Rule.* New York: Oxford University Press. 1996.

Well, T, 'Compassion Is Better Than Empathy', *Psychology Today,* 2017. www.psychologytoday.com/us/blog/the-clarity/201703/compassion-is-better-empathy

Wilkinson, RG and Pickett, K, *The Spirit Level: Why More Equal Societies Almost Always Do Better.* Allen Lane. London, 2009.

Xinhua, Huaxia (ed), 'WHO Calls for Addressing Inequality in Health during the Pandemic', Peking, April 2021.

Other sources

Johns Hopkins University, 'World Bank, UNICEF: Tracker to Measure COVID-impact on Education', Joint Press Release, 2021. www.unicef.org/press-releases/new-global-tracker-measure-pandemics-impact-education-worldwide, accessed April 2021.

Ramey S, 'Benefits of Witnessing Acts of Kindness', 2016. https://exploringyourmind.com/benefits-witnessing-acts-kindness/

UNICEF Data, 'Covid and Children', 2021. https://data.unicef.org/covid-19-and-children/ accessed April 2021.

10 Concluding remarks

Where to Next: Closing Gaps

Rigmor Argren and Jessica Jonsson

Previous chapters have identified the need for an improved application of a child rights perspective in a variety of humanitarian responses. Several authors identify how responses to crises can be improved by means of humanitarian access, directly empowering children through various means of child participation. Taking the chapters of this book as a whole, three areas where there are gaps to fill in order to improve crisis response for children can be discerned. These can be summarised in the following three disparities: first, the gap between internal and external mechanisms of complaints or communication; second, the gap between response at the crisis site and recipient countries' response; and last, the distance between practitioners and academics.

Three areas for improved response

Internal and external mechanisms for individual complaints and communications need to be considered as a whole yet treated as distinctively separate. The acceptance and coming into place of substantial rights were illustrated by Hövelmann, and Argren and Jonsson provided detailed analysis of certain rights that can increasingly be legally enforced. Despite challenges, an important step forward, towards improved feedback, communication, and accountability, was achieved by the coming into force of the Optional Protocol to the Convention on the Rights of the Child on a communications procedure, in 2014. At the 66th session of the General Assembly of the United Nations by Resolution 66/138 of 19 December 2011, children globally were finally recognised as entitled rights holders to a right to redress, through the communication procedure created with the OPIC-CRC. The third optional protocol entered into force 14 April 2014, and the UN Committee on the Rights of the Child issued its first decision in January 2018, in relation to a complaint made under the OPIC-CRC.[1] The OPIC-CRC is, regardless of

1 Views adopted by the Committee on the Rights of the Child under the Optional Protocol to the Convention on the Rights of the Child on a communications procedure with respect to

DOI: 10.4324/9781003187493-10

being only the eighth individual complaints mechanism to enter into force, currently the third in terms of the number of cases adopted per year.[2] It is the fifth both in terms of the number of communications registered[3] and the number of state parties.[4] By April 2020, the Committee on the Rights of the Child had received over 300 individual communications.[5] State signatories to the protocol recognise that children have the right to appeal to a mechanism specific to their human rights when national mechanisms fail to address child rights violations effectively. This establishment is, together with participatory, internal feedback efforts conducted by humanitarians through their various instruments and routines, an essential accountability mechanism.

Efforts of internal and external accountability mechanisms identify the potential establishment of child-friendly, accessible communication and complaints channels. As Hill outlined in her chapter, humanitarian actors need to emphasise the importance of an integrated child rights perspective and the human rights of the child whilst seeking to uphold minimum standards in any crisis response. Ensuring that feedback informs decision-making and closes the feedback loop, that is, providing information of what happened as a result of the feedback given, is important both with regard to beneficiaries and donors. The important external counterpart is foremost the OPIC-CRC, providing the right to redress.[6]

The central theme remains to assess and discuss accountability mechanisms that allow for individual communications and complaints, used by or meant to be used by humanitarians, amongst other duty bearers, in relation to children's rights, in the context of crises response. This includes processes and procedures established by national and international organisations that carry out humanitarian response for children. Such procedures may be put in place internally within organisations with regard to their own response handling. They may also be promoted externally to other actors and partners. Also, formal complaint mechanisms linked to international

communication No. 3/2016, CRC/C/77/D/3/2016, www.ohchr.org/Documents/HRBodies/CRC/CRC-C-77-DR-3-2016.pdf.

2 After CCPR (Human Rights Committee) and CAT (Committee against Torture).

3 After CCPR, CAT, CEDAW (Committee on the Elimination of Discrimination against Women) and CESCR (Committee on Economic, Social and Cultural Rights).

4 After CCPR, CEDAW, CAT and CRPD (Committee on the Rights of Persons with Disabilities).

5 Last update in April 2020 on the number of submitted communications, but an increase can safely be assumed. www.ohchr.org/en/treaty-bodies/crc/individual-communications. The Committee had registered 116 of those cases and adopted decisions on 39 registered cases. www.ohchr.org/EN/HRBodies/CRC/Pages/Decisions.aspx. See Jaap E Doek, 'Communications with the Committee on the Rights of the Child under Optional Protocol to the CRC on a Communications Procedure and Admissibility. Report on the Decisions of the Committee on Admissibility: Summary and Comments', *Leiden Children's Rights Observatory Papers* No. 2, 12 May 2022.

6 As of July 2022, the OPIC-CRC has 58 signatories and 48 parties, https://treaties.un.org/Pages/ViewDetails.aspx?src=TREATY&mtdsg_no=IV-11-d&chapter=4&clang=_en, accessed 30 July 2022.

conventions, especially the OPIC-CRC, are part of the framework for possible avenues for redress.

Bolling, Al Zayani and Vaigè discussed experiences of recipient countries' responses. Clearly, this is not without challenges. But it remains pertinent to recognise the rights of children, regardless of whether the response takes place at the site of the crisis or further away, in a recipient country. Irrespective of where, children have a right to accessible, child-friendly feedback and communication procedures and the right to make a complaint or challenge a decision of a court or other administrative proceeding, formal or informal. This requires accessible, relevant information and independent support provided to all children, in all settings, such as schools and health clinics, to use the procedures effectively.[7]

With varying degrees of often lacking or unused communications procedures handling complaints in humanitarian contexts, a continued importance of an applied child rights perspective becomes apparent. Furthermore, it is here argued that in order to strengthen the impact for the benefit of children, internal and external accountability mechanisms must be aligned as far as possible. Of explicit attention is the situation of often overlooked and marginalised children, such as minorities, gender equalities and children with disabilities; feedback, communication and complaints mechanisms shall be in place and accessible in order to right wrongs that they might experience. Given that these groups may be even more vulnerable in a humanitarian crisis, marginalised children are far too easily overlooked or even ignored in urgent responses. In the book, crisis responses are discussed from two distinctive perspectives. On the one hand, the work in recipient states is discussed from the perspective of national, local organisations that engage in crisis response. On the other hand, the global-level perspective of larger, often international organisations is also discussed, where the work is at the initial emergency or close to it. Considering the number of involved actors, spanning such a variety of knowledge, capacity and resources, there ought not to be any lack of suitable actors. What is required, however, is a clear view of where responsibilities are separate and distinct or joint and shared.

A common concern in the context of human rights is the question about which state has jurisdiction. Although regularly handled as a legal issue, it cannot be ignored that when it comes to children in humanitarian crises,

7 Child-friendly, accessible communication and feedback procedures is part of the 10 indicators the Child Participation Assessment Tool (CPAT) of the Council of Europe, developed to assist member states in assessing their progress towards full implementation of the Recommendation on Participation; Recommendation Rec(2012)2 on the participation of children and young people under the age of 18; Recommendation Rec (2010)7 on the Council of Europe Charter on Education for Democratic Citizenship and Human Rights Education; Recommendation 128 (2003) on the revised European Charter on the participation of the young people in local and regional life; Vanessa Sedletzki and Agnes Lúx, 'Child Friendly Complaints Mechanisms', *National Human Rights Institutions (NHRIs) Series: Tools to Support Child-friendly Practices* (UNICEF, 2019).

the matter also clearly has a moral side. From such a perspective, there should always be someone accountable for the well-being of children. Given that the situation may change rapidly in humanitarian crises, not least when children are on the move, there is seemingly a need to make sure that accountability can be established promptly and also revised, if needed. In this process it is essential to make sure that the geographic whereabouts of children, and the resources attached to where they happen to find themselves relating to this, do not hinder full realisation of their rights. Children, although in need of protection, also carry with them the promise for a better future and, where needed, the necessary social change.

In her chapter, Walther raised the need for social change while underlining that all is connected. In a similar vein, it is noted that there clearly is a connection between practitioners and academics working in humanitarian response and child rights. However, there remains scope for re-enforcing this link between practitioners and academics by promoting closer collaboration and joint research projects.

In advancing an increasingly holistic approach to safeguarding children and children's rights in humanitarian responses, the joint effort of practitioners and academics is required to create the best possible conditions for knowledge production and tangible support. For practitioners and academics to learn each other's languages and become familiar with the respective ways of working does take some effort and perseverance. But when the task is completed and a common language is found, the endeavour is undoubtedly rewarding and well worth the collective effort. Such joint enterprises provide holistic results, based on knowledge and sound analysis, with practical relevance. This book must be considered in the best interest of any child in a humanitarian crisis. The remaining aim of the synthesis is to clarify when crisis response and complaint procedures must connect to each other or may even be reconciled and where they are distinctively separate and should remain so, in the best interest of the child.

List of references

Literature

Committee on the Rights of the Child, 'Views Adopted by the Committee on the Rights of the Child under the Optional Protocol to the Convention on the Rights of the Child on a communications procedure in respect of communication No. 3/2016'. CRC/C/77/D/3/2016. www.ohchr.org/Documents/HRBodies/CRC/CRC-C-77-DR-3-2016.pdf

Council of Europe Recommendation 128 (2003) on the revised European Charter on the participation of the young people in local and regional life.

Council of Europe Recommendation Rec(2010)7 on the Council of Europe Charter on Education for Democratic Citizenship and Human Rights Education.

Council of Europe Recommendation Rec(2012)2 on the participation of children and young people under the age of 18.

Doek, JE, 'Communications with the Committee on the Rights of the Child under Optional Protocol to the CRC on a Communications Procedure and Admissibility. Report on the Decisions of the Committee on Admissibility: Summary and Comments', *Leiden Children's Rights Observatory Papers,* No. 2, 12 May 2022.
General Assembly Resolution A/RES/66/138 Optional Protocol to the Convention on the Rights of the Child on a communications procedure. 19 December 2011.
Sedletzki, V and Lúx, A, 'Child Friendly Complaints Mechanisms', *National Human Rights Institutions (NHRIs) Series: Tools to Support Child-friendly Practices.* UNICEF. 2019.

Other source

Council of Europe, Child Participation Assessment Tool (CPAT). www.coe.int/en/web/children/child-participation-assessment-tool

Index

abuse, reported by children 20, 21
accessibility 119, 125
accommodation centres, detention in 139, 148–149, 150
accountability: accountability mechanisms 9–10, 205–206; accountability to affected people (AAP) 11–12; in digitalised responses 57, 72
action: anticipatory 65; informed by feedback 18–20
Act on the Legal Status of Foreigners (Lithuania) 138–140
Afghanistan 18
agency: concept of 42–43; in context of paternalism 43–44; in digital environment 77; and right to development 51–52
Agenda for Sustainable Development (2030) 2
antenatal/postnatal care 68
applications, mobile 70
artificial intelligence (AI) 57; AI-powered chatbots 67
Association for Solidarity with Asylum Seekers and Immigrants (ASAM) 164, 168
asylum seekers 140–142; *see also* refugees and internally displaced persons (IDPs)

Bangladesh 14, 19, 26
Belarus *see* refugees at Belarus-Lithuania border
beneficiaries: contrasted with rights-holders 10–13; in digital environment 65, 72, 76, 77–78
"best interest of the child" principle 4
Bill of Rights, England (1688) 39
biometric data 71–72; biometric identity management 68–69
body, as individual dimension 183

Cambodia 31
CEDAW (UN Convention on Elimination of All Forms of Discrimination against Women) 134
CERD (UN Convention on the Elimination of All Forms of Racial Discrimination) 134
change, as universal principle 180–181
chatbots 66–67
childhood, concept of 41–43, 59
child marriage 163–166
child participation *see* participatory rights of children
Children and Armed Conflict (Machel) 85
children's comfort with feedback mechanisms 16–18, 20, 22
child rights perspective: background and overview 1–4, 177–180, 200–202; collective principles 180–182; in COVID-19 context 193–200; individual dimensions 182–184; reciprocity 188–193; social interplay 184–187
Cluster Approach, IASC (Inter-Agency Standing Committee) 98–99, 101
coercive reproduction and marriage 163–166
Colombia 17, 31–32
Committee on the Rights of the Child *see* UN Committee on the Rights of the Child
Common European Asylum System (CEAS) directives 168
complaints mechanism 9–10

complementarity, as universal principle 180–182
connection, as universal principle 180–181
connectivity *see* digital access
content control 68–70
continuum, as universal principle 180–181
Convention on the Rights of the Child (CRC) 2, 3, 84; Article 2 45–46, 113; Article 3 113; Article 5 113; Article 6 51–52; Article 12 3–4, 8, 18, 111, 113; Article 13 37, 44, 45–46, 48–49, 113; Article 17 50–51, 113; Article 23 113; Article 28 113; Article 29 113; Article 39 84; conflicting rights within 67–68; and dimensions of human being 194–195; and Swedish law 119
Convention Relating to the Status of Refugees (1951) 84
Core Humanitarian Standard (CHS) 11
Côte d'Ivoire 26–27, 28
Council of Europe Recommendation (2018) 61
countering violence and extremism (CVE) and education 95–96
COVID-19 pandemic: and child participation 30–32; and digital access 73–74; disruption of routine healthcare 196; human rights implications 193–200; and inequality 196–197; and interconnectedness 177, 181; rights and freedoms 61; social interplay 184–187
crowdsourced information 65
CRPD *see* UN Convention on the Rights of Persons with Disabilities (CRPD)
Cyclone Idai 15–16
Cyclone Roanu 22

debate, public and political *see* freedom of expression
decision-making processes 18
Declaration on the Rights of the Child (1959) 38, 42
detention contrasted with "accommodation" 139, 148–149, 150
development, right to 50–51
development cooperation contrasted with humanitarian action 83–84
digital access: background and overview 56–59, 75–78; digitally included children 66–71; marginalisation 73–75; meaningful access 59–66; potential for harm 71–75
digital content, restrictions on 68
digital divide 74; *see also* digital access
digital information-as-aid 68–69
digitalised humanitarianism 66–71
disability: and personal assistance 122; social model of 111; *see also* refugee children with disabilities
Disabled Refugees Welcome (DRW) 110; *see also* refugee children with disabilities
domestic violence *see* gendered violence in Turkey
"do no harm" principle 71

Eastern route states 132, 135, 143, 151; *see also* refugees at Belarus-Lithuania border
Ebola epidemic 24
education, right to: background and overview 83–87, 104–105; data collection and analysis 90–104; refugees in Lithuania 150; theoretical frameworks 87–90
education in emergencies (EiE) 83, 84–85; *see also* education, right to
Education in Situations of Emergency 102
emergency preparedness 65
empathy 190–191
empowerment 113–114, 125, 128
Ethiopia 21–22, 26
e-transfers 68–69
European Civil Protection and Humanitarian Aid Operations (ECHO) 93
European Commission 137
European Convention on Human Rights (ECHR) 39–40, 134; Article 2 138; Article 3 138; Article 15 138
European Court of Human Rights (ECtHR) 40, 142, 151
European Court of Justice (ECJ) 139

facial recognition 71
FARR (Swedish Network of Refugee Support Groups) 111
feedback boxes 16–18
feedback channels 12
feedback mechanisms 12, 13–24
feminist analysis 158–160
forced migration *see* migration, forced

Framework for Access to Education (ICRC) 100
framing/frame analysis 87–88, 89, 92–93; Snow's frame alignment strategies 101
freedom of expression 38–41, 43, 69
Fruchterman, Jim 72

gender-based violence in Turkey: background and overview 156–162, 173–174; and intersectionality 162–173
gender issues 158–160; gender and forced migration (GAFM) 160; gender as binary 173; gender roles and empowerment 127
Geneva Declaration on the Rights of the Child (1924) 38, 42
Global Education Cluster 101
Global South and digital access 75
Grand Bargain 3, 11; Annual Independent Report (2019) 18
Ground Truth Solutions 12–13
Guidance Note on Refugee Claims Relating to Sexual Orientation and Gender Identity 160

Handyside v the United Kingdom 39–40
health, right to 150–151
heart, as individual dimension 182–183
Hêvî LGBT (NGO) 171–172
Humanitarian Accountability Partnership (HAP) 11
humanitarian aid: action contrasted with development cooperation 83–84; areas for improvement 5, 204–207; and changing normative frameworks 86–87; humanitarian programme cycle (HPC) 23–30
humanitarian crises 5; and violation of rights 8–9, 37–38, 43–44, 49–50
Human Rights Council 2
Human Rights Watch 109

ICESCR (International Covenant on Economic, Social and Cultural Rights) 40, 41, 84
"illegal migrant" status 133, 136, 145–146
illiteracy 14
Improving Learning Environments Together in Emergencies 26
inaccessibility *see* accessibility
incest 165–166
inclusion, digital *see* digital access
independent living (IL) for persons with disability 120–122
Independent Living Institute (ILI) 110
India 29
Indonesia 22–23, 24–25
information, right to 30–31; analysis of 44–49; background and overview 37–44, 52–53; further provisions 49–52
InsightShare 28
Inter-Agency Network for Education in Emergencies (INEE) 85, 97–98, 99, 101, 102
Inter-Agency Standing Committee (IASC): Cluster Approach 98–99, 101; Guidelines 23
internally displaced persons (IDPs) *see* refugees and internally displaced persons (IDPs)
International Centre for Transitional Justice 28
International Committee of the Red Cross (ICRC) 100
International Covenant on Civil and Political Rights (ICCPR) 40, 41; Article 19 37, 44, 45, 47
International Rescue Committee 18
Internet access 31–32, 61; *see also* digital access
intersectionality 118–119, 133, 144–145, 162–173
ISIS members and threats of violence 170, 171–172

Jordan 27

Kadmlarla Dayanişma Vakfı (KADAV) 169, 170

language: language barriers 14; minority languages 75
Lebanon 27
LGBTIQ+ persons 157, 170–173; *see also* gendered violence in Turkey
LGBTQIA+ status 145
life-saving intervention, education as 93–94
Lithuania *see* refugees at Belarus-Lithuania border
local partnerships and digital technology 70

m4-matrix (micro-meso-macro-meta) 191–193, 197–201
Machel Report (1996) 90, 101
Malawi 15–16
male/female roles and empowerment 127; *see also* gender issues
Mali 31
marginalisation and digital access 73–75
marriage 163–166
mass media 43, 50–51
migration, forced: migration influx, Sweden (2015) 112, 114–116; mixed migration 136–137; *see also* refugee children with disabilities; refugees at Belarus-Lithuania border
mind, as individual dimension 183
Minimum Standards for Education in Emergencies (MSEE) 96–97; MSEE Handbook 102
mobile applications 60, 64–65, 66–67
mobile phone access 14, 71
morality, innate human foundations 188–193
Movement of African Working Children and Youth 31
Mozambique 15–16
Myanmar 14

National Advisory Council of Children and Youth of Mali 31
National Children's Parliament (Mali) 31
National Coordination of the Working Children and Youth Associations of Côte d'Ivoire 27
National Society for Deaf (Sudan) 31
needs assessment and analysis 24–25
neighborhood parliaments 29
Nepal 24–25, 28
Nicaragua 31
Nigeria 15, 18
normative frameworks 86–90
norm dynamism 94–96
norm emergence 92–94
norm institutionalisation 96–104
Norwegian Refugee Council (NRC) 96

ombudsperson: in Lithuania 139, 143–152; potential for 21, 32
online violence 170
OPIC-CRC (Optional Protocol) 3, 9–10, 32, 144, 151–152, 187, 204–205
opinion contrasted with view 45–47
Organisation for Economic Co-operation and Development (OECD) 12

Palestine 27
participation: full participation 119; Participation Revolution 3, 11; principle of 113; right to 111
participatory rights of children: assessment and analysis 24–30; background and overview 3–4, 8–10, 32–34; beneficiaries contrasted with rights-holders 10–13; Covid-19 pandemic 30–32; digital participation 64–71, 77–78; feedback mechanisms 12, 13–24
paternalism 43–44
patriarchal norms and systems 166, 173
peer review 27–29
peer support for children with disabilities 124
personal assistance 122
Philippines 24
POZE paradigm 178–179, 180
predictive analytics 65
privacy, right to 68–72

Qualification Directives (EU) 160

real-time data 65
Real Time Reviews (RTRs) 28
reciprocity 188–193; reciprocal integration 114, 127
Red Cross/Red Crescent Movement (IFRC) 100
refugee children with disabilities; background and overview 109–112, 128–129; DRW (Disabled Refugees Welcome) in social context 120; DRW (Disabled Refugees Welcome) project design 122–124; DRW (Disabled Refugee Welcome) results 124–128; DRW (Disabled Refugees Welcome) terminology 112–114; independent living 120–122; and international law 116–119; refugee influx (2015) 112, 114–116
refugees and internally displaced persons (IDPs): digital access 64–66; and right to education 85
refugees at Belarus-Lithuania border: background and overview 132–137, 151–152; children's perspective

on 143–151; and human rights violations 141–143; Lithuanian response 137–141
resource mobilisation 25
right to information *see* information, right to
Rohingya people 14, 19
Russia, aggression against Ukraine 57–58, 70, 71, 133; *see also* refugees at Belarus-Lithuania border

Save the Children: child participation during implementation phase 25–26; Colombia 17; and education 99; feedback and suggestions 10, 20–22; foundational rights-based information 48; *Improving Learning Environments Together in Emergencies* 26; Mozambique emergency response 15–16; Real Time Reviews (RTRs) 28; Rohingya Response 14–15
Search for Common Ground 28
self-determination, right to 110, 111, 114, 120, 123
sexual abuse 69–70
sex workers 171–173
Sierra Leone 24–25
solidarity 188, 190–191
soul, as individual dimension 182
Sphere Handbook (2000) 97, 98
Sphere Project Management Committee 97–98
Sri Lanka 22
Stockholm cooperative on Independent Living (STIL) 122
strategic planning 25
Sudan 31
Sweden 110; *see also* refugee children with disabilities
Swedish Agency for Participation (MFD) 114–115
Swedish Migration Agency 110
Swedish Red Cross 110–111
Swedish Refugee National Council 111
Syria 27

Telegram (application) 70
Terre des Hommes 30
Togo 31
transphobia 171–173
Turkey *see* violence, gendered, in Turkey
Typhoon Haiyan 24

Ukraine, Russian invasion 57–58, 70, 71, 133; *see also* refugees at Belarus-Lithuania border
unaccompanied minors 145–148
UN Committee on the Rights of the Child: complaints and accountability 9–10, 187, 204; and digital access 56–57; General Comment (No. 7) 113; General Comment (No. 12) 111, 112, 113; General Comment (No. 25) 57; guiding principles 51
UN Convention on Elimination of All Forms of Discrimination against Women (CEDAW) 134
UN Convention on the Elimination of All Forms of Racial Discrimination (CERD) 134
UN Convention on the Rights of Persons with Disabilities (CRPD) 111, 116–119; Article 19 120–122, 124
UN Declaration on the Rights of the Child (1959) 38, 42
UN Educational, Scientific and Cultural Organization (UNESCO) 85
UN General Assembly: Resolution 64/290 84, 102
UNHCR Need to Know Guidance on Working with LGBTI Persons 160
UN High Commissioner for Refugees (UNHCR) 66, 85
UN Human Rights Committee 63
UN Human Rights Council 62
UN International Children's Emergency Fund (UNICEF) 27, 48, 66, 99; Cryptocurrency Fund 66; guide to using chatbots 67; right to education 85
Universal Declaration of Human Rights (UDHR/1945) 41, 84, 117–118, 179

Venezuela 17
view: children's views and feedback 18; and freedom of expression 113; view contrasted with opinion 45–47
violations and accountability mechanisms 9–10
violence *see* gender-based violence in Turkey
Voluntary Health Association of Kanyakumari 29

war refugees 133; *see also* refugees at Belarus-Lithuania border
women in forced migration (WIFM) 160
World Declaration on Education for All (EFA) 84
World Food Programme (WFP) 66
World Humanitarian Summit (2016) 3, 11
World Summit on the Information Society (2003) 63
World Vision 19; Ethiopia 21–22

Yayasan Sayangi Tunas Cilik (YSTC) 22–23

Zimbabwe 15–16

For Product Safety Concerns and Information please contact our EU representative GPSR@taylorandfrancis.com
Taylor & Francis Verlag GmbH, Kaufingerstraße 24, 80331 München, Germany

www.ingramcontent.com/pod-product-compliance
Ingram Content Group UK Ltd.
Pitfield, Milton Keynes, MK11 3LW, UK
UKHW020007200926
475702UK00015B/2521
* 9 7 8 1 0 3 2 0 3 4 7 7 5 *